Culture and Family
Problems and Therapy

HAWORTH Marriage and the Family
Terry S. Trepper, PhD, Senior Editor

CULTURE AND FAMILY: PROBLEMS AND THERAPY

Wen-Shing Tseng, MD
Jing Hsu, MD

SOME ADVANCE REVIEWS

"This is a consciousness-expanding book. We are led through the virtually uncharted field of comparative family patterns, functions, pathology, and therapy. Although there are many single-culture explorations of families that at least implicitly make contrasts with those of the West, this is a brilliant first attempt at a more comprehensive survey. The authors are experienced clinicians and know what they are talking about. All who work in multi-ethnic settings need this book."

Raymond Prince, MD
Editor, Transcultural Psychiatric Research Review
Professor, Division of Social and Transcultural Psychiatry
McGill University, Montreal, Canada

"A near exhaustive review of the literature in this area. It is notable for the clarity of expression and the organizational sequence of topics that makes it easy for the reader to digest. The book covers an area that has been long neglected and yet is extremely important. No family therapist should be without it."

John P. Spiegel, MD
Professor of Social Psychiatry, Emeritus
The Florence Heller Graduate School for Advanced Studies
in Social Welfare, Brandeis University
Waltham, Massachusetts

Culture and Family
Problems and Therapy

Wen-Shing Tseng, MD
and
Jing Hsu, MD

The Haworth Press
New York • London • Sydney

The Haworth Press, Inc., 10 Alice Street, Binghamton, NY 13904-1580
EUROSPAN/Haworth, 3 Henrietta Street, London WC2E 8LU England
ASTAM/Haworth, 162-168 Parramatta Road, Stanmore (Sydney), N.S.W. 2048 Australia

Library of Congress Cataloging-in-Publication Data

Tseng, Wen-Shing, 1935-
      Culture and family : problems and therapy / Wen-Shing Tseng and Jing Hsu.
          p.   cm.
      Includes bibliographical references and index.
      ISBN 1-56024-058-X (alk. paper). — ISBN 1-56024-059-3 (pbk.)
          1. Family — Mental health. 2. Family psychotherapy. 3. Cultural psychiatry. 4. Transcul-.
tural psychiatry. I. Hsü, Ching, 1937- II. Title.
RC488.5.T79 1991
616.89'156 — dc20
                                                                                              90-21961
                                                                                                   CIP

To our wonderful children:
Chau-Wen, Chien-Wen, and Stephanie Shieh-Wen
for their love, encouragement, and assistance,
and for their growing together with us as a family
in different cultural settings,
which inspired us to write this book.

CONTENTS

ABOUT THE AUTHORS

Wen-Shing Tseng, MD, is Professor of Psychiatry at the University of Hawaii School of Medicine. He has served as Chairman for the Transcultural Psychiatry Section of the World Psychiatric Association since 1981 and is known as an expert in cultural psychiatry both nationally and internationally. Dr. Tseng has conducted extensive research on cultural psychiatry and has also organized numerous conferences on culture and mental health relating to Asia and the Pacific. In addition to numerous scientific articles and book chapters, Dr. Tseng is the author of *Culture, Mind, and Therapy: An Introduction to Cultural Psychiatry* (1981) and the editor of *Chinese Culture and Mental Health* (1985).

Jing Hsu, MD, Clinical Professor of Psychiatry at the University of Hawaii School of Medicine, is in private practice in psychiatry with a subspecialty in marital and family therapy and is Director of the Family Institute of Hawaii. Dr. Hsu is a Diplomate of the American Board of Psychiatry and Neurology, a Fellow of the American Psychiatric Association, a member of the American Family Therapy Association, and is President of the Hawaii Council on Family Relations. The author of the Chinese textbooks, *Modern Psychiatry* (1981) and *Psychotherapy* (1987), she has also published a number of book chapters and scientific articles.

Senior Editor's Comments

When I took my first course in "Culture and Personality" as an undergraduate many years ago, I felt as if I had just been inoculated with the answers to the secrets of psychology. Suddenly all of the inconsistencies in human behavior became "understandable," merely artifacts of cultural determinism and cultural evolution. No longer could I accept even our most strongly held beliefs, since now I knew that for every behavior our culture found abhorrent, there was another which revered it; conversely, even our most cherished activities would be viewed as pathological among some Polynesian culture with an unpronounceable name.

My hypomanic undergraduate enthusiasms for cultural relativism lasted only for a while. As I went forward with my studies in clinical psychology, the "truths" I gleaned from the professional study of personality and abnormal psychology and psychotherapy took precedence over the more "ethereal" culture and personality. After all, if I were going to be a psychologist I had just better accept that, for example, there is indeed psychopathological behavior, Thomas Szasz and other cultural relativists notwithstanding.

Happily, as I moved into the field of family psychology, I was reintroduced to the joys of cultural anthropology. The family studies disciplines and anthropology have had a long history together, being inexorably linked through the common bond of "culture" and "family." After all, one cannot understand a culture without understanding the basic unit of culture: the family. And more and more scientists in the family studies disciplines are becoming aware that to try and study the family without understanding the cultural context in which it resides is like trying to study the individual without understanding the family in which he or she was raised.

When I recently read Tseng and Hsu's *Culture and Family: Problems and Therapy*, I had that same "rush" of excitement I had during that first course in "Culture and Personality." Again it all made sense! I was reminded to explore and understand the cultural context in which my families in therapy experienced the world, each other, and me. Since my own case-load is multi-ethnic, this reminder was particularly useful, and the specific suggestions for doing therapy with families from different ethnic backgrounds was immediately helpful.

Tseng and Hsu's book is an extremely ambitious work. They provide the reader with an understanding of the complex interactions between culture and family in a careful and methodical way. They first describe the dimensions of family from a cultural perspective, providing those non-anthropologists among us with an excellent primer in the anthropology of the family. They then discuss the various aspects of family development, structure, dysfunction, and therapy within a cultural context.

Family studies researchers will find this book an excellent sourcebook for stimulating hypotheses and designing cross-cultural studies. Professors in the family-related disciplines will find this work to be a superb ancillary text for courses in family studies and therapy. And therapists who work with families of different cultures will find the book to be indispensable as a guide for understanding, assessment, and treatment. Tseng and Hsu's *Culture and Family: Problems and Therapy* is indeed a landmark work. I hope upon reading this book you experience the same sense of excitement at "rediscovering" culture and the family that I did.

Terry S. Trepper, PhD, Senior Editor
HAWORTH Marriage and the Family
and Professor of Psychology
Purdue University Calumet

Preface

This book addresses the cultural aspects of the family. It systematically reviews the function of the family from a cross-cultural perspective, examines the problems and dysfunctions which can occur in different cultural backgrounds, and proposes culturally-appropriate assessments and treatments for resolving family conflict. By examining the family from a cultural aspect, knowledge of and insight into the family can be expanded.

"Culture" refers to a unique style of life patterns shared by a group of people. The value and belief systems function as the core of the culture. Countless types of cultural patterns have existed among humankind in the present, as well as in the past. These patterns provide a human laboratory in which to study how the family system and function may vary in different settings and how family problems will differ due to various sociocultural backgrounds. On the other hand, the family is the basic sociocultural unit through which culture is transmitted from generation to generation. It is, therefore, the appropriate place in which to examine the culture.

"Ethnic group" refers to a group of people who are distinguished by a characteristic language, common history, and customs. Theoretically speaking, an ethnic group may or may not be strictly equivalent to a culture system in concern. However, for the sake of convenience, ethnicity and culture will be interchangeably used in this book as people are more or less familiar with the term and concept of ethnicity, and it is easier to identify a particular ethnic group rather than a particular cultural system.

Although there is an increasing interest among family scholars, researchers, and therapists in culture and family systems, there remains a lack of information and literature on this important subject. Recently, there have been numerous publications describing the culture and family aspects of specific ethnic or cultural groups, particularly those found in the United States. Most of these publications are concerned with family mental health aspects of various ethnic or cultural groups, i.e., they review and discuss family systems, functions, and problems of each particular ethnic group. We feel that it is now appropriate to move from that position to integrate systematically existing information and experiences at another level upon which we can build further understanding of the family from cultural perspectives. Instead of dealing with family issues of each particular ethnic/cultural group, we focus on dissecting the various subjects of the family: family systems, subsystems, development, family group and dynamics, problems, assessment and treatment — all the areas which need to be covered comprehensively in family mental health from a cross-ethnic/culture perspective. Thus, we deal with the subjects of family vertically, but integrate the cultural material horizontally. This is a new adventure in organizing knowledge so the scientific and clinical concepts of family can be dealt with on another organizational level.

Since there is a wide degree of variation between different cultural systems around the world, examining diverse culture groups allows the impact of cultural elements to be reviewed more explicitly. A comparison with multiple cultural examples also ensures that a more accurate generalization can be made based on the findings obtained. Therefore, in order to analyze the cultural aspects of family, the focus of this study needs to be expanded beyond our own ethnocultural group to other groups, not only in our society but in other societies throughout the world. Since cultural samples that are quite different from our own will be included, the spectrum of focus on the family will become broader and more comprehensive.

Based on this reasoning, the ethnocultural information in this book has been gathered as broadly as possible, utilizing all available data and knowledge concerning the family. Our search has extended beyond the English-language publications and pertinent literature. Material from the past to the present is included from various cultural settings. This book is not intended to understand or to update the current situation of any particular family system within a specific cultural setting. Rather, by utilizing various kinds of unique examples, it aims to elaborate how families' functions, problems, and therapy can be influenced by cultural factors. The authors' Asian cultural heritage has enabled them to focus on material from the Asian region. In this way, the accumulated knowledge can be derived from both the East and the West.

In order to understand the family cross-culturally, knowledge about the family from cultural anthropology, social and cultural psychology, and international family psychiatry are all utilized, which results in a "cross-fertilization" of interdisciplinary knowledge. The scientific reports from family researchers and the clinical experiences of family therapists concerning cultural aspects of family functions and problems have been extensively reviewed before inclusion.

Trained both in the East and the West, and working in the multi-ethnic society of Hawaii, in areas involving clinical services, training, and research on families of many ethnic groups, we have developed a long-term interest in the cultural aspects of family mental health. As husband and wife, we have also experienced family life and raised our children in a rapidly-changing society and in the different cultural settings of the East and West. Through such transcultural family experiences, we have come to appreciate the impact of the cultural environment on family life and health.

By reviewing the family from a cross-cultural perspective and examining the extensive variations of family systems, we hope that a comprehensive theoretical concept can be constructed in the future which has more universal applications. In the meantime, a set of practical guidelines for the transcultural assessment and management of families of different ethnocultural backgrounds can be developed for clinical application. We believe that by opening our angle of view and examining the cultural aspects of the family, we can acquire more insight into the nature of the family.

Wen-Shing Tseng, MD
Jing Hsu, MD

Chapter 1

Culture and the Family System

DIMENSIONS OF THE FAMILY

The family is the basic sociocultural unit. It is the nest for the growth of an individual, the resource for social support, and the institution through which culture is transmitted. The universal basic functions of the family have been defined by anthropologist Hoebel (1972) as:

> The institutionalization of mating and the channeling of sexual outlets; the nurture and basic enculturation of the young in an atmosphere of intimacy; the organization of a complementary division of labor between spouses; and the linkage of each spouse and the offspring within the wider network of kinsmen for the establishment of relations of descent and affinity. (p. 422)

It is very important to notice that cross-culturally the term "family" has been used with varied concept and meaning, and furthermore it is hard to retain the exact meaning of the English word "family" when translating it into other languages. For example, Japanese synonyms include *ie* (building of house), *uchi* (inside of the house — in contrast to the outside world), *kazoku* (members of family, which may include only nuclear family or all the family clan), and *katei* (the structure and life of family). For these reasons, anthropologists usually avoid the term "family" because it simultaneously implies the concepts of "residence," "household," and "kinship" (Yanagisako, 1979). In this book, for the sake of convenience, the term "family" will be used in a conventional way to

1

refer to a group of people who are brought together and live together through marriage and as the product of mating.

Marriage refers to the customs, rules, and obligations that establish a special relationship between a sexually cohabiting adult male and female, between them and any children they produce, and between the kin groups of husband and wife (Nanda, 1980). From a sociological point of view, marriage is considered to be a socially approved formal sexual union with the intent of permanence of one or more men and one or more women, which is conducted within a set of designated rights and duties expected of them by society and certain rights and duties they expect of each other in their roles. The specific rights and duties that comprise the roles of husband and wife may change from time to time within any one society, may differ from grouping to grouping in the same society, and may also differ from one society to another (Lantz and Snyder, 1969).

The family is a complex institution which can be investigated and understood from various dimensions (Howells, 1971). Methodologically, researchers have studied the family from five perspectives — by examining (1) individual members of the family, (2) the subsystem of the family, (3) the life cycle of the family, (4) the interaction patterns of the family as a group, and (5) the family as a system.

By examining individual family members focus is placed on the personality, psychology, and behavior of each with the conviction that the family is an accumulated result of the individual family members' behavior. It is assumed that a set of well-functioning individuals — father, mother and children — will compose a well-functioning family and vice versa.

The family has also been explored from the viewpoint of a family subsystem. By analyzing the interpersonal relationships that exist in each subsystem of the family, such as husband-wife, parent-child, and sibling-sibling, an attempt has been made to understand the behavior of the family by closely assessing and analyzing the relations, affections, roles, and conflicts that may exist within each subsystem.

By focusing on the chronological aspects, family development has also been reviewed by considering the family as an organization which goes through the vicissitudes of life in various stages (Lidz, 1970; Duvall, 1971; Carter and McGoldrick, 1980). The growth, development, and contraction of the family have been evaluated by stages of family life which are usually in connection with the growth of children — how spouses marry, bear and raise children, and how children leave parents.

Recently, by viewing the family as a group of people, many investigators and therapists have focused on the study of the family group. In such cases, the matters of hierarchy, leadership, communication, role patterns, interaction patterns, affectivity, boundaries, and task performance of the family as a "group" are usually the parameters examined (Lewis, Beavers, Gossett, and Phillips, 1976). Along the same lines, stress encountered by the family, and resources and coping patterns utilized by the family as a group, can be examined.

Finally, based on systems theory, an approach is taken that views the family as existing in a system which is broadly comprised of intrapsychic, interpersonal, intra-family, and extra-family perspectives, which interact and are interrelated as a whole system. The family is examined and understood within the network of each system inwardly and outwardly in ecological and dynamic ways.

Although marriage and the formation of families rest on the biological complementarity of male and female and on the biological process of reproduction, both marriage and family are cultural patterns. As such, they differ in form and function among human societies (Nanda, 1980). As pointed out by Haviland (1978), historical and cross-cultural studies of the family offer as many different family patterns as the human imagination can create. These different family patterns are not just interesting products of human investigation; they are solutions to the different sorts of problems with which people must cope. At the same time, different family forms present certain sets of problems which must somehow be dealt with. By studying families of diverse types that exist among humankind, we are able to construct theoretical concepts which have more universal applications.

In order to provide a culturally-relevant assessment and treatment for families of different cultural backgrounds, it is essential to understand the cultural aspects of family systems and function. When we are dealing clinically with families with ethnic and cultural backgrounds that are different from ours, it is essential to extend our orientation and understanding of family dimensions by considering cultural aspects of the family system. Otherwise, we may suffer from "cultural myopia" — being shortsighted in terms of our views and orientation towards the cultural dimension of the family.

CULTURAL VARIATIONS OF FAMILY SYSTEMS

Based on unique cultural patterns, anthropologists have recognized and described nearly one thousand units of societies that exist around the world. Such descriptions have been recorded and collected as the *Ethnographic Atlas* for the systematic scientific comparison and study of human life patterns, as well as family systems (Murdock, 1967). Cultural anthropologists also describe and distinguish between various family systems by referring to parameters such as marriage forms, descent system, post-marital residence choice, or household structure.

Marriage Forms

Marriage forms concern the number of spouses in a marriage. All societies have rules concerning the number of spouses a person may have at one time. *Monogamy* permits a person to have only one spouse at any given time, while *polygamy* permits more than one spouse in the marriage. If a man has several wives it is called *polgyny*, and if a woman is married to more than one man it is known as *polyandry*. Monogamy is the rule in most contemporary, developed societies, although it is by no means the most common rule among the world's cultures. According to anthropologist Hoebel (1972), who adopted data from Bourguignon and Greenbaum's (1968) study, among 854 societies described in the *Ethnographic Atlas* (Murdock, 1967), only 16 percent consider monogamy exclusively as an expected marriage form, 39 percent prefer monogamy with polygyny, and 44 percent opt for polygyny. Polyandry is found in only 4 of the 854 cultures listed. Thus, more than 80 percent of the world's societies prefer plural marriage. However, as pointed out by Nanda (1980), this preference does not mean that most people in these societies actually have more than one spouse. Even where polygyny is preferred, the ratio of males to females may be such that few men would be able to acquire more than one wife. Furthermore, where men must exchange wealth for wives, many men cannot afford more than one wife and therefore are limited to monogamy.

It needs to be pointed out that the figures presented here deal with percentages of "social units" as identified by anthropologists, and do not reflect population percentages. One social unit may have a small population of at most a few hundred or thousand people, while others may have a large number of people — such as the Chinese society which contains nearly one-fifth of the world's population. Therefore, if social units are considered in terms of number of members, it would be fair to say that the majority of the world population considers monogamy the expected marriage form.

In societies where monogamy is preferred and marriage is considered closely and exclusively tied to sex and emotion, it is hard to understand how polygynous marriages can exist without conflict and jealousy between wives. Actually, much evidence indicates that when a man has many wives, problems usually occur between the wives. However, as explained by anthropologist Nanda (1980), sexual jealousy among wives might not be a great problem in societies which do not idealize romantic love and exclusive sexual rights in marriage. Furthermore, in societies where women are economically important, polygyny can increase a man's wealth and therefore his social position. By having several spouses, an individual may also extend his alliances with different groups. Thus, in some societies, polygyny has important economic and political functions.

Polyandry is basically different in nature from polygyny. It is not brought about by super women having many men-husbands as might be speculated (Berreman, 1980). As observed among the Tibetans, the Todas, and other tribes of India where the practice of polyandry is well-known, several brothers usually marry the same woman (Hoebel, 1972). In societies where land and property are scarce, the division of assets between siblings can be avoided if brothers form a family by marrying a common wife. Thus, polyandry is frequently practiced as a way to cope with an economic situation (Levine and Sangree, 1980).

Choice of Mates

Every society has certain rules pertaining to the choice of a candidate for marriage. Often marriage partners must be chosen from outside one's own kin group or community — this "outside" choice is known as *exogamy*. In contrast, at times one is obligated to marry a person within his or her own culturally defined group; this "inside" choice is called *endogamy*. An example of caste-related endogamy is the social rule in India which requires a person to marry within his/her caste group, so as to avoid becoming "polluted" through marriage to someone outside of the caste.

The prohibition of sex relations between culturally identified relatives is known as the *incest taboo* (Nanda, 1980). It automatically follows that marriage between persons subject to this rule is also forbidden. Incest taboos are universal among all peoples. With rare exceptions, all societies forbid cross-sex relationships within the nuclear family, namely between parents and children and between brother and sister. Yet, no society stops the incest taboo there; additional kin also fall into the incest taboo category. Interestingly, however, in most societies there is no single class of kin outside the nuclear family from which it is not acceptable to choose a sex partner. First cousins, aunts, nephews, and so on, are taboo in some societies but not in others. In most societies, intercourse is permitted with some fairly close blood relatives and prohibited with more distant ones. For instance, within the Chinese culture, cousins and nephews on the maternal side are permitted to marry but those from the paternal side, who have the same family name, are not. The restriction is so extended that a person is not permitted to marry *any* person who happens to have the same family name, even though they are not blood-related at all; theoretically, they are considered to be members of the same patrilineal family. As Chinese have a relatively limited number of family names, caution needs to be exercised to avoid falling in love with someone who has the same family name. As explained by cultural anthropologists, the key to this extension of sex and marital taboos is that the family is perceived as a social group rather than as a biological one. Thus, the extension of incest and marriage taboos tends to be rooted more in sociology than in biology.

Associated with the rule of marital choice is the process of how the marital partner is chosen. Arranged marriage refers to a situation in which marriage partners are selected and decided upon primarily by someone other than the partners themselves — usually by parents or other kin. Marriages may also be arranged through a matchmaker. The marriage partners may or may not be consulted. In extreme circumstances the partners might not even see each other until the wedding ceremony.

The main concerns in arranging a marriage are the compatibility of the family backgrounds and of the prospective partners as well as the partners' physical condition, health, moral character, working patterns, and ability to produce the next generation. In other words, the major considerations stem from the perspectives of the family. Anthropologists remind us that, for many cultural groups, marriage constitutes an alliance between two kinship groups in which the couple concerned is merely the most conspicuous link.

In contrast, the choice of a marriage partner may occur by self-selection or through free love, the method preferred by young members of most contemporary societies. In free love, affection and love are the major concerns, even though other factors such as the character and personal background of the partner may be taken into consideration. The background of the partner's family may also be considered; generally, however, these concerns are superficial ones.

Different modes of acquiring a wife exist around the world. As described by Hoebel (1972), in many societies the prevalent method of obtaining a wife is through the formal exchange of goods considered equal in value to the offspring the woman is expected to produce — progeny price. Progeny price was found to prevail in virtually all tribes in Africa, where 214 out of 238 (90 percent) listed in the *Ethnographic Atlas* practice it. Taking the world as a whole, well over half (58 percent) of all societies in the *Atlas* expect progeny price to be paid to the family of the bride by the kin of the groom. Progeny price may partly represent compensation for the loss of the girl by her kinship group, but it is much more an act of compensation to that group for its loss of a legal claim to the children that she will bear. The social prestige of a married woman is directly influenced by the amount of the progeny price that has been paid on her account.

Another way to obtain a wife and the rights to her future children is to work for the bride's family — suitor service. Scattered tribes in all parts of the world (77 out of 565 cultures) have been found to require service in the bride's household as the price the groom must pay.

The opposite of progeny and suitor service is the custom requiring the bride to bring a dowry to the groom's family. This custom is based on the conception that the woman is going to be taken care of her entire life by the man's family, and relates to the patrilineal system in which lineage is traced only through the male's kinship system. In cultures in which descent is not vested exclusively in either line of kin, but rather through bilateral descent, an equivalent exchange of gifts between the families is an alternative possibility.

When familial or social disapproval blocks a fervently desired marriage, or when a marriage is planned with a distasteful partner, elopement (the act of running away secretly to get married) is a way out. Although elopement is a safety valve of escape from the dictates of formal customs, the status of elopement varies in different societies. In some societies a couples' elopement is ultimately recognized as a marriage, while in others there is never full acceptance by the family or the society. In such cases, couples in love may choose the only way left open for them — to commit double suicide, known in the past as "love suicide" in Japan, Korea, and China.

Post-Marital Residence

In societies in which newly married couples customarily live with or near kin, several residence patterns may be established. If the married couple lives with or near the husband's parents (67 percent of the total World Ethnographic Sample), it is described as *patrilocal residence*; if the married couple lives with or near the wife's parents (15 percent of the sample societies), it is called *matrilocal residence*; if the married couple can live with or near the parents of either side (7 percent) it is addressed as *bilocal*; and if the newly married couple lives apart from the relatives of both spouses, choosing a new place of their own (5 percent of the world sample), it is described as *neolocal residence* — the most common practice of our present industrialized and urbanized society.

The significance of post-marital residential choice is obvious, as it affects the pattern of kinship relations as well as the power distribution and respective roles of the spouses. For example, if the wife stays and the husband leaves the natal family after marriage (matrilocal residence), as observed in Truk, Micronesia, the husband has to disrupt the bonds he has established with his original kinship group and psychologically work out his split loyalties to the family of his origin and his wife's family. One reason for frequent divorces in Truk is the difficulty a husband has in establishing his authoritative role at the matrilocal residence (Tseng and Hsu, 1986).

Why do societies practice different patterns of residence? As elaborated by Haviland (1978), the prime determinants of residence are ecological circumstances. If the man's role in subsistence is predominant, patrilocal residence is the likely result. In contrast, matrilocal residence is a likely result if ecological circumstances make the role of the woman predominant in subsistence, as is found most often in horticultural societies, where political complexity is relatively undeveloped and cooperation among women is important.

Bilocal residence is particularly well-suited to situations where the cooperation of more people is needed, but where resources are limited. Because one can join either the bride's or the groom's family, family membership is flexible, and one can go where the resources look best.

Neolocal residence occurs where the independence of the nuclear family is emphasized. Since most economic activity occurs outside the family in industrialized modern societies, and it is important for individuals to be able to move where jobs are to be found, neolocal residence is the pattern best-suited to this type of society.

Kinship System and Descent Group

A kinship system is a system of terms used to classify different kin. It refers to the totality of relationships based on blood and marriage that links individuals, through a web of rights and obligations, to the kinds of groups formed in a society on the basis of kinship. Although kinship always rests on some kind of biological relationship, as explained by Nanda (1980), kinship systems are actually cultural phenomena — the ways in which a society classifies kin may or may not be based on an accurate assessment of biological ties. The functions of kinship are necessary for the continuation of society. Kinship serves to provide continuity between generations; it also defines a universe of others on whom an individual may depend for aid in a variety of ways. Although kinship is of great importance in structuring social relations and as a basis for the formation of groups in a society, there are also nonkin groups which are based on age, sex, or other factors. These groups include voluntary associations such as those observed in urbanized societies, which are also important in building social groups.

Societies differ in the categories of relatives they distinguish and the principles by which kin are classified. Generation, relative age, sex, and lineality versus collaterality are some of the categories usually considered. Anthropologists have identified six basic systems of kinship terminology: Hawaiian, Eskimo, Iroquois, Omaha, Crow, and Sudanese. These different systems of kinship terminology reflect the kinds of kin groups that are considered most important.

In most societies, where kinship connections are important, there is a rule of descent which defines how individuals are affiliated with sets of kin. As stated by Ember and Ember (1973), *patrilineal descent* affiliates an individual with kinsmen of both sexes through the males. In each generation, children belong to the kin group of the father and carry the father's family name; a person's lineage is traced through the line of grandfather, father, son, and grandson. *Matrilineal descent* affiliates an individual with kinsmen only through females; thus, children belong to the mother's kin group and lineage is traced through the line of grandmother, mother, daughter, and granddaughter. *Ambilineal descent* affiliates an individual with kinsmen through either males or females, so that in the society some children belong to the kin group of the father and others to the kin group of the mother. Consequently, the descent groups show both female and male genealogical links.

The occurrence of different types of descent groups seems related to the dominant type of subsistence base. Patrilineal descent is most often associated with the subsistence base characterized by pastoralism, matrilineal descent with developed agriculture, and bilateral descent with hunting and gathering (Schneider and Gough, 1961).

According to Hoebel (1972), patrilineal organization is the most frequent type of descent system, constituting about 45 percent of all societies in the world (Bourguignon and Greenbaum, 1968). The male members of a patrilineage (who constitute the male population of a single community) can trace their actual relationship through males to a common ancestor. Although societies with matrilineal descent (about 14 percent of the world sample) seem in many respects like mirror images of their patrilineal counterparts, they differ in one important way. As elaborated by Ember and Ember (1973), that difference has to do with who exercises authority in the matrilineal system. In patrilineal systems, descent affiliation is transmitted through males, and it is also the males who exercise authority in the kin groups. Consequently, in the patrilineal system the lines of descent and of authority converge. In a matrilineal system, however, the line of descent passes through females but females rarely exercise authority in their kin groups. Thus, unlike the patrilineal system, the lines of authority and descent do not converge. This presents somewhat of a problem. If the men go too far away from their parents' homes, it will be difficult for them to return to exercise authority in their own kin groups; thus, the decision-makers of the kin group are scattered as they live with their wives' kin groups. In most matrilineal societies, the solution seems to be that males move away to live with their wives but usually do not move too far away, often marrying women who live in the same area. Thus, matrilineal societies tend not to be locally exogamous as patrilineal societies do.

The emphasis of the lineal link of a person and family in its extreme form is expressed in the phenomenon of ancestor worship. Great importance is placed on being able to identify the linkage of the family. It is expected that the deceased will be worshipped and taken care of spiritually by their descendants. In return, the deceased will protect and bless their descendants. Within such a system, it is extremely important to have offspring to ensure the success of the lineage. If continuity is threatened, various efforts will be undertaken to prevent such extinction. For example, a husband is permitted to have another wife to assure the bearing of children if the primary wife has failed to produce offspring.

In a patrilineal society, such as that of Chinese, Japanese, or Koreans, a man is selected to "marry in" to the bride's family as an "adopted son-in-law" if the bride is an only child—her marriage will deprive the bride's family of origin from having descendants carry on the lineage as all the children borne by her will carry the groom's family name and become his descendants. If it is the norm for a man to "bring in" a wife to his family, and it is considered culturally important to have descendants to carry on a man's lineage, then the practice of "adopted son-in-law" will be perceived psychologically by most men as undesirable since it implies that the man has to give up his "man's" right and duty to have descendants from his own side. However, since there are many women without siblings, efforts will usually be made to find a potential candidate to "marry in" as an adopted son-in-law. Usually the candidate is not the eldest son of a family, as the eldest son is considered the primary person with an absolute duty to have descendants to continue the family line. Since most men tend to shy away from becoming an adopted son-in-law, the bride's family may offer irresistible inducements, such as land, in order to attract candidates. Sometimes these marriages do not work out well and the husband is placed in a "parasite" position in the bride's family. He may also feel he has no authority as a man.

Another peculiar custom still observed occasionally in Taiwan is ghost marriage, which is rooted in the problem of the descent system, as pointed out by Li (1968). Ghost marriage refers to a marriage that takes place between a living person and a deceased person—usually between a man and the ghost of a deceased woman. According to the traditional Chinese patrilineal system, all women eventually belong to their husband's lineage after marriage. After their death, they will be worshipped by the descendants of the husband's family. However, a problem arises if a woman dies before she marries, for there is no room for a girl in her family of origin as she is expected to become a member of her husband's lineage. In other words, in the system of ancestor worship, if a woman dies before marriage, she will become a "wandering ghost" who is unattached to any lineage and therefore has no descendants who will care for and worship her. If frequent undesirable events occur in the woman's family, they might be interpreted by a fortune-teller as a sign that the deceased unmarried woman feels neglected by her family and is causing them trouble. In such circumstances, an effort will be made to marry the ghost of the deceased unmarried woman to a living man so that she will belong to a proper lineage and family.

Household and Family Structure

Household refers to all the persons who live in one house. Usually it implies that they are related either by marriage or blood and they share the work, financial responsibilities, and food. Although a household may be equivalent to a "family," such a description may not always hold true from a cross-cultural perspective. For instance, as described by Berkner (1972), nearly half of all the peasant households in eighteenth century Austria included some nonfamily members such as servants and lodgers. Servants were employed by the family in whose house they dwelt, sharing their food and shelter as part of their wages. Lodgers were also residents, but were not usually steady employees of the householder, and paid for their lodgings. Therefore, in a strict sense, a household consists of more than a family.

On the other hand, a family may imply more than a household — as in the case of the Chinese. As pointed out by Li (1982) and Cohen (1976), the Chinese word *Jia* usually refers to the nuclear family but may also mean a family in a larger sense, including an extended family or even a clan having the same family name. In contrast, the Chinese word *fu* refers to a household. In certain circumstances, a nuclear family may be split into more than one household (*fu*) at different geographic locations for occupational or educational reasons — for example, if the husband is working in another city and some grown-up children are studying at schools away from home. Therefore, at times, several households will compose a nuclear family, and many families may compose a clan-like organization, which is still literally and conceptually addressed as a "family." Thus, the boundary of household and family may not overlap exactly in some societies as is customarily believed.

In spite of such complications, several terms address various forms of a household. *Nuclear family* refers to a family composed of the basic family members: parents and their (unmarried) children. It is the most frequently observed form of a household in most industrialized societies. If a household is composed of a nuclear family plus the parent (or parents) of either the husband or wife, it is called a *stem family*. If in addition to the stem family, a spouse's unmarried siblings are living with them, it is referred to as a *joint family*. If the married siblings (and their children, if any) are living in the same household (usually with the presence of their parent or parents) it is recognized as an *extended family*.

The nuclear family may exist as a relatively isolated and independent unit, as it does in our industrialized society, or it may be embedded within the larger kinship units. As pointed out by Nanda (1980), the independent nuclear family is considered ideal in only a small percentage of the world's societies, primarily among hunters/gatherers and in modern industrialized societies — both of which require a high degree of mobility.

In contrast, the extended family is clearly adaptive under certain kinds of economic and social conditions. Murdock's survey (Nanda, 1980) indicated that the extended family prevails in all types of predominantly cultivating societies. The main advantages of this type of family are economic; the extended family can provide a larger number of workers than the nuclear family. In stable agricultural societies, ownership of land becomes important. A system in which land is subdivided into small parcels through inheritance becomes relatively unproductive. The extended family is a way of keeping the land intact, which produces more security for the family. There is also the value of companionship as daily activities are carried out jointly by a number of kin working together. The extended family also provides a sense of participation and dignity for older family members.

In spite of these advantages of the extended family for the aged, in practice, the lives of individuals past their prime are not always enviable. For example, in Fiji, as noted by Sahlins (1957), the ideal is that an old father should be properly cared for by his younger brothers and sons. Actually people say: "His time is up" — thus an old man sinks into a pitiable position, literally waiting to die.

The extended family system in China has been idealized and described as if it were the prevalent style of household in all of traditional China. In reality, the extended family household was observed primarily among the affluent; census surveys of households conducted about a half century ago revealed that the average size of a household was about 5-6 persons (Chen and Rai, 1979). The census indicated that most households consisted of the nuclear family or at most the stem family.

However, it should be pointed out that although the household was seldom composed of the extended family, in daily living the relations among kin and family clans were crucial and there were frequent and close interactions between married siblings functioning within the framework of the extended family kinship. The extended family system could therefore be termed functional relations rather than actual household structure.

One-parent families, particularly female-headed households, are found to be widespread in various cultures. Bilge and Kaufman (1983), when examining this type of family cross-culturally, took the view that the one-parent family is neither pathological nor inferior. They concluded that whether or not the single-parent household becomes a personal or social disaster depends upon the availability of sufficient material resources and supportive social networks, as well as the culturally-structured attitudes toward it. However, in some societies such as ours, there are no adequate institutionalized support systems for children of single-parent families, and the social conditions of genuine single-parent families are generally not as good as those of two-parent families. This situation is also reported as being true in European societies in Denmark (Koch-Nielsen, 1980) and France (Lefaucheur, 1980).

Associated with the increase of divorce and remarriage, the number of stepfamilies is rising remarkably in our society. As pointed out by Visher and Visher (1982), stepfamilies differ structurally from biological families in several ways. Namely, all stepfamily members have experienced important losses, all members come with past family histories, parent-child bonds predate the new couple relationship, there is a biological parent elsewhere (either living or deceased), children often are members of two households, and no legal relationship exists between stepparent and stepchild. Thus, from a developmental point of view, stepfamilies need to work on the reintegration of the family.

Family Authority

In many societies, the authority and power to make major decisions in family matters is explicitly given to a particular family figure. A *patriarchal system* refers to a family in which the authority is customarily delegated to the father (or grandfather). He alone has the final say about family issues. In general, a patriarchal system comes about in association with patrilineal and patrilocal systems in developing man-centered societies (Pelzel, 1970).

In contrast, in a *matriarchal system*, the mother (or grandmother) has the privilege of making major decisions in the family, such as the division of property and land usage. However, as pointed out by anthropologists, in actuality no true matriarchal societies exist, and chances are good that none have ever existed. Even in societies organized around women that follow matrilineal descent/inheritance and matrilocal residence, power tends to be held by males in the female lineage. Power is usually held and exercised by the women's brothers (the maternal uncle from the viewpoint of "ego").

In practice, many families' decisions tend to be made jointly by parents of both sides, a *biarchal system*. There are many women in any society who are as strong, intelligent, and ambitious as their husbands, if not more so. Even in the most patriarchal societies wives may influence their husbands indirectly in making major domestic decisions, and strong wives may dominate their weak husbands. Therefore, it is important to recognize the cultural pattern that is emphasized in public while, at the same time, closely examining the mode that is actually practiced in private.

The egalitarian family implies an equal and complementary distribution of power and authority between husband and wife. The Western family—particularly in the United States—has tended for many decades toward an egalitarian form of family membership. In some families, the children are frequently invited to participate in discussions and decision-making in significant family matters; these families may be termed *democratic systems* in terms of power execution.

Primary Axis

From the perspective of loyalty and affection bonds, a particular dyad may be molded culturally as the prominent and recognizable axis in some family systems. The axis may be built on husband-wife, father-son, mother-son, or brother-sister dyads. The presence of any particular primary axis can be recognized only when conflict and competition occurs between different dyads in a family. For example, if an open conflict develops between a man's relationship with his wife (husband-wife axis) and his obligations toward his parents (parent-child axis), placing him in a position where he must make a choice to fulfill an obligation to one while sacrificing an obligation to the other, then the axis that is the primary one will become the most explicit. Such a primary axis is referred to as an obligation bond.

Based on this concept of a primary axis, psychological anthropologist F. L. K. Hsu (1972) has hypothesized that the different emphases of the primary dyad will result in different family systems which have specific, varied influences on the individuals reared in them. Consequently, many characteristic thought- and behavior-patterns shown by family members can be attributed to the existence of different primary bonds within a family system.

For instance, Hsu speculated that within patrilineal, patrilocal, and patriarchal family systems exemplified by the majority of the Asian peoples, including the Chinese, Japanese, Koreans, Thai, and others, the most elevated dyad is the *father-son* dyad. Characteristics associated with the father-son dyad are inclusiveness of other individuals and continuity, over generations, as well as mutual dependence and mutual obligation.

Although the Hindu societies of India (and possibly the Moslem groups of this subcontinent as well) also exemplify patrilineal, patrilocal, and patriarchal family systems, their most important structural relationship is that of the *mother-son* dyad. Associated with this primary dyad are the attributes of exclusiveness and discontinuity. As a continuation of the mother-son relationship, unilateral dependence is encouraged and dependence upon an all-answering figure becomes the pattern.

Among the majority of Africans south of the Sahara, kinship structure is dominated by the *brother-brother* dyad, across lines of descent, inheritance, and succession. The characteristics associated with such systems are horizontal orientation and vertical dissociation over the generations. Because of competition between siblings, men are perceived as being unreliable.

In contrast to these types, the kinship structure of the majority of Western peoples (i.e., of European origin) is usually patrilineal, patrilocal, or neolocal, and in many instances, nominally patriarchal with an egalitarian family. The most elevated dyad is *husband-wife*. The characteristics attributed to the husband-wife dyad are exclusiveness of other individuals and discontinuity over generations. Individualism and self-reliance are emphasized and the independence of the children is valued.

Although Hsu's way of categorizing and analyzing the family systems that exist in various parts of the world is subject to criticism, his attempt to explore the potential relation between the family systems and patterns of life associated with each type of primary dyad is nonetheless deserving of further investigation and validation. Awareness of a family's primary axis will at least help us understand the dynamics of behavior observed in that family.

Alternative Ways of Forming a Family

Group Marriage

Group marriage refers to a special marital form in which a relatively small number of adults live together, share labor, goods, and services, raise children in common, and engage in promiscuous sexual relations. In spite of speculation that group marriages may have been relatively common throughout history, group marriages are not customarily observed in any society. According to Ember and Ember (1973), the Marquesans of the South Pacific and the Toda seem to have developed group marriages out of polyandrous marriages. For example, if a polyandrously married wife has not produced a child, another wife may be co-opted with a view to remedying the situation.

Several decades ago, small-scale group marriages were observed in various parts of the United States. Despite the fact that some people are quite devoted to this kind of living arrangement, such a special form of family does not usually remain viable for any considerable length of time. As Ellis (1974) points out, a group of four or more adults of both sexes find it difficult to live together harmoniously. Problems involving sexual or other relationships are almost certain to arise among the group's members. In our present society, fewer females than males appear to be interested in group marriage.

Collective Commune

The collective commune as the basic living organization has been observed in different parts of the world. Communes may emerge as a result of political ideology, as in communist societies, or as a reaction to sociocultural change. As indicated by Shey (1977), Western society has witnessed much social unrest and change. Traditional norms and values are being challenged and a liberalizing trend in social relationships questions the basic foundation upon which society rests – the nuclear family. Twenty years ago, the so-called commune movement arose in the United States as well as in Denmark. The movement attracted literally thousands of predominantly younger followers; most communes, however, failed after a short time. Investigation revealed that poor planning, a general lack of organization, over-idealism, excessive individualism, diversity of the members, and internal conflict were among the major factors that led to the dissolution of the communes in both countries.

The kibbutz community in Israel, a collective agricultural commune, has special historical significance and is the type most frequently studied and reported on in scientific literature. According to Miller (1969), about 80,000 people in Israel live on 230 collective communes known as kibbutzim, in which there is no private ownership. The first kibbutz appeared as a unit of Jewish land settlement in the Jordan Valley. It was settled by a group of young unmarried Jews who emigrated from Eastern Europe. They believed that only through a national revival would a dignified future life be assured for the Jewish population of Israel. The plan evolved for the kibbutz family called for a relationship of complete equality between husband and wife and for the economic independence of women. It was also felt that children should be reared and educated outside of the family. They felt that such an environment would engender in children values of group loyalty rather than the egotisms produced in the family setting. As a result, children in a kibbutz do not live with their parents, but live instead in the "children's house" where they are organized according to age group. Full responsibility for their care is undertaken by the children's nurse who acts as a housemother.

Although the inhabitants of kibbutzim comprise only 4 percent of the total Jewish population of Israel, they have played a cardinal role in the resettlement of the country, in its defense, and in the establishment of its social values and institutions. From a scientific point of view, these collective communes illustrate an alternative way to organize life which has an interesting impact on the life of the family.

SUMMARY

From the review of various patterns of family systems that exist around the world, it becomes clear that the patterns of family systems tend to be molded by economic, political, and sociocultural factors outside the family system rather than determined merely by emotional and psychological factors within the family. It is also clear that the family system with which we are most familiar and which we tend to view as the "typical" form of family life in our contemporary society is merely a minority pattern rather than a prevalent form when compared with other family systems that exist around the world.

Based on our own projections, we have pointed out numerous ungrounded past speculations by laymen as well as professionals about the nature of the family system. For example, promiscuous group marriages were not necessarily the historical prototype for the monogamous marriage. The patrilineal family did not develop evolutionarily after the matrilineal family. Also, the family has not been inclusively the "extended" one in traditional times in contrast to the "nuclear" family of contemporary times. Finally, various family systems have developed not through simple chance or fixed evolutional paths, but rather as basic responses to different social environments as well as solutions to the problems of the psychological world in which they exist. Therefore, it is essential for us to understand various family systems from the point of view of how they function. It is also useful to understand the advantages and disadvantages, or assets and problems, inherent within each system, as this knowledge can broaden our perspectives as well as that of our patients.

Since many kinds of family systems exist among humankind, it is also important that we, as family researchers or therapists, should have a culturally-oriented understanding of the family, utilizing broad perspectives which go beyond the typical family pattern we are familiar with. Theoretically, by examining the diversity of these variations, we will be able to develop more relevant and valid concepts of the family for universal application. Practically, by knowing the different systems of family, we will be able to deal with families of various cultural backgrounds in terms of assessments as well as intervention. After becoming oriented with the cultural aspects of family systems, we are ready to go further and review the cross-cultural aspects of family development and function.

Chapter 2

Culture and Family Development

Families, like individuals, go through predictable growth stages that can be understood both in terms of the development of the individual family members and of the family as a whole. Family development is one important way to understand the family as it keeps the family in focus throughout its history and highlights critical periods of personal and family growth (Duvall, 1971; McGoldrick and Carter, 1980). Family researchers have conventionally conceptualized the process of family development with the landmarks of establishment of a marriage, bearing and rearing of children, and launching of young adults to begin their own families.

It is obvious that this way of dividing the stages of family development is based on the assumption that the nuclear family follows a universal pattern and that bearing and raising children is the main focus of family life. This perspective is convenient, but also limited, as the life of the family is more complicated, particularly from a cultural viewpoint. In some cultures, the family is not nuclear in structure, marriage goes beyond monogamy, and developmental stages do not merely evolve around the production of the next generation. Before we discuss cross-cultural differences of family development patterns let us first discuss the cultural factors that may critically affect the milestones of family development.

CRITICAL ISSUES CONCERNING
FAMILY DEVELOPMENT MILESTONES

Premarital Interactions

Although it is customarily thought that the starting point of the family life cycle is when a couple marries, it is more appropriate to

22

discuss the couple's relationship (which may include premarital sexual relations and premarital marriage arrangements) even before marriage takes place.

Premarital Sexual Relations

Attitudes toward premarital sexual relations vary greatly between different cultural groups. Anthropologist Hoebel (1972) tells us that, taking human societies as a whole, the majority accept premarital sexual experimentation without serious disapproval. According to Bourguignon and Greenbaum (1968), of the 863 societies in Murdock's *Ethnographic Atlas*, 67% impose little restrictions on premarital sexual behavior. The greatest proportion of permissive societies is found in the Pacific areas, while the most restrictive area of the world is the Circum-Mediterranean, the home of the Semites and Muslims.

The course of premarital heterosexual development in the Marshalls of Micronesia provides an illustration of how the cycle of marriage may start in a unique way (Iamen, 1986). In contrast to societies with strict taboos governing both speech and behavior linked with sex or excretory functions, the Marshallese in the atoll society have few inhibitions about sexual intercourse. Sexual activities begin around the age of puberty. After youthful sexual experiences with several partners, young men and women are ready for a somewhat more serious love relationship. A young man goes to live with a young woman and they begin relations of *koba* (cohabitation) without religious or legal ceremonies. If the woman becomes pregnant and gives birth, her parents raise the baby. If the couple decides to separate, no legal measures or rituals are involved. Many young couples have several more-or-less temporary *koba* arrangements before settling down with a more permanent mate. Thus, there is no clear point in life when the marriage (as defined in the customary sense) starts, as there is in other societies. In this pattern of life, there is no stigma attached to being an "illegitimate" child or an "unmarried" mother. A young girl with babies does not jeopardize her future mate relations; in fact, as children are treasured, the young women with children usually have a better chance of remarrying than those without. This example from the Marshalls supports anthropologist Malinowski's (1931) viewpoint that premarital activity may function among people with a simple lifestyle to prepare young people for marriage. It can provide an intimate test of the compatibility of mating pairs before marriage, with all its social and economic responsibilities.

Premarital Marriage Arrangement

In a society where marriages are arranged by the parents, marriage negotiations may occur very early, even before the prospective partners have grown up. In extreme cases, as in early China, marriages were sometimes arranged by the family before the children were born. This type of marriage was called "marriage by pointing to the abdomen" in Chinese operas. In these dramas the implication was that by pointing to the abdomen of a pregnant women, a marriage was promised to take place between two families sometime in the future after the as-yet-unborn child came of age.

The practice of a special form of marital arrangement, called "little bride" (or adopted daughter-in-law) in Taiwan in the past, was studied and described by American anthropologist Wolf (1966). In this form of marriage, the parents of a little girl—seldom more than three years old and often less than a year old—would dress her in the traditional red wedding costume and send her to live in her future husband's home. She would then be raised, trained, and educated as an adopted child by her parents-in-law, and grow up together with her future groom. The actual marriage ceremony would not take place until she was old enough to fulfill her duties as a wife; in the meantime, the prospective couple would be free to behave as though they were siblings. As the bride and groom are raised as members of the same family, experiencing a prolonged period of intimate association, a unique opportunity to examine the theory of the incest taboo and study how the shared childhood may affect their later marital life is provided. According to Wolf's survey, most of the grooms (after growing up) were very reluctant to marry such sister-like brides. In fact, out of 19 arranged marriages between 1910 and 1930 (when such patterns of marriage had already been officially prohibited), in 15 cases the young couple refused to go through with the match. As for those couples whose marriages were arranged in an earlier period when there was less chance to object to such an arrangement, Wolf found that the husbands tended to visit prostitutes more frequently and were involved in extramarital affairs more often than husbands whose marriages had been arranged in an ordinary way. These observations indicate that there are potential obstacles to forming intimate husband-wife relations when the couple enters a conjugal union after being raised in a sibling-like environment.

Mate Selection and Arrangement

Although marriages are conventionally categorized as either arranged marriages or love marriages, in actuality such distinctions have limited application, as pointed out by Lebra (1978). For example, in Japan, the so-called arranged marriage often involves love generated prior to or subsequent to the arrangement, and love marriages usually go hand-in-hand with the process of arrangements. Nevertheless, such labelling is useful to elaborate two extreme ways for processing marriage formation, particularly concerning the major factors considered and emphasized in mate selection.

In so-called arranged marriages, the selection and decision of the subjects are carried out mainly through a third party, such as a professional or amateur matchmaker. In extreme cases, the potential marital partners may never have the opportunity to meet until the wedding ceremony. In traditional China, when the binding of women's feet was still practiced and when women with small (bound) feet were considered to be better educated and more cultivated, the matchmaker would ask to see the bride-to-be's feet which were exposed under a Chinese style door screen which hid the body and face of the bride-to-be. Thus, a responsible matchmaker could confirm that the candidate bride certainly had small bound feet and so report to the potential groom's family. Even the matchmaker, however, would be denied a glimpse of the girl's face. Under such circumstances, the background and origin of the families, the physical condition of the candidates, and the absence of particular physical deformities or mental problems would be major concerns of the parents. The point of the marriage was for the whole family to gain a new member to produce the next generation. Whether the young people were interested in each other or felt affection for each other were not considerations. It was assumed that a marital relationship as husband and wife would eventually develop after the marriage took place. Associated with such customs of arranged marriage was the belief that most young couples would not need to worry about developing heterosexual social skills in searching for mates and competing with eligible peers. Also, as marriage would be almost automatically arranged by other people when the young person reached a certain age, most of the young people would be able to get a mate and very few would be left unmarried. Further, as pointed out by Gupta (1976) about the situation in India, since arranged marriages are made for the continuity and unity of the extended family, any possible problems that emerged from the couple's marital life became problems for the whole family, and would be addressed by the whole family rather than by the couple themselves.

With the introduction of modern communication media, greater physical mobility, and concomitant changes in the village economy, Dissanayake (1982) reported that the institution of marriage broker in Sri Lanka began to lose its importance. Instead, its function was taken over by the modern newspapers, which carry many matrimonial advertisements. The same phenomenon is observable in India (Kurian, 1976). Interestingly, despite technological changes and socioeconomic development, the traditional concerns about caste, horoscopes, and dowry are still paramount for mate selection.

In contrast to arranged marriages, the selection of the partner in love marriages is in the hands of the young people themselves. They have to learn how to search and how to select an appropriate partner for marriage. In general, affection between the partners is the major concern, although the personal background of the partner as well as that of the family may also be taken into consideration — either consciously or subconsciously — but with relatively lower priority.

An ideal process of mate selection may progress through the steps of acquaintance, dating, mutual exploration of interests and compatibility of a potential mate, and establishment of a stable and lifelong relationship. Yet the opportunity for going through such experiences is not necessarily available in societies even when autonomous mate selection is preferred. As revealed by Khatri's (1980) analysis of pre-1912 fiction in India, most of the progressive stages of exploration of a potential mate are lacking in Hindu self-selected betrothals, since unrestricted personal mobility and uninhibited interaction with members of the opposite sex are taboo in traditional Hindu society. Consequently, when chance clandestine contacts of two concupiscent adolescents of the opposite sex take place, a flood of love impulses may be released.

Similar situations can be observed in the past among the Chinese. Analysis of man-woman relations as described in classic traditional Chinese opera stories (Hsu and Tseng, 1974) has shown that "love at first sight" was a common occurrence in Chinese traditional society, where encounters between young men and women were not culturally permitted and therefore young people had little experience in relating to persons of the opposite sex. Regarding possible relations between family structure, type of mate-selection, and the cultural endorsement of romantic love, Lee and Stone (1980) have reviewed data from a sample of 117 societies. They found that autonomous mate selection based on romantic attraction is more likely to be institutionalized in societies with nuclear family systems than in those in which families are typically extended.

As indicated by Udry (1966), a sociological survey disclosed that despite the American idealization of self-selection of mates based on romantic love, most young Americans marry someone who lives near them, whose family status is not too different from their own, and whose educational level is similar to their own. This finding represents a considerable departure from the myth of romantic love and the values of individualism and egalitarianism. It also means that an individual's choice of a mate is influenced by a series of factors in social organization.

Childbearing

Fertility Behavior

Hassen (1980) surveyed cultural differences in fertility behavior and beliefs among three ethnic groups — Chinese, Malay, and Indian groups in Singapore — to illustrate how cultural factors affect fertility behavior among different racial groups living in the same society. Results indicated that among the Chinese, sexual intercourse is linked with "energy" or life-forces: an over-extension of one's sexual energies could shorten one's life. Women, in general, are not expected to express sexual desire. Traditional Chinese society encouraged the formation of large families as the number of children in a family was linked to the notion of prosperity.

In contrast, the Malay group regarded sexual intercourse as a pleasurable experience for both men and women. Despite this, premarital and extramarital intercourse is forbidden, principally on religious grounds. Malay families also prefer several children — a house without children is said to be without good fortune from the gods.

The Indian group believed that men are not supposed to have strong sex drives and women should not have any sexual desires at all. Indulging in frequent sexual intercourse is discouraged.

Among most of the modernized societies, the number of children in a family has decreased substantially over the past decades. Based on the concern that an increase in voluntary childlessness is likely to lead to extremely low fertility rates in the United States, Blake (1979) conducted a Gallup survey of voting-age adults in 1977 about American attitudes toward childlessness. He found that there is a strong consensus that childless couples do not have an advantaged status. Although offspring are not regarded as economic investments, they are viewed as being socially instrumental — not solely as consumption goods. Children are viewed as giving meaning to life, providing women with important status, and as a means of guarding against loneliness in old age. By examining the relationship between voluntary childlessness and marital adjustment in the United States, Housekenecht (1979) revealed that women who were childless by choice and women with children differed significantly in their overall marital adjustment. However, the difference was comparatively small and resulted mainly from variations in the area of "cohesion," one of four components in Spanier's Dyadic Adjustment Scale, which also includes the components of "consensus," "satisfaction," and "affection expression."

Abortion

The ethical aspects of abortion have been controversial in the United States in the past decade. Ebaugh and Haney (1980) disclosed that while there has been increasing liberalization of attitudes toward legalized abortion in the past 15 years in the United States, as early as 1975 the trend began to reverse and attitudes became slightly more conservative, with the reversal becoming more pronounced in 1978. They reported that several studies in the 1960's presented evidence indicating that contrary to what might be expected, younger people were more opposed to abortion than older ones. By 1972, however, younger people had become significantly more liberal in their attitudes than older groups. From the point of religious groups, it was found that Jews are distinctly liberal in their attitudes — even more so than those without any religious group. In general, Protestants are slightly more liberal than Catholics.

Attitudes toward and the practice of abortion varies greatly among societies of different cultures. For example, in many societies (Japan, Korea, and the Philippines are examples in Asia) abortion has been practiced routinely as a way of controlling childbirth, even though such practices may not be legal (Singer, 1975). In contemporary China, in order to prevent the expected population explosion, abortion is used as a legalized method for carrying out family planning. It is estimated that many women in China have at least two or three abortions during their reproductive period.

Pregnancy Taboo

Bearing children becomes a serious matter if the demand to maintain or expand the population is high while the methods and facilities assuring the success of childbearing are limited. In order to cope with anxiety-causing situations during pregnancy, rituals and taboos have been elaborated and practiced in certain societies. In early Micronesia, from the time a woman became pregnant, she was guarded at night and outside the house from ghosts or spirits. During pregnancy and for varying periods after childbirth, sexual intercourse between husband and wife was forbidden to assure the health of the fetus and the mother. The wife returned to her family of origin during her pregnancy. The husband's sisters assumed her household chores. The husband could visit his wife as often as he wished and usually brought nourishing food to his pregnant wife, but physical relations were prohibited. The practice of sexual abstinence was continued even after the baby was born. Not until the baby reached a certain stage of development—when he/she was able to jump across a ditch or to hold its breath under the water, demonstrating its ability for survival—would the mother (and her grown-up "baby") be permitted to return to her husband's home and resume sexual activity. As soon as she became pregnant again, the same practice of separation and sexual abstinence would be repeated. Lengthy periods of sexual abstinence served to space out births and to improve both infant nutrition and maternal health, but also served to increase mistrust and suspicion between husband and wife. The theme of a husband's infidelity appears frequently in Micronesian folk stories (Tseng and Hsu, 1986).

Preference of Child's Sex

Williamson (1976) has suggested that parents may have a preference for either sons or daughters if children of one sex are considered to be more economically valuable or productive, perform a more important social function, or provide greater psychological rewards. Furthermore, children of one sex may be preferred when there is strict segregation by sex in the performance of economic, social, and psychological functions.

Despite the common image of male dominance in Latin America, the predominate family sex composition preference among Latino-Guatemalan men and women is for equal numbers of sons and daughters, as found by Pebley, Delgado, and Brineman (1980). This is consistent with the findings in Puerto Rico (Myers and Roberts, 1968) and Argentina (Inkeles and Smith, 1974) which indicate that sex preference is not widespread in Latin America.

In Asia, several societies strongly prefer having sons. Data collected in Taiwan show a clear inverse relationship between the desire to have an additional child or current use of contraceptives and the number of living sons (Freedman, Cooms, and Chang, 1972). In Korea as well, the number of living sons appears to strongly influence the use of contraceptives. Some of the factors contributing to the strong preference for male children among Korean wives are ancestor worship, lineage continuity, and security in old age (Lee, Ong and Lee, 1973).

In contrast, the evidence for Thailand suggests that most Thai couples lack a strong preference for sons (Prachuabmoh, Knodel and Alers, 1974). This trend is interpreted in terms of the social and cultural patterns characteristic of Thai families; there exist weak feelings for lineage and of ancestry and slight interest in descendants beyond living children or grandchildren (Blanchard, 1958). Marriage in Thailand frequently involves paying a bride price to the wife's parents. In rural areas, the newlywed couple usually resides with the wife's parents for at least an initial period following their marriage, thus adding the labor of the son-in-law to that of the household. In comparison to most other developing countries in Asia, in Thai society women play important economic roles (Sharp, 1970-71). However, a detailed study by Knodel and Prachuabmoh (1976), which compared the preferences of Thai husbands and wives concerning the sex of their children, revealed that considerable differences in both rural and urban samples exist. A noticeably strong preference for sons was evident in the husbands, in contrast to the rather moderate preference for sons expressed by the wives.

The situation in the Philippines varies by geographic location even in the same country. According to Stinner and Mader (1975), an emphasis on balance, or son-daughter equivalence, is strongest in metropolitan Manila. General egalitarianism exists in male-female roles; daughters carry the same obligations for parental support as do sons.

Sharply in contrast to this, son preference is highest in rural Mindanao and Sulu, due to the high concentration of Muslims as well as the pioneer environment, in which sons may be seen as providing the means to exploit a new and promising environment.

Khan and Sirageldin (1977) reported their findings from Pakistan, where they found strong son preferences in both husbands and wives.

Birth Order Consideration

Substantial evidence is available to suggest that parental expectations for their children vary from child to child, with the resulting parental behavior affecting the personality development of each child. As summarized by Stainton (1980), the first born is raised by parents inexperienced with each stage of development a child goes through. The eldest child therefore tends to develop a greater conscience as a result of being vigorously trained for an adult role by the parents. The first born child may be less affectionate and have lower self-esteem than his/her siblings, as well as more extreme psychological reactions to stress. The middle child may receive less attention from the parents and tends to develop the values of cooperation and responsibility, growing up in a relatively pressure-free environment. The youngest child tends to become the least studious, the least achievement-oriented, and the most peer-oriented.

From a cross-cultural perspective, some societies are more conscious of the birth order of children than other societies. Japanese parents are quite concerned about sibling order, particularly among boys. This is illustrated by a commonly practiced method of naming boys: The eldest son is often named *ta-ro*, literally meaning the first or great son; the second son is called *ji-ro*, meaning the second son; the third son *sabu-ro* (third), and the fourth son *yobo-ro* (fourth) and so on. By using a number as part of the name, the parents explicitly indicate each son's position in the birth order. By recognizing such obvious tendencies, Caudill (1963) studied the possible correlation between types of emotional disorders and the sibling order among Japanese. He reported that schizophrenia and obsessive neurosis are found to occur most frequently among eldest sons, while hysteria is most prevalent among youngest daughters.

Practice of Adoption

In a society where family succession and care of the aged parents are important, the custom of adoption is practiced among couples unable to have their own children. An adoptive child can be chosen from anywhere, but if blood ties are considered important, attempts will be made to secure a child from relatives so as to continue the bloodline. Adoptive parents may try to keep the fact of their child's adoption a secret, and such information may be kept from the child even after he/she reaches adulthood in fear that the child will not become as close as a blood related child would.

The practice of adoption observed in most of Micronesia has different implications. Micronesian families (particularly those in Belau) which already have five or six children of their own may still adopt two or three more. Adoption serves to strengthen and widen the family support system; for example, a family in need of help may look to the biological parents of their adopted child to provide assistance. The local saying, "To adopt a child is to fertilize the banana!" reflects this concept of increasing sources of support by expanding and tightening the family's resources. Adopted children may sometimes be treated even better than natural-born ones, thus causing tension and conflict between biological and adopted children in a family (Tseng and Hsu, 1986).

Child-Rearing

Cultural variations in child-rearing patterns and their impact on child development attracted substantial interest among behavioral scientists at the beginning of the century. Many investigations were carried out, focusing on different cultural groups. Whiting and Whiting's (1975) systematic investigation and comparison of child-rearing patterns in six countries (India, Japan, Kenya, Mexico, the Philippines, and the United States) and Mead's (1928) investigation of Samoa, both contributed to our understanding of the cultural aspects of child development in different social environments.

Concerning maternal care and infant behavior in Japan and America, anthropologists Caudill and Weinstein (1969) conducted a comparative study utilizing well-designed methodology. They selected a matched sample of 30 Japanese and 30 American three-to-four-month-old infants — equally divided by sex, all first borns, and all from intact middle-class families living in urban settings — and carried out an observational study in the homes of these infants from 1961 to 1964. In making observations, they used a time-sampling procedure; four observations were made each minute, two and one-half hours in the morning of the first day and two and one-half hours in the afternoon of the second day, leading to a total of 800 observations during five hours for each case. The behavior of both the infant and the caretaker (the mother) was recorded using coded categories during each observation period. Results of the overall observations were statistically analyzed. The findings indicated that the American infants were more happily vocal, more active, and more exploratory of their bodies and their physical environment than the Japanese infants. In direct relation to these findings, the American mother was found to engage in greater vocal interaction with her infant, thereby stimulating him/her to greater physical activity and exploration. The Japanese mother, in contrast, was found to be in greater physical contact with her infant, thereby encouraging physical quiescence and passivity in regards to the environment. The authors pointed out that the patterns of behavior learned by the infants correspond to the differing behavioral expectations faced by children growing into adulthood in each of the two cultures.

Objective observations were repeated at two additional points in the lives of these children — at 2-1/2 years of age, and 6 years of age. The results of the two follow-up observations showed the same cross-cultural behavioral differences in infants and mothers that were present in the first study (Caudill and Schooler, 1973). The cross-cultural differences in the behavior of the parents and the children mirrored each other at each of the age periods observed. The authors pointed out that based on such findings it is tempting to try to demonstrate a causal relationship between the parents' behavior and the children's behavior — a theory to be investigated by further studies.

Child-rearing in the commune setting of the kibbutz in Israel has been investigated by numerous behavior scientists. As described by Miller (1969), the kibbutz is a collective agricultural commune in which there is no private ownership. Rearing and education of the children are carried out outside of the family, in a "children's house" where the children live together. This is because kibbutz dwellers believe that the education of a child in a group environment engenders values of group loyalty rather than the egotistic attitude produced within the family setting.

The kibbutz mother spends a great deal of time with her infant in the common nursery during the first year. The toddler is then transferred to a new house with a group of other children and the full responsibility for the care of each group is given to a nurse, who also acts as their housemother. Because of its special social structure and method of child-rearing, child development in the kibbutz has been studied frequently. For example, since the child has emotional attachments to both biological mother and housemother, Rabin (1958) found that in comparison to infants from noncommunal villages in Israel, the kibbutz child tends to be retarded in his early ego development. By age 10, however, the kibbutz child's ego is no longer impaired. Nagler (1965) stressed that powerful pressures for conformity operate on the individual child in the kibbutz group, as he/she cannot "escape" to any other group. The threat of exclusion therefore arouses strong anxieties that may have lasting effects on the child's personality. Caplan (1953) observed that while kibbutz children below the age of five reveal a great deal of thumbsucking and aggressive behavior, they have a smoother adolescence and later become stable, cooperative, and brave.

Adolescent and Family

An adolescent has tremendous impact on other family members. The family members must recognize that the adolescent is entering adulthood and adjustments must be made to accommodate the new, upcoming adult role.

Initiation Ceremony

In many societies—particularly in Africa and the Pacific regions—initiation rites for adolescents are practiced about the time they reach puberty. These prescribed ceremonial events are mandatory and considered a part of the life cycle, indicating a transition in development and a change in the social role from childhood into adulthood. Based on their observations of the male initiation ceremony in Africa, anthropologists Whiting, Kluckhon, and Anthony (1958) hypothesized that such rites are associated with the cultural custom that young boys sleep with their mothers and the women practice postpartum sexual abstinence for more than a year. Thus the rite has functional implications—that is, it symbolically forces the young man to be separated from his mother and to enter his manhood. Later, Young (1962) reviewed the societies that practiced such ceremonies and pointed out that such initiation rites are actually associated with societies with strong male solidarity, usually observed in conjunction with the system of polygyny. Assurance of their sex role is very important in such societies (Hsu, 1977).

Regarding female initiation rites, Brown (1963) reviewed many societies that observed such ceremonies. He found that female initiation rites tend to occur in areas where the young girl continues to reside in her mother's home after marriage (matrilocal). The purpose of the rites appears to be an announcement of status change. Further, Brown pointed out that the few female initiation rites that subject the initiate to extreme pain occur in societies where conditions in infancy and in childhood result in a conflict of sex identity; thus, special measures must be taken to force both sexes to accept their respective roles. Finally, female initiation rites are found in those societies in which women make notable contributions to subsistence activities. Because of her future importance to the life of the society, the young girls are given special assurance of their competence through the rite.

In most of modern Western society, as well as some of the Eastern societies, the individually-oriented initiation rite for adolescents is no longer practiced. Instead, events such as birthday celebrations, the acquisition of a driver's license, high school proms, and graduation become substitute markers of approaching adulthood. These events are not family-oriented, but rather school or society-related.

Launching Grown-up Children

Associated with different cultural backgrounds, the autonomy of children and their departure from the family home is dealt with in various ways among different societies. In some societies there are no expectations for adolescents to become rapidly independent from parents and family, either psychologically or physically. In others, it is considered crucial that adolescents become autonomous emotionally as well as financially; they are required to physically leave their parental home in order to prove their maturity.

For example, the traditional Hindu family in an agricultural setting does not permit the offspring to leave the extended family household even after marriage or even after reaching middle age as long as the father is still alive. In many Asian societies, it is normal for unmarried children in their thirties to continue to live with their parents. In contrast, college-age children in the United States encounter peer pressure to move out on their own, even if they attend classes in the same town where their parents live. Almost all the parents of high school graduates feel that their children should get out of their house after the age of 18 — the time for launching!

Adulthood and Family

Work and Family Life

As pointed out by Skinner (1980), a significant influence on contemporary family living is the increased rate of (married) female participation in the labor force. The extent to which wives work outside of the home varies tremendously in different societies in association with socioeconomic and cultural background. For example, among the Asian countries of China, Japan, and Korea, Korea has the lowest rate of married women working outside of their home. Although young unmarried Korean women in cities or towns frequently work either in offices or factories, they are usually dismissed once they marry, since their employers prefer that married women do not work for them. Husbands do not want their wives employed outside the home either. Therefore, the rate of working housewives is as low as 15-20 percent despite the fact that housewives in a modern home do not have too much to do. As a matter of fact, the so-called "housewife's syndrome," labelled by Korean psychiatrists (Chang and Kim, 1988), describes those housewives who, bored and even depressed by their monotonous lives at home, came to visit mental health clinics with multiple-somatic complaints.

Although the rate of full-time working housewives in Japan has been increasing gradually, it is still estimated to be less than 20-30 percent. The factors behind this low rate are similar to those found in Korea; due to the fact that employers and husbands mostly do not welcome married females in the workforce, most women work only part-time if at all. Housewives' daily routine is therefore often described as "three meals plus taking a nap." In contrast, in Socialist China (in line with their political ideology), more than 95% of housewives work full-time outside of the home; the two-career family is therefore a majority norm (Tao, Qiu, Yu, Tseng, and Hsu, 1986).

Although it is difficult to determine accurately the number of married women in the workforce in the United States, it seems reasonable to assume that it has increased significantly in the past several decades. Whether the dual-career lifestyle produces stress and strain on the family has become of interest to social and behavioral scientists. By reviewing the existing literature, Skinner (1980) points out that strain in a dual-career family can be attributed to various problems of work and role overload. The identity dilemma for dual-career participants as a result of discontinuity between early gender-role socialization and current wishes or practices, the difficulty of meshing individual career cycles with the cycle of the family, and limitations on the availability of time to interact with friends and relatives all produce strain on the family.

As stated by Rapoport and Rapoport (1976), the presence or absence of children, as well as the current stage of the family life cycle, seem to affect the complexity of the dual-career lifestyle. By studying working wives, Orden and Bradburn (1969) found that a woman's choice of employment strained the marriage only when there were preschool children in the family. Ridley (1973) mentioned that tension in the marital relationship may occur when either partner becomes so highly involved in a job that family obligations are excluded. He found marital adjustment highest when the husband was "medium" and the wife "low" on job involvement. In spite of speculation that marital stress would be attendant if working wives had higher occupational prestige than their husbands, Richardson (1979) found no support for this hypothesis. Burke and Weir (1976) reported that while working wives were found to be more satisfied with their lives, marriages, and jobs than nonworking wives, husbands of working wives were less satisfied and performed less effectively than husbands of nonworking wives. However, when Booth (1977) replicated their study, he found that the wives' employment had little effect on the stress experienced by their husbands. Booth concluded that the dual-career husband may actually experience less stress than his conventional counterpart, since the added income and personal fulfillment of the wife outweigh temporary problems in lifestyle adjustment.

Retirement and Family Life

Family members' retirement from the workforce is a transitional change for the family. There are numerous investigations concerning the reactions of housewives to the retirement of their husbands, many resulting in controversial reports. Some studies have found that participation of husbands in household tasks contributes to the satisfaction of their wives (Kerckhoff, 1966), while other research suggests that newly shared control of homemaking activities may be problematical, with some wives actually resenting the increased presence of their husbands (Fengler, 1975). By interviewing thirty-six housewives whose husbands had recently retired from a university, Hill and Dorfman (1982) found that most of the housewives appreciated the new time available to do what they wanted (81%), the "increased companionship" (67%), and the increased participation of the husband in household tasks (28%). Nevertheless, some complained that their husbands did not have enough to do (31%); the problem of "too much togetherness" also surfaced (22%), particularly in the early years of retirement.

In contrast to male retirement, very little attention has been given to female retirement. By studying a small sample of female retirees from low to middle white-collar positions at a university, Szinovacz (1980) made several discoveries. Namely, the wife's retirement does not necessarily lead to changes in the couple's already rather traditional division of labor in the home, even though the wife may now perform her household tasks more thoroughly. Some women reported difficulties in "settling down" to household work. Finally, the amount of leisure time available to employed wives to develop hobbies and leisure time interests is often very restricted. Unless their husbands are able and willing to share some of their free time with their wives, the only alternative may be an increased involvement in household tasks. The recent increase in working housewives highlights the need for more extensive investigation of the impact of female retirement on spousal roles and marital adjustment.

Divorce and Remarriage

Separation, divorce, and remarriage are practiced differently in various cultures, with reactions to each of these happenings also varying from culture to culture (Albrecht, 1980; Yoder and Nichols, 1980; Tcheng-Laroche and Prince, 1983). In some societies, such as the Marshall Islands of Micronesia, separation and remarriage are viewed without prejudice, and in fact are so common that almost every couple goes through several such experiences. In other societies, these deviations from marriage occur only under exceptional circumstances and are regarded very negatively (Whitehurst, Frisch, and Serok, 1980; Jones, 1980). Divorce and remarriage may be discouraged for either religious or cultural reasons, leading to a very low divorce rate. In China, for example, the divorce rate is estimated to be less than one percent (Tao et al., 1986). Moskoff (1983) reported an extraordinary increase in the Soviet divorce rate, which has become the second highest in the world. He attributed the increase to alcoholism, adultery, and incompatability, as well as housing problems and the changing role of Soviet women.

Divorce and remarriage have far-reaching psychosocial effects on the life of a family (Spanier and Furstenberg, 1982). In the United States, the crude divorce rate doubled (2.5 to 5.3 per 1,000 population) between 1965 and 1979 (National Center for Health Statistics, 1980). From a demographic point of view (Prince-Bonham and Balswick, 1980), marital dissolution is negatively correlated to income and education and positively correlated with premarital pregnancy and multiple previous marriages.

Concerning adjustment to divorce, the period of separation has been described as the greatest period of stress during the divorce process (Hunt and Hunt, 1977). The degree of stress experienced during separation is related to legal problems, concern about children, family, jobs, and money (Salts, 1979); loss of familiar activities and habit systems, and the loss of a love object (Weiss, 1975). Three hundred newly-separated men and women were examined by Chiriboda, Roberts, and Stein (1978) and it was found that the men experienced a lower overall sense of well-being while the women experienced greater emotional turmoil, indicating that men and women react to separation in different ways. Research data indicated that divorce has greater negative economic impact on women than it does on men (Brandwein, Brown, and Fox, 1974); the fact that women usually receive custody of the children often contributes to financial difficulties and role strain. Indirect evidence suggests that from a psychological point of view, marital dissolution constitutes as severe a crisis for men as it does for women. Hetherington, Cox, and Cox (1978) reported that due to the loss of children and home and possessions, men spent less time at home and more time at work, often had a frenzied social and recreational life, experienced problems in everyday living, and underwent changes in self-esteem and identity.

Family and Aging

Adult Children and Aged Parents

Social and biological changes during the twentieth century have influenced the development of the distinctive stage in the family life cycle often referred to as the "empty-nest" or the "postparental" period (Borland, 1982). With life expectancy increasing from about 45 years at the turn of the century to about 70 years in the 1970's, the average couple can now expect to live alone without their children more than 15 years after the last child leaves home permanently, provided that they have a nuclear family household. Williams (1977) suggested that the empty-nest period will most likely have the most serious impact on women who are housewives, who are experiencing maternal role loss, who have been overprotective and overinvolved in the lives of their children, and who have believed that if they subjugated all their own needs to their children's needs, they would one day be content. In contrast to this, Back (1971) found that men may be affected more negatively than women when children leave. Freedom from family obligations may allow women greater ease in accepting themselves for what they are, while men may become more dependent on their work role, in which they have difficulty presenting their real self-image.

Borland (1982) brings out the socio-cultural and historical circumstances that may affect the impact of the postparental period on aged couples. By comparing different cohort groups at various times among several ethnic groups of women in the United States (White, Black, and Mexican-American), he hypothesized that a particular cohort of white middle-class women, born between 1920 and 1939, are more vulnerable to the development of the empty-nest syndrome. This group of women had been socialized by early life teaching and mother-role modeling to believe that in order to be feminine and happy, one had to be married and become a mother dedicated selflessly to family needs. In the years 1960-79, these women found that their education was outdated and their homemaking skills had little marketplace value. Furthermore, they were competing for jobs with experienced men and with the recently-educated and skilled younger women and young mothers of another cohort who were born later from 1940 to 1959. Therefore, different experiences of postparental adjustment were found among white women of different ages who faced different historical circumstances. Borland's theoretical position was that because of the unique set of social circumstances in which they live, with a unique set of family values and social norms concerning women's "proper" roles, the impact of emptiness will occur differently for cohorts of different ages and ethnicities.

In order to test a widely-held American myth that the elderly are isolated from their families in the United States, Shanas (1973) used national sample data to compare the family composition, living arrangements, and family contacts of persons aged 65 and over in the United States with those of the elderly in Denmark, Britain, Yugoslavia, Poland, and Israel. Surprisingly, Shanas found that in the United States, as in other countries, the elderly find their primary support in the family and kin network.

Considering television as playing an important role in the shaping of children's attitudes and beliefs, Holtzman and Akiyama (1985) made cross-national comparisons of the Japanese and American television programs most often watched by children. By evaluating the frequency and quality of the portrayals of older characters in the programs, they unexpectedly found that American television portrayed older characters more frequently and more positively than did Japanese television. In response to the methodological question regarding the validity of this type of investigation, they explained that the pervasive belief in the high status of elderly Japanese compared to their American counterparts may be a cultural myth.

Death and Widowhood

Becoming widowed—the difficult and sometimes devastating life transition associated with losing one's spouse to death—is a process encountered by an increasing proportion of the U.S. population. According to Balkwell (1981), in 1960 there were 9 million widowed persons in the United States; by 1975 this number had increased to 12 million, with 11 million of the widows being women. Twenty percent of American widows lived alone in 1940; this figure had increased to 50 percent by 1970 (Arling, 1976).

As stated by Balkwell (1981), the death of a spouse is an event that leads an individual through the transition from married person to widowed person, which includes the formation of a new self-identity and the taking on of new social roles. Without doubt the transition to widowhood varies greatly in different cultures, depending on family structure and attitudes toward widowhood. In a traditional Hindu family, if a husband dies his widow is expected to observe traditional customs of seclusion. She is not permitted to have encounters with any men except her father-in-law and brothers-in-law and is not allowed any social life outside of the family. No matter how young she may be, she is not permitted to remarry ever and is expected to care for her children and live the remainder of her life as a widow. Under such sociocultural restrictions, the depression which is a normal reaction to the loss of one's spouse may be aggravated and prolonged.

In contrast, after the death of a man in the Trobriand Islands of New Guinea, his wife is expected to observe a certain mourning period. Once this period has passed, a special ceremonial ritual is performed in public, during which the wife is expected to perform a dance and to remove her mourning clothes. Underneath her dark mourning attire, she wears a colorful dress to show that her life has started again and she can once again engage in social life. She is encouraged to participate in and conduct a normal family and social life, with the possibility of remarriage and starting a new family life cycle (Mathison, 1970).

FAMILY DEVELOPMENT AS A CYCLE

The stages of the family life cycle have been clearly defined and described for intact nuclear families in contemporary Western societies in terms of the landmarks of marriage, and bearing, raising, and launching children. However, in societies of different time periods (Berkner, 1972), ethnic groups (Falicov and Karrer, 1980), or geographic locations, the stages of family development are much less clearly defined and the changes in the phases of family life are more subtle. Also, as pointed out by Rossi (1972), increased longevity and improved birth control have led to remarkable changes in family development. Women now devote a smaller proportion of their adult life to the rearing of children; maternity has become a very small part of the average adult woman's life. Women have also achieved higher levels of education, which has facilitated more egalitarian relations between husbands and wives, and also increased the participation of married women in the labor force. These are remarkable changes in family life and development in contrast to a half century ago.

In order to demonstrate how the family life cycle can vary in different cultural settings, two examples from other culture groups are presented in addition to the "conventional" family life cycle described for the urban nuclear family in Western societies (Type A in Table 1).

As described by Collver (1963), a nuclear family's life in rural India (Type B) is blurred within the larger family, so that the family life cycle is much less clearly defined than in the United States. The extremely young age of marriage in the villages accentuates the couple's dependence on the joint household. This youthful marriage is followed by a long childbearing period and complicated by the high mortality rate of both the children and their young parents—the life expectancy of the couple barely runs to the end of the fecund period. More than half of the couples are dissolved by the death of the husband or wife before the spouse reaches age 45. This results in a large proportion of orphans and widows with dependent children who are supported by a larger kinship group. This situation certainly brings about a different pace and course of family development from that in the United States, where the family cycle goes through certain distinct states: a very short period from marriage to the first birth, a short childbearing period, a long period in which the children are growing up, and an extended postparental phase in which the parents live without any children in the home. In the Indian villages, the family cycle flows continuously with little disruption to mark transitions from one stage to another.

The family life cycle for the Marshallese in the past (Type C) is also unique. Life is characterized by premarital sexual encounters and several *koba* (living together) experiences with different partners—including bearing several children. Eventually, men and women begin a formal union with a particular partner. This formal union may or may not be permanent; frequently there will be disso-

TABLE 1

EXAMPLES OF FAMILY LIFE CYCLES IN DIFFRENT CULTURES

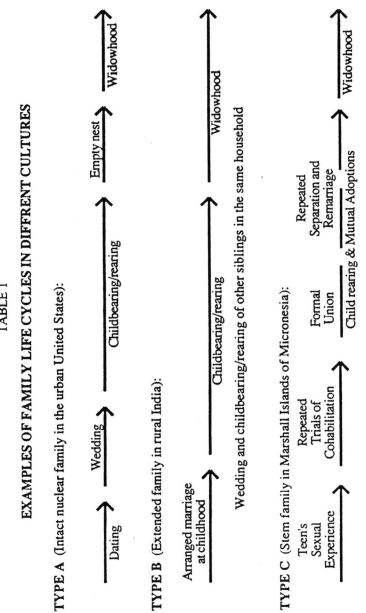

TYPE A (Intact nuclear family in the urban United States):

Dating → Wedding → Childbearing/rearing → Empty nest → Widowhood

TYPE B (Extended family in rural India):

Arranged marriage at childhood → Childbearing/rearing → Widowhood

Wedding and childbearing/rearing of other siblings in the same household

TYPE C (Stem family in Marshall Islands of Micronesia):

Teen's Sexual Experience → Repeated Trials of Cohabitation → Formal Union → Repeated Separation and Remarriage → Widowhood

Child rearing & Mutual Adoptions

lution and reunion of the couple's relations. While the couple continues to have children (an average of five to ten), to adopt some from others, and to give up some of their own for adoption by other relatives, their teenage children have already begun their own *koba* phase in the same household. These teenagers bear children who will be raised by their parents (as grandchildren). Under the same roof, there is a constant coming and going of family members, including the spouses, children, adopted children, teenagers living together, and relatives who come to live there temporarily. Thus, the membership of the household is frequently in flux. From the view point of a family cycle, there is no clear-cut starting point; premarital sexual encounters gradually evolve into a formal union. The childbearing phase is complicated by the practice of mutual adoptions between families as well as by the addition of the grandchildren produced as a result of the *koba* experiences of their teenage children. Since the household always has some family members in residence, the aged parents may never experience the so-called postparental or empty-nest period.

In summary, the family life cycle varies among families of different cultural backgrounds in the following ways.

1. In addition to marriage and the bearing and rearing of children, there are many other milestone factors relating to family system and structure. These factors may include the pattern of getting married, ways to bear and adopt a child, and cohabiting members in the household, all of which affect the total configurational pattern of the family life cycle.

2. Due to numerous variations (such as differences in premarital experience, patterns of childbearing, the life span of the parents, and the structure of the household), the rhythm of family development may vary; the transition between phases may be clear-cut or blurred, and each stage may be short, long, or even absent.

3. Associated with the different cultural implications of critical issues concerning developmental milestones (such as the formal marital union, dissolution of marital relations, launching of children from the home, and widowhood), the impact of such milestones of family development on the life of family members has different meaning and effects. Therefore, it is necessary to examine the meaning of family development in the context of cultural background.

Chapter 3

Culture and Family Subsystems

One way to look at the family is to examine its existing subsystems: husband-wife, parent-child, and sibling-sibling. In this chapter, cultural aspects of the family will be examined by analyzing cultural variations on each subsystem of the family.

THE HUSBAND-WIFE SUBSYSTEM

Marriage between husband and wife has various implications. From a psychological functional point of view, the purposes of marriage have been described by Lidz (1974): to gain the security afforded by a union; to complement and complete one another; to find a common purpose sexually and by having and rearing children; and to find diverse ways of achieving reciprocity with one another. From a socio-anthropological point of view, marriage is considered a way to constitute an alliance between two kinship groups in which the couple concerned is merely the most conspicuous link (Hoebel, 1972).

The basic nature of marriage can be considered a fulfillment of ethical/moral expectations; marriage is a means of achieving membership in a society, or a means of meeting a partner's biological, psychological, and social needs. In other words, marital relations can be seen either as an obligatory lifelong commitment or as a functional unit based on affectional needs and relations. For the latter case, if the relationship is unsatisfactory, the spouses can choose to terminate the commitment and search for other partners.

The Marital Life Cycle

From a longitudinal perspective, marital relations are closely related to the personal life cycle and go through different stages of development in terms of the nature of marriage. The marriage life cycle has been systematically reviewed in the context of the nuclear family in contemporary American society by Pollak (1965), and Carter and McGoldrick (1980), focusing primarily on the tasks of childbearing and child-rearing. Utilizing such a framework, the marital cycle can be compared with marital life within the nuclear and extended families to illustrate how family systems may affect the life cycles of marriages differently. *Nuclear family* refers to a family made up of a couple and their children. *Extended family* refers to a couple, their children, their parents, and their married siblings and siblings' children.

Table 1 illustrates the marital life cycles which can occur within the nuclear family and within the extended family, and is intended to indicate how the marital cycle may differ between different family structures.

Parameters of the Marital Dyad

Cross-sectional examination of the husband-wife dyad as a major subsystem has been elaborated from many angles by family researchers. These include interpersonal relationships, communication, expression of affection, sexual experience, power distribution, role division, bond formation, conflict-solving patterns, adjustment, and mutual satisfaction. Some of these parameters of the marital dyad will be analyzed and elaborated from a cross-cultural point of view as follows.

Communication

Based on clinical experience, family therapists tend to take the view that the capacity to communicate is closely correlated with marital adjustment (Lewis, Beavers, Gossett, and Phillips, 1976). Family therapists place emphasis on teaching each partner to communicate effectively: speaking for themselves, articulating their own feelings rather than blaming others, engaging in calm negotia-

TABLE 1

COMPARISON OF MARITAL LIFE CYCLE
WITHIN NUCLEAR FAMILY AND EXTENDED FAMILY

Within Nuclear Family	*Within Extended Family*
A) *The newly married couple* (before arrival of children)	
Formation of marital system	Formation of marital system within the context of a larger family system
Learning to be separated from family of origin	Learning to readjust relations with family of origin, as expected by culture
Learning appropriate roles for husband and wife	Learning appropriate spousal roles in relation to other roles within large family (i.e., relations with in-laws)
Confirming own marital identity	Confirming marital identity within the surrounding kin-family-social system
B) *Couple begins to have children*	
Greater harmony in biological completion	Greater harmony in biological completion
Realization of self, and fulfillment of culturally expected mature adult role through reproduction	Fulfillment of culturally expected mature adult role through reproduction of members for larger family
Learning parental role	Learning parental role
	Readjusting and establishing new status as parents with children in a larger family system (i.e. increased status as a daughter-in-law with a child to continue the large family)
C) *Couple with adolescent children*	
Adjustment of flexibility of family boundaries to meet children's increasing tendency toward independence as permitted in culture	Adjustment of relations and roles in association with sister-in-law if they exist.
Developing family group solidarity of their nuclear family	Developing family group solidarity within the context of larger family

TABLE 1 (continued)

D) *Couple with children getting married or leaving*

Development of adult-adult relations with grown children	Development of adult-adult relations with grown children
Establishing relationship with married children as parents-in-law	Establishing relationship with married children as parents-in-law including acceptance and adjustment to children-in-law
Work on sense of loss over departure of children if it has occurred	
Renegotiation of marital system as dyad including the adjustment of husband-wife status which may gradually change	

E) *Couple with grandchildren or after children have left*

	Adjustment to the culturally expected role as grandparents
Adjustment to the departure of all children if it has occurred (empty-nest phase)	Adjustment of parental role in association with grown and married adult-children
Readjustment of marital role as husband and wife after retirement	Transfer of authority to next generation
Maintaining own and/or couple functioning in face of physiological decline	
Preparation for or acceptance of loss of spouse if it has occurred	

tions with each other, and listening to each other with emphatic understanding. After surveying ordinary American couples, Navran (1967) pointed out that happily marrieds differ from unhappily marrieds in several respects. The happily married couples more frequently talk over pleasant things, discuss matters of shared interest, talk to each other about personal problems, and feel more frequently understood by their spouses.

Based on the parameter of low or high disclosure and closed or open exploration, Hawkins, Weisberg, and Ray (1977) have categorized communication into four styles: conventional (inhibition of explicit verbalization in low disclosure), speculative (open to exploration in low disclosure), controlling (inhibition of explicit verbalization in high disclosure), and contactful (open to exploration in high disclosure). Using this set of categories, they examined marital communication styles and social class. They found that the higher the class level of the couples, the more the "contactful style" is preferred and the less the "conventional style" is preferred. Despite these variations, all classes have the same general rank order with regard to styles, suggesting that class differences are matters of degree rather than kind.

To investigate cross-cultural differences in marital communication, Winkler and Doherty (1983) studied Israeli couples living in New York City, along with socially-similar American Jewish couples in order to compare the conflict-related communication styles of these two groups. They found that Israeli couples were more apt to be verbally aggressive and less apt to behave calmly during marital conflicts. These communication styles did not relate to marital satisfaction as strongly for the Israelis as for the Americans, who tend to view calm, rational approaches to communication as important for a happy marriage.

Marital Power

The power relationship between husband and wife is only one aspect of their total relationship, yet it has attracted extensive investigation by family researchers. Many methodological questions have been raised regarding the study of this subject. For instance, the method by which information is obtained may influence the results; in addition, decision-making centering around the possible delegation of power not only varies from decision to decision, but also changes from time to time.

The resource theory of marital power hypothesizes that the partner's comparative participation in the external system determines his/her power position in the internal system of marriage (Lupri, 1969). This theory is generally supported by findings from many industrialized societies that indicate that the husband's status is positively associated with his power. For example, data on the United States and France show a positive association between the husband's authority score and such variables as the husband's educational status, occupational status, and income level (Rodman, 1967). A study from West Germany indicated that while the power of the German husband is positively related to social status, the wife's working status was also significantly associated with her position in the power structure. The husband's authority was significantly reduced if the wife made a comparatively equal or greater financial contribution to the marriage (Lupri, 1969). However, the resource theory of marital power is not always validated cross-culturally—there are a number of reversals in this tendency. For instance, data from Greece and Yugoslavia show negative correlations with these variables (Rodman, 1967). As elaborated by Safilios-Rothschild (1967), a Greek husband's association with a high level of education, a skilled or prestigious occupation, and a high salary level tends to diminish rather than increase his authority in the family. In Greece and Yugoslavia, the more education a man has, the more likely he is to grant his wife more authority, despite a traditional patriarchal culture. Thus, marital power is not as dependent on resources as on the learning of a new role (Rodman, 1967).

Expression of Affection

Concerning emotional expressiveness and marital adjustment, Ingoldsby (1980) conducted a cross-cultural analysis comparing couples from the United States with couples from Colombia. In spite of his original hypothesis that a positive relationship would be found between emotional expressiveness and marital adjustment, Ingoldsby came to several unexpected conclusions. First of all, he found that Colombian females were not more emotionally expressive than their male counterparts, as was the case, with American couples. This finding indicated that sex differences in expressiveness are due to cultural conditions rather than genetic factors. Second, the positive relationship between emotional expressiveness and marital adjustment was found in the United States couples, but not the Colombian ones. For the United States couples, high emotional expressiveness was important to marital adjustment, whereas for Colombian couples it was important that the couple be compatible in their level of expressiveness, whether high, medium, or low. Ingoldsby concluded that the relationship between emotional expressiveness and marital adjustment differs, based on the different marital styles in different cultural settings. For "companionate" marriages like those of the American couples, high positive emotional expression is essential for satisfactory marital adjustment. For "traditional" marriages, like those of the Colombian couples, a similar level of emotional expression is more important for a happy marriage.

Marital Satisfaction

Various terms, such as "marital success," "marital adjustment," and "marital satisfaction" are commonly used to describe the condition of marriage. However, as pointed out by Winch (1963), it is important to distinguish between these terms in order to avoid confusion. According to Winch (1963), "marital success" describes the achievement of one or more goals of marriage by the marital dyad, while "marital adjustment" refers mainly to the expectations, knowledge, and performance of marital roles and psychic adjustment to marital life, and "marital satisfaction" can be determined only by the emotional responses of a spouse.

Marital satisfaction can be focused on specific aspects of marital life such as expressions of affection or communication, or on overall married life. Regarding American couples, Synder (1979) reported that measures of communication are the best single predictors of global marital satisfaction.

Some studies have shown that husbands and wives have similar degrees and patterns of marital satisfaction (i.e., Rollins and Cannon, 1974). Rhyne's 1981 investigation of couples in Canada, however, revealed that men and women assess various aspects of marital life differently; for example, men are more satisfied with their spouse's help and time spent with children, while women are more sexually fulfilled.

Spanier, Lewis, and Cole's 1975 study of marital satisfaction during the course of the family life cycle resulted in contradictory findings. Their inconsistencies have been attributed to methodological effects including their choice of measurement instrument and mode of investigation (longitudinal design versus cross-sectional design). Schram (1979) offered a proposal to reformulate the developmental aspects of Spanier's study in light of relevant cultural changes. Concerning the issue of spouses' value similarity, Medling and McCarrey (1981) reported that such a variable was only peripherally related to the level of marital adjustment during the early part of the family life cycle. However, spouse value similarity did appear to have a significant impact upon adjustment in the latter years of marriage, when the couple's priorities shifted away from the children and back to themselves, and the dyad once again became the family's nuclear unit.

Cross-ethnic comparisons have been made in several investigations regarding marital satisfaction. Bean, Curtis, and Marcum (1977) compared the effects of family size, the wife's labor force participation, and conjugal power on marital satisfaction among Mexican-Americans living in Austin, Texas. They reported that husbands and wives were found to be more satisfied with the affective side of their marriages when there were fewer children present and when the conjugal power structure was more egalitarian. In addition, affective satisfaction was lower for the husband when the wife worked, and lower for the wife when she worked voluntarily. Bean et al. pointed out that these findings paralleled those generally reported for Anglo samples in other studies. They further indicated that levels of marital satisfaction are products of marital conditions per se rather than products of culturally based values about familism.

Glenn and Weaver (1981) used data from nation-wide surveys done in the U.S. to estimate the contribution marital happiness made to the overall happiness of black and white men and women.

They reported that, except in the case of black men, the estimated contribution of marital happiness is far greater than the estimated contribution of all other kinds of satisfaction, including job satisfaction. They concluded from their findings that Americans depend very heavily on their marriages for their psychological well-being.

By comparing marital situations in the United States, France, Greece, and Yugoslavia, Buric and Zecevic (1967) reported that marital tendencies in Yugoslavia differ considerably from those found in the other three countries. In Yugoslavia, the wife's marital satisfaction does not increase in relation to her husband's educational background as might be expected, but instead actually decreases as her husband's educational accomplishments grow. This phenomenon is interpreted as being affected by the wife's employment and her family ideology. That is, a wife whose husband has a high educational background tends to work outside the home. Yugoslavian working wives tend to report less marital satisfaction than nonworking ones, since they have higher expectations for their husbands—expectations which frequently remain unfulfilled.

By utilizing the instruments of the Areas of Change Questionnaire (Weiss and Birchler, 1975), a self-reported inventory that assesses marital partners' complaints, Rabin, Margolin, and their colleagues (1986) studied Israeli couples and compared them to previously studied American couples. They disclosed that the finding that American women desire more changes in their marriage than men do was not replicated in the Israeli sample. In general, Israeli men and women were more similar to each other than were the American men and women, at least in regards to the number of requests for changes in their marriage.

Marital Relations Beyond Monogamy

Anthropologists have informed us that in many cultures spouses are not united as "one husband and one wife." Unfortunately, anthropological studies of such marriage systems have long suffered from a lack of descriptive accounts of extant, fully functioning polygamous systems (Levine, 1980). Furthermore, there are virtually no studies that intensively examine and report on the emotional aspects of such spouse relations.

One Husband with Several Wives

According to Hoebel (1972), 44 percent of cultural groups around the world favor polygynous marriages and an additional 39 percent favor polygyny with monogamy. A majority of the world's existing cultural groups can therefore be described as either preferring or practicing polygamy. However, the extent to which men in any particular society actually practice polygyny varies greatly among different societies. For example, although polygyny in Iran predates the Islamic period, Momeni (1975) found that national census reports done in 1966 indicated that only one percent of Iranian men had more than one wife. The frequency of polygyny in Iran is thus not only much lower than generally believed, but has steadily declined over the past decade in association with increased education, modernization, and urbanization. In the past, wealthy men in many Asian countries kept concubines in addition to having a wife, but since the turn of the century such customs have become illegal and have mostly disappeared.

In contrast, Welch and Glick (1981) studied the frequency of polygamy in selected African countries in the period from 1960 to 1977, and reported that the frequency rates ranged mainly from 20 to 35 percent of married men in most of the contemporary African countries. Furthermore, it is predicted by the local people in Africa that polygamy will continue in the future as an alternative form of marriage, in spite of the modernization process.

The reasons and motives for a man to marry several women vary. An uneven ratio of men to women (as the result of war casualties) was one practical reason for some societies. In others, a man is permitted to marry another woman if his primary wife is found to be infertile, as having a child to continue the family is considered very important. In some societies, multiple wives or concubines are a sign of success, privilege, authority, or wealth. The nature of spouse relations within a polygamous marriage may differ according to various factors, such as the degree to which polygyny is prevalent in a society, cultural attitudes toward such a marriage system, or the underlying cause of having many wives.

Ware (1979) conducted his investigation in a transitional urban society in western Nigeria where polygyny is quite common; nearly half of the married women are living in a polygynous marriage. As explained by Ware, this high incidence of polygyny is demographically possible because men, on the average, marry seven to eight years later than women, which leaves a large number of females of marrying age free to participate in polygynous unions. Another fact that might encourage men to take other wives is that in this culture women customarily space births by abstaining from sexual intercourse for years after the birth of a child. In theory, there should be a strong relationship between religion and the incidence of polygyny, since traditional followers of religion are allowed as many wives as they can afford. Moslems are limited to four wives at any one time, while members of Christian faiths are supposed to remain monogamous; however, in practice, religious prohibitions have limited effect in this culture where polygyny is so widely accepted.

An interesting point is the women's views toward polygyny. Ware found from in-depth interviews that some 60 percent of wives said that if their husbands took another wife, they would be pleased to share the housework, husband care, and child-minding, and to have someone as company to gossip. Only 23 percent openly expressed anger at the idea of sharing marital and sexual resources with another wife. The remainder expressed some ambivalence, stating that such a marriage would be acceptable if only the wife could choose her new co-wife. As for questions about the negative side of being the wife of a man who has several wives, 85 percent reported feelings of envy, jealousy, hate, chaos, devilishness, or murderous intentions.

In traditional China, some men would have several wives for various reasons. Wealthy or successful men were permitted to have concubines. If a man's family arranged his marriage while he was very young and he was not happy about this union, it was possible for him to have a second marriage later if he could afford it. No matter what the reasons for such polygamous unions, the system was socially enforced to maintain order and harmony within such multiple-wife situations. A clear-cut hierarchy by seniority was maintained within the co-wives: the primary wife was always recognized as the "orthodox" wife while others held "secondary" or "tertiary" positions. Children borne by the primary wife were regarded as "orthodox" children while those born to succeeding wives were regarded as "non-orthodox." For some families the first names of all the children from all the co-wives would be similar to indicate that they belonged to the same generation of the family, in an effort to establish the solidarity of the family members. In spite of applying such measures to maintain domestic order within polygynous marriage, there were frequent emotional conflicts and turmoil associated with favoritism among co-wives as well as among the children of the wives.

Several Husbands with One Wife

As pointed out by Berreman (1980), our culture-orientation tends to regard "one husband and one wife" (monogamy) as the expected or even moral norm, "one husband and many wives" (polygyny) as reasonable or even enviable, and "one wife and many husbands" (polyandry) as puzzling or even disturbing. Polyandry has fascinated anthropologists largely because it is exotic and, particularly from the male perspective, problematic. Despite this, anthropological studies about polyandry are scant, and interpretations of the husband-wife relationship are rarely consistent from one study to the next.

There are several structural subtypes of polyandry, as indicated by Levine and Sangree (1980). "Fraternal polyandry" is a form of marriage in which two or more brothers marry the same woman and form a single household. This type of polyandry was found among Tibetans and is still found among people in Nepal, Sikkim, and Tadas.

"Associated polyandry" is a system of marriage in which a women may marry two, and rarely more than two, men who need not be brothers. The marriage is not begun as a joint venture, but rather begins monogamously, with additional husbands being incorporated into the pre-existing union later. One of the husbands, usually the primary one, holds the dominant position in the marriage. This type of arrangement was found in Ceylon.

"Secondary marriage" refers to the marriage of a woman, during the lifetime of her first or primary husband, to one or more secondary husbands which neither necessitates nor implies divorce or annulment of previous or temporarily co-existing marriages. Secondary marriage implies sequential marital rites and serial cohabitations, without the severance of prior unions or the cessation of the rights and duties associated with these prior unions. This form of polyandry is found only in Northern Nigeria and the Northern Cameroons.

Levine (1980) has made an insightful analysis of the marital relationship of fraternal polyandry practiced by Nyinba in Nepal. Namely, the characteristic features of polyandrous marital relationships may be explained by three basic principles which pervade Nyinba social life and underline domestic relations: (1) the equality and unity of brothers, (2) seniority within a sibling group, and (3) respect accorded to individual differences.

According to Levine (1980), the ideological emphasis on the equality of brothers is central to the Nyinba perception of polyandrous marriage. All co-husbands are said to have identical rights concerning the common wife or wives and equivalent obligations to them. It is considered wrong for any brother to try to gain a monopoly over the women's attentions and services. Meanwhile, the polyandrously married woman is expected to perform domestic chores for all of her husbands and to defer to their wishes equally.

The full equality of brothers is compromised by two competing factors, namely their relative age and individual proclivities. In the society of Nyinba, the overall status of men in their domestic groups depends upon their age position within the sibling group. Such respect of relative age in the social system is extended to the polyandrous marriage. For instance, the eldest brother acts as the principal figure and represents the household both at elaborate weddings and informal celebrations, while a younger brother's participation may be minimal. Associated with this respect for age is another principle: the acceptance of individual differences together with recognition of individual rights in the marriage. This recognition of the rights of the individual may be illustrated by the way in which wives are chosen. As pointed out by Levine, while the eldest brother inevitably selects the first wife, this is not the case in later marital unions. If the first wife dies, is divorced, or proves infertile, younger brothers are expected to take on the task of introducing new wives into their household. The brother who has taken the predominant role in the arrangements for a particular marriage is known as the "bringer" of the wife. As such, he may expect a certain degree of affection from the woman he has brought in.

Thus, Nyinba polyandrous marriage is influenced by these complementary and competing principles. As a result, the stress on equal status, unity, and cooperation among co-husbands stands in strong contrast to the disunity and competitiveness of co-wives in polygynous marriages observed in the same Nyinba society studied by Levine (1980).

In Africa, several different structural subtypes of polyandrous marriage exist. As described by Sangree (1980) in Irigwe, Nigeria, a form of secondary marriage is practiced that leads to polyandrous marital relations. A "primary marriage" is usually arranged by the parents while the couple are still infants or small children. Substantial farm labor is performed by the groom-to-be's agnates for the girl's father over a period of several years prior to consummation of the marriage. Although the primary marriage unions seldom lead to co-residence of more than a few weeks, labor service is provided by the boy's parents to the girl's parents. The real payoff for the boy's family from a primary marriage is the kinship or friendship alliance it helps affirm and strengthen with the girl's father and her family.

In contrast, second marriages are initiated by the couple themselves and involve minimum expenses. After a man gives a small gift of money to the marriage guardians (the woman's father and mother), the prospective secondary wife is obliged sometime thereafter to cohabit with her new husband for a minimum of three or four nights at his compound, but she is not obligated to remain longer. Usually, a good and devoted daughter will attract and accept engagements to a half dozen or more secondary husbands during her early and middle teens. However, once she becomes pregnant, a wife is expected to remain with the husband with whom she is then residing until after the infant's successful delivery; that husband becomes recognized as the legitimate father.

A similar but slightly different version of the second marriage is observed in Abisi, Nigeria. According to Chalifoux (1980), a young Abisi girl is ideally betrothed to three young men who belong to three different clans. She is formally married to her three grooms on the same day, but she goes to live with each of them separately on different days according to a fixed order. These three marriages are recognized as "work prestation marriage," "love marriage," and "home marriage."

The groom of the first marriage, or "work prestation marriage," is chosen neither by the girl nor by her parents; rather the bride is selected by the parents of the young man. The boy's father tries to get a wife for his son from a patrilineal group to which his patrilineal group has already given a daughter; this is considered by the local people as a matter of "taking back a girl" from where a woman of their group has been given in marriage. A particular set of work prestations performed by the groom and his family for the bride's family confers special rights and duties upon both spouses.

After the young girl is betrothed to the youth who will become the husband with whom she will first reside, she is then able to choose her second groom in accordance with her own preferences; her choice is recognized as a "love marriage." The third groom is chosen by the girl's parents, and thus this marriage is called "home marriage" since it is members of the girl's home who arrange it. A "home marriage" ranks below the first two.

A woman is normally married to her three grooms on the same day. The three grooms-to-be all arrive on the day chosen to receive their bride. She thereupon sets out for her first husband's home and must remain with him for at least a month. After a year has elapsed, she must go—if she has not already done so—to her second husband. She is then required to stay a minimum of a month with her second husband, but most wives remain for several years. At the end of the second year of a woman's marriage, the third husband is theoretically entitled to claim his wife. In reality, more than half of the Abisi women refused to go to their "home husband," as reported by Chalifoux (1980). After staying with their husbands according to the expected lengths of cohabitation, women can go back and forth among their husbands or take advantage of a fourth marital possibility. Both men and women are entitled to contract a "grass marriage" in addition to the others. This type of union is the least valued by the society, and therefore is undertaken in secret, literally "in the grass." By the time the wife reaches middle age and has had ample contact with her various husbands and has undergone various shifts of residence between them, the husband of the "love marriage" is usually the most favored. According to Chalifoux's (1980) report, more than 40 percent of all women resided with their love husbands at this stage in their lives; another 30 percent lived with their first husbands; approximately 20 percent of the women were widows, and only a very small portion lived with their "home marriage" husbands.

Having multiple husbands serves several purposes in an integrated way: it solves the socioeconomic situation, it fulfills the social need to unite clans, to strengthen interfamily relations, and to meet the affectional need of the partners (Levine & Sangree, 1980). Within such multiple marriages, expectations and rules within the social system are set up to stabilize such a complicated marital system. At the same time, the husband and wife must adjust their emotional relationship to limit, confine, and shift their emotional bond in an appropriate way to avoid and minimize potential complications. Potential marital problems could occur, usually in the form of jealousy, favoritism, and the conflicts of loyalty and faithfulness. The occurrence of such difficulties is seldom investigated in-depth and deserves future study.

Swingers (Mate Swapping)

Many of our contemporary social institutions are facing the challenge of changes. These changes include the marriage system as well. In spite of the traditional emphasis on faithfulness and monogamy in Christian society, the past two decades in the United States (as well as in some other countries in Europe) have seen the rise of couples who, in a semi-public fashion, have explored and practiced extramarital sex in the form of co-marital sex. Those indulging in this type of behavior are popularly known as "swingers" (Smith and Smith, 1973).

Extensive study of American marital education literature for the period from 1883 to 1940 by Gordon (1972) revealed that there has been a dramatic transformation in the prevailing conception of female sexuality, and marital sex in general. Throughout most of the nineteenth century, the commonly held attitude toward sexual intercourse was that it was, unhappily, required for the perpetuation of the species. Later, acceptance of marital sex for something apart from its procreative function, which was beneficial to the marriage, was considered. Starting at the turn of the twentieth century, there was growing realization that women experience sexual desire and that this desire should be satisfied. This increasing acceptance of the pleasure aspect of marital sex, as pointed out by Denfeld and Gordon (1974), seems to have had an impact on a number of areas, as evidenced by the decreasing amount of premarital contact with prostitutes for men and the increasing amount of premarital sex for women.

As explained by Denfeld and Gordon (1974), the current concept of female sexuality as legitimate and gratifying, coupled with enlarged opportunities for women to pursue sex without unwanted pregnancy (due to the revolution in contraceptive techniques), has greatly increased the incentive for women, like men, to seek sexual variety outside marriage. Among the available ways for both husbands and wives to find such variety, mate swapping is the least threatening and the one most compatible with monogamy. Thus, the emergence of marital deviancy in the case of swingers is a consequence of the high personal and social value placed on sexuality. The highly formalized and routinized quality of the swinging subculture is interpreted as essential for the maintenance of conventional commitments along with the deviant ones (Walshock, 1974). In other words, swapping is a particular attempt to institutionalize the extramarital sexual adventures among those co-marital sex practitioners.

In spite of the notion voiced by some sociologists that swinging may support rather than disrupt monogamous marriage as it exists in our society, swinging carries with it many psychological complications and may create emotional problems between husband and wife. Denfeld (1974) has conducted a questionnaire survey of marriage counselors for information regarding dropouts from swinging. The results indicated that the reasons for dropping out are not surprising and are what one might expect: jealousy and guilt were the most common problems. Husbands reported more jealousy than wives. A number of husbands became quite concerned about their wives' popularity, their own sexual performance, and the fact that their wives were having more fun than they were. Although some swingers attempted to protect themselves from developing emotional attachments by avoiding swinging with the same couple more than once, some swinging couples became emotionally attached to people with whom they have had sexual relations. In general, the men initiated the swinging and the women forced the termination. Wives expressed feelings of disgust or repulsion and were considerably more troubled by swinging than their husbands. Swinging, for many couples, did not always provide the excitement that the couple had fantasized. Dropout couples report that swinging weakened rather than strengthened the marriage.

PARENT-CHILD SUBSYSTEM

Parenthood implies continual adaptation to physiological and psychological changes within the self, parallel to and in conjunction with changes in the child and the child's expanding world (Benedek, 1974). Parents who enjoyed their own childhood will treat it as an enjoyable period for their children, while parents who experienced great difficulties in childhood are more likely to expect, and perhaps create, difficulties for their own children (Petersen and Offer, 1979).

Parent-Child Relations
in Life Cycle Perspective

Although child development has been reviewed extensively by developmental psychologists and child psychiatrists from psychological (Petersen and Offer, 1979; Duvall, 1971) as well as psychosocial points of view (Erikson, 1963), most of the studies have been more or less focused on the perspective of the child rather than on dyadic and triadic relations between parents and children.

In accordance with the life cycle, parent-child dyadic relations will be examined from both the functional pattern and the dysfunctional pattern. While the functional pattern refers to the usual and optimal conditions that can occur, the dysfunctional pattern points out the possible problems that can be faced and need to be coped with even though the appearance of such patterns does not necessarily imply that they are pathological. Table 2 outlines the functional and dysfunctional patterns of parent-child relations which can occur in life cycle perspectives.

TABLE 2

PARENT-CHILD RELATIONS IN VARIOUS STAGES OF THE LIFE CYCLE:

FUNCTIONAL VS DYSFUNCTIONAL

A) *Infant and Parents*

INFANT	PARENTS
Functional Patterns	
Total dependency on parents	Nurturing, protection and care of infant
Dysfunctional Patterns	
Regression and withdrawal from forming relationship with parents	Rejection, negligence or abuse of child

B) *Young-Child and Parents*

YOUNG-CHILD	PARENTS
Functional Patterns	
Achieving psychological separation from parents	
Achieving autonomy	
	Adjustment to triadic relation to child
Mirroring and imitating of parents' behavior	Provision of behavior model for child to imitate
Mastering omnipotent wish	Provision of appropriate restrictions and limitations
Dysfunctional Patterns	
Prolonged symbiotic relation with parents	Inability to let child gradually separate from parents

C) *Old-child and Parents*

OLD-CHILD	PARENTS
Functional Patterns	
Search for individuality	Sensitivity to children's growth needs
	Provision of opportunities for the child to do things for self which are within child's abilities
	Letting child go and grow

TABLE 2 (continued)

Enjoying life through children's eyes

Dysfunctional Patterns

Failure to seek individuality

Insensitive to child's growth needs

Inhibition or limitation of child's individuality

D) *Adolescent and Parents*

ADOLESCENT	PARENTS
Functional Pattern	
Development of self-image and identity	Provision of assistance in establishment of role and identity
	Can tolerate and compromise the cultural gap which may exist between generations
Dysfunctional Patterns	
Adolescents believe that parents depreciate them	Parents feel that their children undervalue them
Adolescents rebel against parents	Unwilling to negotiate cultural gap with adolescent

E) *Adult-child and Parents*

ADULT-CHILD	PARENTS
Functional Patterns	
Relative independence from parents	Letting grown-up child go and be independent
Develop adult-to-adult relationship with parents	Accepting adult-to-adult relationship with grown-up child
Seek guidance and support from parents whenever it is needed	Standing by with encouragement, reassurance and appreciation
Dysfunctional Patterns	
Fail to develop adult-to-adult relations with parents	Unable to let grown-up child go and be independent

F) *Adult-Child and Aged-Parents*

ADULT-CHILD	AGED-PARENTS
Functional Patterns	
Reverse role to take care of aged and incapacitated parents	Reverse role to be taken care of by child
Dysfuctional Pattern	
Unable to take the reversed role, still expecting parents to be omnipotent	Resistance to giving up authoritative role toward grown-up child
Rejection and negligence of incapacitated aged parents when they need help	Refusal of help from adult-child when its needed

Cultural Variations on Parent-Child Relations

The nature of the society and the cultural system will influence the nature of parent-child relations. For example, cultural emphasis on conformity, relative to self-reliance, has a substantial effect on parents' disciplinary behavior towards their children (Petersen, Lee, and Ellis, 1982). Kohn (1959) has disclosed that both in the United States and elsewhere, the degree of close supervision by authority figures in a job setting led blue-collar parents to place greater value on conformity than on self-direction for their children; the opposite was true for white-collar parents. As an extension of Kohn's finding, Olsen (1974) revealed how family structure as an antecedent of socialization values extrapolates the variable, closeness of supervision. She noted that mothers in patrilocal extended families in Taiwan are typically closely supervised by their mothers-in-law and, in turn, emphasize conformity for their children in discipline. This contrasts with nuclear families in Taiwan where mothers are not subject to the direct supervision of their mothers-in-law, and accordingly emphasize self-reliance for their children.

Many family researchers have paid attention to how different family structures such as family size, number of children, sibling order, or sibling configuration, may affect parent-child relations (Fishbein, 1981), yet there are no congruent findings to support various speculations (Bell and Avery, 1985; Kidwell, 1981). In order to prevent a potential population explosion, China has vigorously enforced its "one-child per couple" family policy since 1980. As a result, among young couples, nearly 95 percent in urban areas and about 60 percent in rural areas have only one child. Traditionally, Chinese (especially farmers) felt that many children constituted a treasure and that it was very important to have a son to continue a family clan. The extent to which such compulsory restrictions on the number of children in a family may affect child-raising is therefore an interesting subject. In collaboration with Chinese colleagues, Tseng, Tao, Hsu, Chiu, Yu, and Kameoka (1988) have conducted a questionnaire survey of child behavior problems among preschool children in the Nanjing area. Results indicated that a comparison of behavior problems in the single child and the nonsingle child (usually with one sibling) does not reveal any differences for boys, but reveals significant differences for girls. The single female child, in contrast to the nonsingle girl, tends to score higher on the subscales of moodiness, temper, and depression. Results suggest that Chinese parents who have only one girl are not satisfied and the parents' reactions influence the single girl's behavioral development.

Various Family Systems and Parent-Child Relations

In contrast to the simple nuclear family system, parent-child relations within different "family systems" can be modified in many ways. Cultural variations in parent-child relations will be explored by the following situations.

Parent-Child Relations in a Matrilineal Family

In societies where the descent group is identified through mother-daughter linkage — the matrilineal system — children will develop a close relationship with the father and with the mother's brother (maternal uncle). While the father, who actually lives with the children, will provide affection and discipline, the maternal uncle has the ultimate authority over guidance and control of the children. Children have to learn how to relate to these two male parenting figures in their different roles.

Parent-Child Relations in a Polygamous Family

One of man's concerns in marriage (whether monogamous or polygamous) is his wife's childbearing capacities. In the case of a polyandrous marriage, all husbands may hope to have children by their common wife. As pointed out by Levine (1980), "having children" includes not only children born to the conjugal group, but children who are attributed to each of the men. How is each child attributed to a particular father when the wife has several husbands? As reported by Levine (1980), the Nyinba in Nepal who practice polyandry, believe that only one man is responsible for the conception of a child, and the attribution of a child's paternity is critical in establishing rights to inheritance and social position. In Nyinba, the wife designates the father of her unborn child shortly after she becomes pregnant. Based on the particular time she engaged in sexual relations with her husbands, the pregnant woman in a polyandrous marriage will try to determine the genitor—the physical father—of a particular child. In Nyinba, all of a woman's husbands are rarely at home simultaneously. Some spend most of the year on trading expeditions, while others are away pasturing the herds. Thus, it is usually not difficult for a woman to determine the genitor of the child. If the issue is in doubt, the parents will wait for the birth of a child to compare its appearance with that of possible genitors. The family will eventually reach a consensus about the child's parentage and specify one of the co-husbands as genitor.

Levine (1980) states that in Nyinba a child regards all the men of the parental generation in his household as fathers and refers to them accordingly. There is no special term for the genitor. The genitor who legitimates and thus acts as *pater* may be seen as "his own" and show his child special affection; children often express special emotional response in return. This interaction does not lessen the children's respect for their co-fathers, who also played a significant part in their upbringing.

The situation in Africa appears to be different. Concerning parent-child relations in a polyandrous family, Levine (1970) studied an African family and pointed out that in many societies there is considerable strain between father and son, who have a culturally prescribed avoidance pattern. Levine further notes that intergenerational male homicides are the most common form of murder in many African groups. He explained that part of the reason may stem from the cultural custom that forces a firstborn male to wait until his father is dead before he can share any of his father's accumulated wealth. As there are not too many other opportunities to acquire possessions, this custom can provide a focus for considerable conflict. In the Iatmul, fathers and sons were culturally forbidden to become intimate. Opposition between father and son is further reinforced by the close ties of sons to their mother's brother's clans. Hoffman (1981) emphasizes that cultural variants of the triangular relations between parents and children exist. The triad will differ depending on the way families are organized within a society.

Parent-Child Relations in Stepfamily

Associated with the increase in the frequency of divorces and remarriages in many societies (particularly in western, modernized countries) is an increase in the number of reconstructed families with stepparents and stepchildren in one household. This brings about new kinds of experiences for families in terms of relationships between stepparents and stepchildren. As listed by Visher and Visher (1979), the problem areas resulting from stepfamily structure are numerous. The biological parent outside the stepfamily unit very often continues to exert a strong psychological force within the stepfamily. This may be true even when the biological parent is far away or even after the biological parent has died. Most children in stepfamilies hold membership in two households—that of the reconstructed family and that of the family of the original parent. This dual family membership may lead to considerable discomfort and ambiguity for the children in terms of how family life is run and how the children are raised, cared for, and disciplined, as they shift and adjust to these two "cultures" of family. The stepparent and stepchild relations are new and untested, not "given" as they are in intact families, and need time to build and develop. Stepparents usually have ill-defined roles and do not clearly know what to expect of themselves; meanwhile, other family members do not know what to expect of the stepparents. The stepfamily has not yet been fully institutionalized, so even society has no idea what to expect.

Situations where "blended" families come together from diverse historical backgrounds accentuate the need for tolerance of these differences. The stepfamily usually has complicated financial arrangements which can take on many emotional overtones. Finally, children in stepfamilies have an extra set of grandparents, increasing the risk of destructive coalitions. Thus, in a way, reconstructed families share similarities with extended families in that family relations become "complicated." However, stepfamilies differ from traditional extended families in that there is a lack of an institutional system for the reconstructed family, which is a product of the contemporary society.

Triangular Relations in Cross-Cultural Aspects

The concept of triangular parent-child conflict was introduced by Sigmund Freud. This refers to the triangular relations that occur between the parents and the child — affinitive relations with the parent of the opposite sex versus repulsion of relations with the parent of the same sex. This conflictual relationship between father, mother, and son or daughter during the stages of child development is called the Oedipus complex, recalling the Greek myth in which a young man kills his father by mistake and marries his mother. When he discovers what has happened, he harshly punishes himself.

To what extent this triangular complex is a universal phenomenon has been the subject of debate among scholars (Hoffman, 1981). Some cultural anthropologists have speculated that such triangular tensions will be less likely to occur in certain family systems. For instance, within the extended family, the presence of multiple adults (i.e., uncles and aunts) in addition to the father and mother make it less likely that a father-mother-child conflict of competition, favoritism, or attachment will develop. In a society in which the father tends to be relatively less available to the family, such as in Japan where the father is often occupied with his work and colleague-related socialization, the mother tends to focus on her children, particularly the eldest son. Such a situation creates a close relationship between the mother and son while the father becomes more distant. In African society, when the family practices polygynous marriage, such as in Nigeria (Ebigbo and Ihezue, 1982), the father is not physically available for the children. The mother usually develops intensive ties with her children, particularly her sons, serving as a husband-substitute from an emotional viewpoint. The father's absence may also enhance father-son tensions. As already pointed out by Levine (1970), fathers and sons in some African families were "culturally" forbidden to become intimate. This opposition is reinforced by the close ties of sons to their mothers and mother's brother's clans, and therefore led to strains between father, mother, and son.

Attitudes toward parental authority among traditional Chinese, as expressed in children's stories, were reviewed by Tseng and Hsu (1972). Findings showed that despite the patrilineal system emphasized by anthropologists for the Chinese family (Hsu, F.L.K., 1949), the close mother-son relationship of filial piety was greatly encouraged in the *Classic 24 Stories of Filial Piety*. In the popular children's story "Sun Wu-Kong," or "The Western Journey," an omnipotent monkey who is full of magic, power, and egocentrism (symbolizing a "phallic child") attempts to defy (male) authority in the form of the king/Buddha. As a result, the monkey is punished and taught how to atone for his unacceptable behavior. The triangular conflict theme has been dealt with in many classical Chinese operas. The stories usually end with the child, rather than the parent, being either punished or killed. This ending is the more appropriate solution to parent-child triangular conflict in traditional Chinese culture. As pointed out by Hoffman (1981), there are cultural variants on triangular conflict, in terms of how tension is created and intensified and how culturally appropriate solutions are provided.

OTHER SUBSYSTEMS

Sibling Subsystem

Sibling interaction is an often overlooked aspect of family functioning, as pointed out by Bank and Kahn (1975). Despite the fact that siblings are a powerful subsystem of the family, sibling status is generally underemphasized in our culture, as well as by family therapists. As elaborated by Bank and Kahn, Europeans and Americans emphasize the romantic aspects of life, namely husband-wife relationships and the product of that union, the children. Further, current theories of family interaction focus almost exclusively on the influence of the parents and on the psychosocial development of their children. Sibling relationships have, at best, been seen only as products of the interaction between each child and the parents rather than "among the children themselves." In technologically advanced Western societies, brotherhood, sisterhood, and siblingship in general no longer have the real status they once had. In addition, shrinking family size has made the sibling subgroup less visible.

By studying slum families — disorganized, fatherless, and poverty-stricken — Minuchin, Mantalvo and their associates (1967) have observed that siblings give reflected self-appraisal, which is crucial for the development of identity for children. Siblings can and do form cohesive defensive groups when one is attacked by an outsider. Siblings can thus act as socializers and interpreters of the outside world for each other.

Interested in examining kinship in Italian-American families with a special emphasis on sibling relationships, Johnson (1982) studied three family subgroups: Italian-American families with both spouses of Italian background, families with only one spouse of Italian background, and families of European Protestant background. The subjects were couples who had lost both parents but still had surviving siblings. It was found that 73 percent of the Italian in-married respondents still contacted their siblings at least weekly, while only 58 percent of the out-married group and 52 percent of the Protestants did so. Sources of sibling solidarity are traced to the hierarchical structure of the Italian immigrant family, which has facilitated the formation of coalitions among siblings.

The traditional Chinese ethic, as based on Confucian thought, emphasized the importance of both filial piety toward the parents and benevolent relations between brothers as the basic forces for maintaining a family system. In actual Chinese society, however, filial piety was practiced but mutual respect and love between brothers and sisters was not successfully achieved (Chin, 1970). Analysis of sibling relations as described in classic Chinese opera (Hsu and Tseng, 1974) revealed intense hostility between siblings.

Reasons for conflict between siblings which were given in the operas were jealousy because of parental favoritism, competition for parental wealth, and plundering of family property. The study suggested that the source for such conflicts was rooted in the traditional Chinese practice of primogeniture—the family's main resources were transmitted to the first born male—which created potential problems between siblings.

As pointed out by Caplow (1968), the husband-wife dyad is the primary axis for contemporary European and American families, yet for families in other cultures, the bond between siblings can be the primary axis for the family. For example, in the South of Sahara, paths between generations are de-emphasized, fraternal solidarity is considered more important than romantic love, and loyalty and the control of rivalry among brothers are the cornerstones of family stability (Bank and Khan, 1975).

As exemplified by matrilineal families in Micronesia, the brother-sister dyad is the backbone of the family relationship. As descent is recognized through the lineage of mother to daughter, women hold an important role in the kin system. However, since actual power and authority are executed through men (the women's brothers), the dyad of brother and sister becomes the main axis of family relations throughout their lifetime. Any important and significant decisions are carried out by a woman's brother. As a result, a careful brother-sister avoidance taboo is practiced from childhood. Brother and sister are not permitted to meet alone under the same roof if no one else is present. This is a measure taken to protect the solidarity of the brother-sister dyad with respect and distance.

In-Law Subsystem

Mother-in-Law and Daughter-in-Law

It is commonly recognized that the relationship between mother-in-law and daughter-in-law is one of the most difficult within the family system. It is the subsystem especially susceptible to problems in the larger family. As pointed out by Duvall (1954), the mother-in-law who can wholeheartedly and enthusiastically welcome her children-in-law has been a good mother all along in the developmental sense, while a selfish, possessive mother finds it hard to be a good mother-in-law.

In a society in which a close mother-son relationship is permitted and is a primary dyad of the family, such as traditional Hindu society, intense strain exists between the son's wife and his mother. This relationship is highly charged with potential conflict. As reported by Ross (1970), the young wife in a Hindu family is in a particularly difficult position. After marriage, she leaves her family of origin to live with her husband's family and is then subject to the absolute power of her mother-in-law. If she is persuasive enough to elicit her husband's support in her new family, her position in the family becomes even more difficult. If her husband agrees with her, the delicate balance of family relationships is upset, and she may suffer repercussions from the tensions created. The daughter-in-law can expect redress of her grievances only by living long enough to become a despot in turn to her own son's wife.

Sister-in-Law

After the mother-in-law/daughter-in-law relationship, the relationship between sisters-in-law is usually described as the most difficult in-law subsystem. In general, sisters-in-law within an extended family, that is, the sisters of the husband, are depicted as possessive, meddling, and intrusive. This situation is always complicated by a considerable amount of competitiveness, jealousy, and bickering, which has its roots in sibling rivalry but continues into adulthood (Duvall, 1954). The same situation applies to the wives of brothers—that is, a competitive and jealous relationship may exist either subtly or overtly.

Grandparents-Grandchildren Subsystem

The relationship between grandparents and grandchildren has not yet been fully examined by either family researchers or therapists in our society where the nuclear family is the predominant household structure, but can be an important subsystem of an extended family. Grandparents can function within a family as either the ultimate authority figures, or as benign adult figures who tend to indulge their grandchildren. Grandparents can also interfere in the chil-

dren's upbringing, especially if their relationship with the daughter-
or son-in-law is a difficult one.

SUMMARY

Subsystems are one arbitrary way by which to examine and understand the complicated family. It is clear that in frameworks of
subsystems, such as the marital dyad and the parent-child dyad,
many variations can be observed across cultures in terms of relations and functions. There are, however, many subsystems that are
not normally included for consideration but still play an important
role in other systems, e.g., the brother-sister dyad in many matrilineal families, stepparent-child relations in reconstructed families, or
grandparent-grandchildren relations in extended families. Also, the
subsystem which serves as the dominant family dyad varies among
various cultures (Falicov and Brudner-White, 1983) as do subsystems which impact differently on family relations and the development of interpersonal behavior patterns (Hsu, F.L.K., 1972). Nevertheless, for the sake of understanding, we should not only dissect
the family into subsystems for analysis, but also learn how to examine the family as a whole in order to obtain a total configuration of
the family as a group.

Chapter 4

Culture and Family-Group

The marital dyad is the backbone of a family, and many family issues can be addressed from this perspective. Once a couple begins to have children, however, the components and structure of the family are changed, and it becomes relevant and necessary to deal with the family as more than just a marital dyad plus children. Since a family functions as a result of the mutual interactions of all the family members, it becomes a group beyond dyad relations. The family thus needs to be addressed, studied, and understood as a "family-group." This is particularly true of families where the children have reached an age where they have significant input and impact on the function of the whole family. Within an extended family, for instance, the newlyweds find that they are part of a family-group even before they have children of their own, since their marriage takes place within the context of a pre-existing family-group which includes the parents/parents-in-law and siblings/ siblings-in-law.

As elaborated by Lidz (1974), the family has a number of characteristics common to all true small groups. First, the action of any member affects all group members — and to function properly, the group requires unified objectives and leadership towards these objectives. Further, the maintenance of group morale requires that each member give the needs of the group some precedence over his/ her own desires. Also, the family needs to have group structure with clarity of roles and leadership to carry out the group function.

The family, however, is a special kind of group in that it is determined by biological background and sociocultural expectation, and consists of members of different genders and generations who undergo intense relations for a prolonged period of time, resulting in a unique kind of commitment, bonding, and identification. The family as a group is also the basic social unit within which a society's culture is maintained and transmitted. Thus, viewing the family as a small group is another way to examine the function of the family in cultural perspectives.

PARAMETERS OF THE FAMILY GROUP

The behavior and function of the family as a group can be studied using various parameters: leadership, dominance, family boundaries, affectivity, communication, and task/goal performance (Fleck, 1980). The structure of the family (including overt power, parental coalitions, and closeness), mythology, goal-directed negotiation, autonomy, and family affect are the main parameters used by Lewis and his group to assess the psychological health of the family (1976). Based on these suggested parameters, the various functions of the family-group will here be defined, elaborated, and examined as follows.

Cohesion

The degree to which family members are connected to each other within a family is addressed as cohesion. As suggested by Olson, McCubbin, Barnes, Larsen, Muxen, and Wilson (1983), the spectrum of cohesion can range from "disengaged" or "separated," to "connected" or "enmeshed." Based on the concept of family structure, Minuchin (1974) has pointed out that enmeshed families reflect dysfunctional structure. According to Minuchin, the "enmeshed family" is characterized by several phenomena: over-involvement with one another, over-responsiveness to one another, diffuse interpersonal boundaries, confusion of roles, discouragement of individualization and autonomy, and low stress tolerance.

Some people have loosely used the term "enmeshed" to describe families of certain cultural groups, such as Italian or Hawaiian families, which emphasize closeness among family members. However, in actuality neither confusion of roles nor low stress tolerance exists within close families of these cultural groups. Instead, there is always clear role division and a clear hierarchy associated with such close families, as well as high stress tolerance. Apparently, there is a need to clarify and distinguish between culturally-sanctioned "intrafamily closeness" and dysfunctional "enmeshed" family structures.

The possible cultural ramifications of perceived family cohesiveness as opposed to individual autonomy among adolescents have been addressed by Sundberg, Sharma, Wodtli, and Rohila (1969) in a questionnaire survey of male and female ninth-grade students in agricultural towns in northern India and the western United States. Their results clearly showed that the adolescents in India perceived cohesiveness while the adolescents in America perceived more self-decisiveness, indicating that the importance of family cohesion and individual autonomy varies in different cultural groups.

Boundary

A boundary means the border or territory maintained between subjects. A boundary in a family may refer to the border maintained between individual family members or between subgroups that exist within the family; it may also refer to the distance kept by the family as a whole in relation to people outside the family. No matter whether the boundary referred to separates individual members, subgroups, or the whole family, concerns about the nature of the boundary may include whether or not the boundary is clearly established, open or closed, receptive to others, or prone to outside invasion.

The degree to which the boundary is emphasized between family members differs greatly among different cultures. Within a family which culturally values individualization and autonomy, there is frequent emphasis on each family member having his/her own boundary, speaking up for his/her self, and protecting his/her own territory, both psychologically and physically. However, within a family which culturally values group-togetherness, the boundary between family members is not essential. One family member may speak up for another, and anyone overly concerned with his/her individual rights or territory would be seen as acting disgracefully.

The boundary between two families or between a family and all those outside the family also shows variation cross-culturally. For example, for Pacific cultural groups which value mutual help and coexistence within the island society, the boundary between families as well as towards the outside of the family is relatively blurred. Food is usually shared between families and many belongings are lent easily from one family to another family. Building a high wall between family residences to ensure territorial rights and privacy would be a foreign custom to them.

Alignment

A prominent line or lines of alliance formed among particular members of a family is referred to as an alignment. When a particularly strong union is formed between parents, it is called a parental coalition. If the alignment involves a parent and a child, it is called a parent-child coalition or a cross-generation coalition. Oppositional relations involving three family members, such as father-mother-son, are referred to as triangulation.

Although the husband-wife alignment is the primary axis in most families in Western society, a spouse coalition is not necessarily the most prominent axis in other cultures. For instance, the brother-sister alignment is the most important one for Micronesian families which are characterized by the matrilineal system and which trace inheritance through the mother-daughter line while actual power is executed through the brother-sister connection.

Power

Power has been defined by sociologists and family scholars as the ability of an individual to carry out his or her will within a social relationship, even in the face of the resistance of others. It is conceived of as a dynamic process rather than as a static phenomenon, and also as a system property rather than an individual attribute. As pointed out by McDonald (1980), family power includes subunits of marital power, parental power, offspring power, sibling power, and kinship power, even though past studies have mostly focused on marital power, and to a lesser extent, parental power.

Power is regarded as a multidimensional phenomenon. According to Cromwell and Olson (1975), power can be divided into three distinct domains: power bases, power processes, and power outcome. Power bases refers to the sources of power. The resources of family power can be viewed as economic, as proposed by Blood and Wolf (1960) or as normative and noneconomic. The sources of power might include normative resources (cultural definitions of who possesses authority), affective resources (the level of involvement or commitment and the degree of dependence), or personal resources (personality, physical appearance, and role competence).

Power process refers to the interactional techniques which individuals employ in their attempts to gain control in the negotiation or decision-making process. These techniques include control, assertiveness, negotiation, persuasion, and influence. Lastly, power outcomes refer to the results of power exercised in decision-making and implementation.

From a cultural point of view, efforts have been made recently to clarify the power structure of black and Chicano families and their respective stereotypes involving "black matriarchy" and "Chicano patriarchy." In reviewing several classic studies of power relations in black families, Willie and Greenblatt (1978) pointed out that, in general, black families appear to be more egalitarian than white families. They concluded that black matriarchy is a myth and that egalitarian decision-making patterns predominate in black families. Hawkes and Taylor (1975) explored the power structure in Mexican and Mexican-American families by conducting standardized interviews. They found that egalitarianism was by far the most common mode in both decision-making and action-taking for migrant farm labor families in California, indicating that the commonly-held view of husband dominance in Chicano families is an unsubstantiated one. When Cromwell and Cromwell (1978) studied perceived dominance in decision-making among three groups representing Anglo, black, and Chicano couples, they also concluded that the stereotypic labeling of matriarchy for blacks and patriarchy for Chicanos should be rejected.

Decision-Making

Decision-making patterns, closely related to power relationships, have also been studied in detail by family researchers. Cooney, Rogler, Hurrell, and Ortiz (1982) studied decision-making patterns among the spouses of parent generations and child generations of Puerto Rican families in the United States. His findings disclosed that while the sociocultural norms of the parent generations (born and raised in Puerto Rico) reflected those of a modified patriarchal society, the sociocultural norms of the child generations (born and raised in the United States) reflected those of a transitional egalitarian society. Thus his research illustrated how assimilation had modified the sociocultural norm of decision-making patterns between generations.

Safilios-Rothschild (1969) carried out a cross-cultural examination of perceived decision-making between American families and Greek families, with special attention to the differences that existed between husband and wife. Results disclosed that while Detroit (i.e., American) husbands frequently saw decision-making as wife-dominated, Detroit wives had an equal tendency to perceive decision-making as husband- or wife-dominated. In marked contrast, Athenian (Greek) wives frequently reported a wife-dominated power structure, while Athenian husbands reported equal instances of husband- and wife-dominance of decision-making. This indicated not only that spouses' self-reported data was incongruent, but that the pattern of discongruence between spouses differed cross-culturally between American and Greek families.

Decision-making patterns of American and Danish urban families were compared by Kandel and Lesser (1972), who found that the most common modal pattern in both countries was the shared pattern of marital authority, in which husbands and wives participate equally in making a variety of family decisions. They also scrutinized theories of resources in marital decision-making, and found that in both countries the correlation between marital power and the resources (family income or occupation) brought into the marriage by each spouse was neither consistent nor always positive. However, results did indicate that wives' employment contributed to their increased power within the household. Interestingly, Kandel and Lesser speculated that the importance of socioeconomic resources in marital decision-making may not derive as much from the availability of financial and status rewards as from the opportunity for gaining interpersonal and decision-making skills outside the family circle which can then be utilized within the family.

Role Division

Many personal factors such as age, gender, birth-order, or family system type determine role division within a family. Parson and Bales (1955) have proposed that a universal feature of the nuclear family is sex role specialization of tasks along instrumental-expressive lines. Specifically, the more instrumental role in the subsystem is taken by the husband-father who has the primary adaptive responsibilities relative to concerns outside the scope of the family, while the more "expressive" role in the family is taken by the wife-mother who is primarily the giver of affection. However, as pointed out by Adamek (1982), such a family role complementarity model has not been adequately tested and validated by the utilization of cultural data from the *Ethnographic Atlas*.

As for role conflict within the family, Spiegel (1957) has listed five causes for failure of complementarity in the role system within the family. First is cognitive discrepancy; one or both persons involved in the role system may not know or be sufficiently familiar with the required roles. Second is discrepancy of goals; the goal associated with the role cannot be attained due to a motivational problem. Third is allocative discrepancy; the role which is to be ascribed, achieved, adopted, or assumed is not done so adequately. Fourth is instrumental discrepancy; deprivation or insufficiency of instrumental prerequisites interferes with role transactions. Fifth is discrepancy in culture value orientations.

The differential role of parents in the family as perceived by adolescents was investigated by Tashakkori and Mehryar (1982) in Iran. Their findings indicated a considerable degree of parental role differentiation, with mothers being dominant in the supportive-emotional areas and fathers taking responsibility for the authoritative-punitive aspects. Certain differences between the male and female respondents with respect to their perceptions of the relative roles of mothers and fathers were also noted. Specifically, girls on the whole attributed a larger share of parental decision-making to their mothers than did boys.

It was Lopata (1971) who found that in the United States, better-educated mothers showed greater awareness of the importance of their role in the development of their children's personalities and abilities than did less-educated mothers. Additionally, Jewish mothers tended to define role competency in terms of how the mother's personality related to and affected the other family members, while Catholic mothers specified the qualities of an ideal mother in terms of how well she carried out household tasks and duties.

When Smith and Schooler (1978) asked Japanese women to rank their various roles as mother, wife, individual, and female, they found—as expected—that by far the greatest importance was attached to the maternal role. In contrast to American women, contemporary Japanese mothers place much greater emphasis on their personal relationship with their children than their relationship with their husbands, although this emphasis may be gradually shifting.

Because of their interest in the change in marriage roles accompanying the acculturation of the Mexican-American wife, Tharp, Meadow, Lennhoff, and Satterfield (1968) examined the Mexican-American wife population of the Southwest United States. Two groups of roughly equivalent age, but representing more-acculturated and less-acculturated, populations were compared. Their results generally confirmed the hypothesis that during acculturation to the hosting society of the United States, marriage roles shift towards an egalitarian-companionate pattern or change from a segregated to a joint conjugal role pattern.

Haas' study (1981) concerning domestic role-sharing in Swedish couples found that while Swedish couples appear to engage in domestic role-sharing to a greater extent than American couples, the actual practice of sex-role equality lags considerably behind official ideology as well as couples' own ideas on the subject. However, the results of this study also suggest that domestic role-sharing may become more widespread in the future for Swedish couples.

Male dominance in the Chicano family was re-examined and new conceptualization of the male role was suggested by Mirande (1979). He found that the traditional view of the Chicano family as patriarchal and authoritarian is erroneous and based on unsupported myths and stereotypes held by both social scientists and the public at large. Although "machismo" was once thought endemic to Mexican or Latino culture, machismo has taken an interesting turn in its transference from Latino to Anglo culture. Namely, the powerless, colonized man is seen as compensating for feelings of inadequacy and inferiority by assuming an overly-masculine and aggressive response. The male is thought to be motivated by an insatiable sex drive and a lifelong struggle to prove his masculinity and sexual prowess. The authoritarian and patriarchal pattern is assumed not only to engender passivity and to stifle independence and achievement in children but to generate family violence. In spite of this stereotypical view, a review of recent research studies suggests that the Chicano family is not male-dominated and authoritarian but egalitarian. Husband and wife share not only decision-making but also share in the performance of household tasks and child care; sharp sex role segregation appears to be the exception rather than the rule among Chicano families.

Concerning sex roles, Balswick and Peek (1971) indicated that emotional inexpressiveness is a culturally-produced temperament trait which is characteristic of many American males, since they have been raised with the belief that emotional expressiveness is not masculine. From the point of view of the family, especially in light of the increased importance of the companionship and affection function of marriage, across-the-board inexpressiveness of married males (that is, inexpressiveness in all women including their wives) can be highly dysfunctional in their marital relationships. However, selective inexpressiveness (inexpressiveness toward women other than their wives) in males can be just as functional in maintaining these relationships.

Communication

Expression and exchange of ideas among family members can be examined from various perspectives: clarity, amount of communication, style of communication, congruence of communication (affect versus verbal, or statement versus context), and responsiveness (how messages are received, whether empathetic or not).

The extent to which open communication among family members is encouraged varies greatly among families of different cultural groups. In Hawaii, for example, traditional Hawaiian family custom has it that children are to be seen but not to be heard when in the presence of their parents at family occasions such as meals. The children are expected to listen to and learn from the adults' conversation, speaking only when they are actually invited to express their opinion. In marked contrast, Caucasian families commonly value conversation carried out among all family members, encouraging even the youngest children to speak up so that their opinions can be heard.

Cultural traditions greatly affect the extent to which families feel comfortable about revealing their private lives to outsiders. A comparison of families of different ethnic groups in Hawaii showed that, generally speaking, Caucasian families discussed family problems with outsiders with relative ease, while Hawaiian families did so less easily, and Asian families did so with the most strain. This indicates that there are different rates at which families feel ready to disclose their internal lives and private feelings to evaluators or therapists.

Affection

Families of different ethnic groups tend to manifest specific patterns of affection expression. For example, whereas Italian or Latin families tend to show full emotion, Japanese or British families tend to be more reserved and constrained. Therefore, there is a need for different baselines in evaluating the emotional responsiveness of families.

For the purposes of assessment, it is very important to be aware that expression of family behavior may differ greatly depending on the families' cultural background. As pointed out by Japanese psychiatrist Doi (1973), Japanese tend to distinguish between public (front) and private (rear) situations, and accordingly behave and react differently. While they tend to be very polite and restrained in public, observed situations, they tend to become relaxed, natural, and unrestrained in private settings. This type of two-fold behavior also applies to family groups, so this type of discrepancy in family reactional patterns should be recognized and interpreted perceptively.

Relations

Within the family, the nature of interpersonal relationships between members can be observed and analyzed by several parameters: complementary or symmetrical, conflicting or harmonious, disengaged or over-involved, and dependent or independent. Such relationships between family members are dynamic ones and will be subject to frequent change, depending on changes in the familial situation.

Based on the nature of family relations, the quality of relations for the family as a group may be described as warm, close, friendly, distant, uninvolved, antagonistic, sarcastic, or hostile. The total configuration of existing family relations can also be drawn as a map to indicate the distance and closeness of various relations occurring among family members. Such a family map can be drawn by any of the family members or even by an outside observer. Since such a map is very much based on subjective impressions, it is relatively unsuitable for cross-cultural comparisons.

Organization

The organizational structure of the family group as a whole in maintaining its organization and performing its functions and tasks varies among different families. Some families are overstructured while others are disorganized, some pathologically integrated, while others are detached and fragmented as a group. This overall assessment of family-group organization pattern is another way to evaluate the structure and function of the family, but mainly from the perspective of the family as a group.

FAMILY-GROUP INTERACTION PATTERNS – CROSS-ETHNIC COMPARISON

Beginning in the 1950's, a group of family researchers became interested in studying families with schizophrenic patients. Their intention was to explore the intrafamilial environment in which the schizophrenic patients grew up (Wynne and Singer, 1963; Litz, Fleck, Cornelson, and Terry, 1965), and to identify the transactional characteristics which differentiated groups of families that produced certain types of children—schizophrenic, delinquent, or normal (Stabenau, Tupin, Werner, and Pollin, 1965). Through such research attempts, a method of observing, describing, and analyzing a family as a group emerged.

In order to understand the interactional variables necessary for healthy family functioning, Lewis, Beaver and their colleagues (1976) at Timberlawn, Dallas, studied optimally functioning families. The interactional patterns of a group of healthy Caucasian families with middle-upper class socioeconomic backgrounds were observed and rated by a group of trained clinicians, using the Beavers-Timberlawn Family Evaluation Scale. This scale was designed to assess family-group behavior patterns on multiple family interactional variables such as power structure, autonomy, affect, and negotiation for problem solving. For each interactional variable, the family is assessed within the range of a spectrum. For example, under the power structure variable, a family would be assessed within the following spectrum: Chaos—Marked dominance—Moderate dominance—Led—Egalitarian. Under communication of self-concept (as a part of assessing autonomy), a family would be scored in the following spectrum: Very clear—Somewhat vague and hidden—Hardly anyone is ever clear. In addition to the variables, a family would be evaluated on the Global Healthy-Pathology Scale (ratings ranging from Most Pathological to Healthiest) to assess the overall degree of competence of the family.

As a result of their investigation, Lewis and Beaver reported that optimally functioning families present flexible structures, demonstrate respect for subjective views, explore numerous options in approaching problems, and are open in the expression of affection. They concluded that a healthy family contains individuals who demonstrate high levels of personal autonomy, and a healthy family as a whole shows strikingly affiliative attitudes about human encounters. They emphasized that optimally functioning families' success did not depend on one single quality, but rather on the presence and interrelationship of a number of variables.

One decade later, Lewis and Looney (1983) used the same family assessment scale to study well-functioning working-class black families. Their intention was to understand the family functioning pattern of black families and compare the optimal functional pattern of black families to that of the Caucasian families previously examined. They claimed that despite the difference in socioeconomic circumstances of the two groups (one group middle-class, the other much more affluent), the most competent families looked much alike when their relationship processes were studied in family interactional testing. From the methodological point of view, such a conclusion deserves careful consideration as a cross-ethnic study. Examining the whole sample of families disclosed that the upper-middle class Caucasian families and the working-class black families differed significantly in the interactional variables of structure, closeness, negotiation, empathy, mythology, and conflict. Out of concern that such differences might derive from socioeconomic factors rather than from ethnic factors, Lewis and Looney studied the families in a different way, comparing only the families of the two ethnic groups which were rated as the "most competent" ones. Since the raters used the subscales in the family assessment to decide the overall degree of competence, those families rated as "most competent" would naturally be similar in family interactional variables, regardless of their ethnic background.

In order to examine cultural aspects of family interactional patterns, families of four ethnic groups in Hawaii were compared (Hsu, Tseng, Ashton, McDermott, and Char, 1986): Caucasian-American, Chinese-American, Japanese-American, and Hawaiian. The basic method of investigation adopted was similar to that of the Timberlawn study (Lewis, Beavers, Gossett, and Phillips, 1976), with videotapes of structured family activities being rated by the Timberlawn Family Evaluation Scale. By design, all the scores on the Family Evaluation Scale fell within the normal range, as only "functioning" families were included for study. However, results still revealed significant differences between the ethnic groups in most family interactions, such as power distribution, parental coalition, closeness, clarity of self-disclosure, and responsibility. The study indicated a need to establish a culturally relevant family interaction profile, so that normal interactions in families outside the mainstream would not be misinterpreted as dysfunctional.

Among the four ethnic family groups investigated, the most divergence occurred between the Caucasian-American and Japanese-American groups, with the other two groups falling in between. Specific comparison of the Caucasian-American and Japanese-American families (Hsu, Tseng, Ashton, McDermott, and Char, 1985) revealed several things. In regard to the distribution of power between parents, the Japanese-American couples were rated as interacting with slightly more dominance and submission than were the Caucasian-American couples. The Caucasian parents were rated as having stronger parental coalitions. The two groups of families were seen as quite different in regards to variables thought to influence the development of individual autonomy: clarity, responsibility, invasiveness, and permeability. The Caucasian-American families were rated as significantly clearer in self-disclosure than the Japanese-American families, who were seen to be somewhat vague and reticent in expressing individual thoughts and feelings. The Caucasian-American families were seen as open and direct in expressing their feelings, while the Japanese-American families were seen as more restricted and more uncomfortable. The characteristics of the Japanese-American family interactional pattern were thought to be rooted in Japanese culture. It is important for a Japanese person to conform to the group norm and to refrain from expressing disagreement (Lebra, 1976). The Japanese also value implicit, nonverbal, intuitive communication over explicit, verbal, and rational exchanges of information. As pointed out by Doi (1973), Japanese have a twofold structure of psychological functioning, conveyed by two Japanese words, "Omote" (front, public) and "Ura" (rear, private), which they use to indicate contrasting attitudes in dealing with social situations. This partially explains why the raters saw the Japanese-American families as having difficulty in expressing affection and revealing private matters, and as displaying incongruity between their stated and observed family behaviors.

Instead of having observers objectively assess family interactional patterns, some studies have relied on self-reported data, asking family members to respond to questionnaires. The Moos Family Environment Scale and the Dollas Self-Report Family Inventory are two examples of instruments designed for this purpose. Another example is the Family Adaptability and Cohesion Evaluation Scale (FACES), created by Olson and his colleagues (1985). FACES is designed for use by the family in assessing their perception of their family function in the two most significant dimensions: Adaptability and Cohesion. For each dimension, the family is assessed on a spectrum of low to high. For the Cohesion dimension, the range is Disengaged — Separated — Connected — Enmeshed, while for the Adaptability dimension, the range is Rigid — Structured — Flexible — Chaotic. As there are four levels of cohesion and four levels of adaptability on each dimension, putting them together forms sixteen cells or family types on the Circumplex Model. Within this Circumplex Model, balanced, healthy, and functional types are considered to be centrally located while extreme or dysfunctional types are located on corners, with the mid-range types scattered in between.

Using this instrument and concept, Caucasian-American, Japanese-American, Chinese-American, and Hawaiian families were surveyed in Hawaii (Hsu, Tseng, Lum, Lao, Vaccaro, and Brennan, 1988). Results indicated that family function in terms of cohesion and adaptability, as perceived by the family members, did not differ among four ethnic groups of non-clinic (functional) families. However, family satisfaction as examined by the Family Satisfaction Scale (Olson, McCubbin, Barnes, Larsen, Muxen, and Wilson, 1982) showed that the Caucasian-American families, in contrast to the three other groups of ethnic families, were slightly but significantly less satisfied. This illustrated that studies of family interaction and function, whether subjective or objective, have different outcomes, indicating that family function needs to be assessed from multiple approaches.

Questionnaire surveys have been conducted in India and the United States concerning family cohesiveness, decision-making, and autonomy (Sundberg et al., 1969). The subjects for the surveys were ninth-grade students of each sex chosen from agricultural towns in northern India and the western United States. The results disclosed that whereas Indian adolescents perceived greater cohesiveness, American adolescents perceived more self-decisiveness.

The American students also did not regard their fathers as influential as the Indian students considered their fathers.

CONCLUSION

Observation and analysis of the structure and function of the family-group have been examined in this chapter. From the perspective of cross-cultural comparison, there are several issues that deserve full attention. Since parameters of the family function are so numerous, the use of different sets of parameters in assessing families will result in different observations. Some parameters are sensitive to the characteristics of the structure and function of families of a particular cultural group, while other parameters are not. Selection of the criteria, parameters, and instruments for cross-cultural examinations and measurements therefore needs special attention (Forman and Hagan, 1983).

Families of various cultural groups tend to perform their family function differently under varied circumstances. This is typified by Japanese families who will interact remarkably differently in public (*omote*) or private (*ura*) as elaborated by Doi (1973). It will also be true for families of many other cultural groups who will not behave naturally in artificial or public settings. Therefore, whether the family is observed in a clinical setting or in the home setting will make a tremendous difference for families of some cultural groups. The existence of such incongruous behavior patterns should be kept in mind, particularly when comparisons are to be made cross-culturally.

Finally, the cultural background of the observer may significantly affect the results of an examination. The observer's bias on interpretation of the family interaction pattern has already been illustrated clearly in transcultural investigation (Tseng, McDermott, Ogino, and Ebata, 1982). All these considerations must be viewed when we are examining the family-group in a transcultural situation.

Chapter 5

Culture and Family Adjustment

Some special functions of the family, including family values, rituals, and socialization, will be discussed here. This will be followed by elaboration of relations between sociocultural issues and the family, with emphasis on the impact of cultural change, migration, or minority status on family life. Finally, the concept of family stress and coping patterns will be reviewed from cultural perspectives.

FAMILY VALUES

A set of family values forms the value system commonly held within a family. Family values concern how events and experiences need to be interpreted, believed, and performed in certain ways in relation to family life. The process by which families and family members develop their value orientations emerges out of multiple factors — including environmental, educational, and experiential. Yet, as pointed out by Trotzer (1981), parents serve as carriers, monitors, developers, reinforcers, and interpreters of their children's values. Children, in turn, merge their experiences with the expectations of their parents and significant others to mold a set of values that will later be passed on to their own children.

From a cultural point of view, maintenance and transmission of values within the family are aspects of family function that deserve careful attention. Methodologically, however, there is not yet a suitable way to conduct comprehensive and practical evaluation and research of family values.

Papajohn and Spiegel (1975) have attempted to describe the

value-orientation held by different ethnic families by utilizing anthropologist Kluckhohn's (1951) view of value-orientation as a behavior influencer. According to this view, value-orientation is a generalized conception of nature and man's place in nature, of man's relation to other men, and of the desirable and nondesirable as they relate to man-environment and interhuman relations. In comparing Puerto Rican and American values, Papajohn and Spiegel found profiles that differed in many ways. One difference concerned time-orientation: the Puerto Rican working class was most oriented to the present, then to the future, and least oriented to the past, while the American middle-class was most oriented towards the future, then the present, and least oriented to the past. Another difference concerned relational-orientation: Puerto Ricans oriented first towards collateral relations and then lineal relations, while Americans oriented first towards individualist relations and then towards collateral relations.

While this method is one way of examining a value system, it has several shortcomings. It deals with value-orientation in a very general way, including orientation to areas such as nature and time without focusing specifically and directly on the matter of a family. It also deals with a "person's" orientation to the universe and life. Additionally, orientation is subject to change depending on its associated circumstances. For example, concerning time orientation, Chinese place great emphasis on the past in worshipping their ancestors but simultaneously emphasize the future in bearing and raising children to continue the family line. This technique therefore needs to describe orientation more specifically instead of inclusively, and should focus primarily on family-related issues.

As a part of Lewis and Looney's (1983) investigation of black families, family members were asked to respond to the Rokeach Value Survey — an instrument for the respondents to rank eighteen items in order of importance based on their own value judgements. They found different patterns of response between the "most competent" families and the "least competent" families. The members of the most competent families generally ranked "salvation" as first, "happiness" as second, "wisdom" as third, and "family security" as fourth in importance as a terminal value. In contrast, individuals from the least competent black families ranked "family security" as first, "happiness" as second, "a comfortable life" as third, and "a world of peace" as fourth in importance. Interestingly, "salvation" (ranked first by the most competent families) was ranked as eighteenth or least in importance by the least competent and most economically deprived families. "Wisdom" (ranked third by individuals from the most competent families) was ranked as fourteenth in importance by members of the least competent families. These results indicated that, even within the same ethnic group, family members' set of values were associated with the competence of the family.

Specifically addressing the generation difference in values, Berrien, Arkoff, and Iwahara (1967) compared the value systems held by "mother and daughter" and "father and son." With the hypothesis that the magnitude of difference of values held between parents and children (of the same gender) would be associated with the degree of sociocultural change, they examined the generational differences in three different settings: Japanese in Tokyo, Japanese-American in Hawaii, and American in New Jersey. The subjects of the study were college students and their parents, and the instrument used was the Edward Personal Preference Schedule. The Schedule provides fifteen scores with various labels such as Achievement, Deference, Order, Exhibition, Autonomy, and Affiliation. The results revealed a remarkable similarity in direction of differences between the generations of the three ethnic groups examined in this study, with dissimilarities only in the magnitude of difference between parents and children of the same gender. For example, Japanese (unlike Japanese-American or American) sons scored lower on Achievement and Dominance but higher on Introception than their fathers, while Japanese-American (unlike Japanese or American) sons scored significantly higher on Exhibition and Change but less on Nurturance than their fathers. The study did not support the investigator's original speculation that the magnitude of generational differences in values would be greatest in Tokyo, where the family faced the greatest degree of sociocultural change. However, it did illustrate that, at least for the three groups studied, the direction of difference of values between the young-adults and their middle-aged parents of the same gender was similar regardless of where they lived or their ethnic background.

FAMILY RITUALS

"Family rituals" refers to the repetitious, highly valued, symbolic occasions or activities observed or undertaken by a family. Family rituals are considered a part of family culture through which enduring values, attitudes and goals are transmitted (Bossard and Boll, 1950). Family rituals can be further subdivided into culture-related family celebrations, family-observed ritual activities, and patterned interactions practiced by the family. Family rituals certainly can promote a sense of family identity, pride, cohesiveness, solidarity, and continuity (Shipman, 1982).

Family celebrations are those holidays and occasions which are widely recognized within a cultural group, and which hold a special place in the mind of the family. Examples include rites of passage such as weddings, funerals, baptisms, or initiation rites; annual religious celebrations such as Christmas; and secular holiday observances such as Thanksgiving. These family rituals are characterized by their relative standardization across most families in a society, and by the universality of the symbols which pertain to the ritual.

Family-observed traditional ritual activities are less culture-specific and more idiosyncratic for each family. They occur in most families with some regularity but not necessarily annually. The family chooses the occasions and activities it will embrace or emphasize as traditions; these may include birthdays, anniversaries, or family reunions.

Patterned family interactions are frequently enacted but less consciously planned by the participants. Examples are a regular dinner-time, the customary treatment of guests in the home, the discipline of children, or everyday greetings.

Family rituals serve as an index to a family's integration level. Wolin, Bennett, Noonan, and Teitelbaum (1980) reported in their study that when one or both parents in a family are alcoholics, their children are more likely to become alcoholics if family rituals are disrupted during the period of heaviest parental drinking.

FAMILY SOCIALIZATION

Every family has its social network and relations outside of the family. Such family socialization may primarily involve kin-related groups or non-kin-related groups, depending on the sociocultural custom.

An informative study has been conducted by Salamon (1977) concerning family bonds and friendship bonds in Japan and West Germany. Families of similar background (all middle-class, residing neolocally in urban apartments) were selected for intensive study in Tokyo, Japan and Munich/Tubingen, West Germany. All the husbands and wives were in their thirties and had two or three children, most of whom were of school age. The husbands all had at least four years of college level training and held middle-level executive positions in either business or government bureaucracies. The wives all had at least two years of college level training and were all housewives, although some also worked additional part-time jobs in their home. The wives were interviewed and asked to give life histories. To get an idea of ordinary family life and its association with family socialization patterns, the families were also observed for an ordinary day in their homes.

The results disclosed that within the Japanese nuclear family there exists a very clear division of labor between husband and wife which places them in separate relational worlds. For example, the wives were often not aware of their husbands' work duties, while the husbands did not know the price of fish or what the children were doing in school. As for socialization patterns, the husband usually socialized with his colleagues at work and related to old friends from college and high school. The wife associated with old friends from college and high school, as well as friends from the PTA and the neighborhood. The children associated with friends from school and the neighborhood. The most characteristic point was that each individual in the family could and did have intimate relationships of his/her own which were not shared by other family members. The Japanese say that loading one relationship with the full range of one's cares and woes is too intense. Thus, a woman might complain to her neighbor about peevish things such as prices and the children, to her husband about the neighbors, to her mother about her husband's drinking problem, and about "everything" (meaning her life) to her best friends from high school. Each relationship serves different emotional needs and in this way the Japanese are able to gather and spread out support through many sources.

In contrast, division of labor is less clearly defined in middle-class West German families. The husband is the economic provider and the wife is in charge of the home and children. However, when the German husband is home, he is an active participant in the family and unlike the Japanese husband who is seldom home, the German husband seems to be always there. Parents in Germany keep up their joint active social life. A German wife is drawn into the social life which evolves out of her husband's work relationships. While a Japanese wife may never have met her husband's work companions, this social life may be the German wife's main source of social contacts.

It is apparent from this study that the family is viewed as being at an intersection of the set of interpersonal bonds of members. Japanese families are found to encourage individualized sets, while West German families favor overlapping sets and a highly integrated system. As pointed out by Salamon, this variety in systems is seen to stem from the factor of choice in relationships, as such families are not economically dependent on their kin.

An insightful point about family socialization was brought up in Cohler and Lieberman's 1980 investigation. Maintenance of close ties with relatives and friends is generally believed to foster personal adjustment, acting to reduce the impact of otherwise stressful life events through provision of increased support and care in times of personal crisis. While such use of primary group or face-to-face relations may reduce the otherwise adverse impact of life stress and strain, less consideration has been given to circumstances in which the maintenance of such face-to-face relations might in itself become an additional source of strain, thereby adversely affecting personal adjustment and morale. In order to examine this, trained field interviewers used a survey research format to interview middle-aged and older men and women from three European ethnic groups in the United States. The subjects were all first- or second-generation Irish, Italian, or Polish, and all lived in urban settings. Life-event stress was measured by the life events scale of Pakel, Prusoff and Uhlenhuth (1971), which assessed a particular event which had taken place in the preceding year, so that a total stress score could be measured. Information was obtained from each respondent regarding patterns of social relations.

Analysis of the resultant data revealed that the presence of an extensive social network and an increased number of persons available to be significant. The increased involvement with significant others appears to have an adverse impact on mental health (particularly among Italian and Polish women) as measured by the total score of life stress experience. This indicated that although it has been assumed that social relations are inherently satisfying and act to reduce the impact of life stress and strain, it appears that at least in some instances (for some ethnic groups), such enduring social ties may enhance rather than reduce feelings of distress.

As a matter of fact, in some ethnic groups (including some Asian or Micronesian groups) in which family socialization with kin is highly emphasized and exchange systems (in the form of gift giving or burden sharing) are expected, maintaining such excessive social bonds and networks and fulfilling such cultural expectations can be the primary source of family strain (Tseng and Hsu, 1986).

FAMILY AND SOCIOCULTURAL ISSUES

There are numerous kinds of unique sociocultural situations or phenomena which have particular impact on the lives and functions of the family. Some of the special sociocultural situations or phenomena which need family adjustment will be examined here.

Sociocultural Change

A society is a dynamic organization which, from a historical perspective, usually undergoes change in certain areas such as its cultural system and family system. For instance, Herz (1967) reminds us that the eighteenth-century American family had several distinctive characteristics. It was a rural family unit that emphasized cooperation and self-sufficiency as well as the economic arrangement aspect of marriage, and viewed familism and authoritarianism as two basic principles to govern internal organization. As pointed out by Cherlin (1983), family life changed greatly in many Western developed societies after World War II, with the United States being no exception. In America, phenomena observed after the sixties included a sharp decline in fertility rate, an equally sharp rise in the divorce rate, a large increase in the labor force participation of married women, and the growth of nonmarital cohabiting relationships. Associated with the emphasis on individualism and democratic organization, the contemporary American family must face transitional conflicting values from authoritarian familism to democratic individualism, changing values that challenge marital stability and the need for a meaningful marital relationship, the pressure of the romantic love concept, the economic independence of women, and parental confusion and conflict about child-rearing. This indicates that a society's family system will change in association with its historical path.

By comparing Indian families in India with Indian families who have migrated to Trinidad in the Caribbean islands, Nevadomsky (1980) has examined how changes over time and space may affect the family system. It was noted that in India and Trinidad, and perhaps in other places throughout the world, a number of similar family changes are taking place. Nevertheless, although the direction of change is approximately the same, the degree of change seems to vary. In Trinidad the process is occurring at a rapid rate among the East Indians, whereas similar changes in India are taking place at a much slower pace. The traditional Indian family is supported and sanctioned by a particular caste and religious system. Associated with the process of migration and social change, this caste system has disappeared in Trinidad, where the majority of marriages are now based entirely on free personal choice. The undisputed hierarchy of the family has been replaced by ambiguity and rebellion.

Sometimes the magnitude of change is so great or the speed of alteration so rapid in a society that there is tremendous impact on family life within that society. Generally speaking, when a society undertakes great or rapid sociocultural change in terms of social structure, hierarchy, lifestyles, common beliefs, and value orientation, the parents' traditional value systems are challenged and their power of authority is frequently shaken. Unlike the older generation, the younger generation is usually able to absorb changes quickly and to develop a new way of seeing things which is remarkably different from that of their parents. A wide generation gap is thus created, with potential tension and conflict between generations. It is a common observation around the world that social change in the form of modernization and urbanization tends to undermine parental authority, reduce respect for the elderly, and weaken male authority in the family (El-Islam, 1983; Moos, 1988).

As for gender differences between the young people, young males are particularly sensitive and vulnerable to the disorganization and confusion of family life that occurs as a result of rapid cultural change. They tend to feel greater impact than young females. When deprived of parental guidance and support, threatened by the gap that separates them from their parents, and frustrated by the absence of direction and goals for their lives, young males tend to react by manifesting openly conflictual and rebellious behavior towards their parents. Some of them turn to alcohol or substance abuse and violent behavior (Rubinstein, 1986).

Migration

When a family undertakes migration to a new place where the sociocultural system differs significantly from the one they are leaving behind, they not only need to adjust to the new environment in terms of residence, occupation, financial resources, and social network, but also to the new ways of thinking.

Generally, the process of adjustment to migration is influenced by various factors. These include the motives for migration, the attitude of the host society toward the migrants, the background of the migrants (educational, occupational, etc.), and the nature of the cultures of the migrants and the host society (i.e., are the cultures compatible or do they clash with each other?).

The adjustment process will further be affected by variables of the family such as the age of the children and the family's life cycle and structure. Each family member (parents, grandparents, and children of different ages included), has his/her own difficulties in adjusting to the new life associated with migration. For example, adolescents tend to be more sensitive towards the situation of migration if they have to make gross adjustments in the areas of language, school system, and peer-relation patterns in addition to changing their general value system. The middle-aged father also frequently has difficulty in adjusting to the new environment if he has to change his pattern of work. The protection of the domestic setting may lessen the housewife's strain of adjustment, but she may still suffer from a degree of social isolation. Thus, family members may face different kinds and degrees of strain in association with migration.

By examining the socialization of children of immigrant Indian and Pakistani families in a city of western Canada, Wakil, Siddique, and Wakil (1981) reported that as traditional social control measures weaken and the demands by children for greater freedom increase, many immigrant parents fall back on traditional concepts of respect for age and authority. According to Wakil et al. (1981), almost all the parents viewed their teenage children's involvement with "dating" and "romantic love" with great alarm and horror. In contrast, the children saw "dating" and "courtship" as socially acceptable ways to gain popularity in their peer groups, and as a part of growing up in Western society. The nervous and somewhat confused parents always failed to find any "solution" to this problem.

It was Sluzki (1979) who pointed out that families face different problems in association with the various stages of the migration process: the preparatory stage, the actual act of migration, the stage of adjustment by overcompensation, the stage of decompensation, and the stage of integration and balance. It is clear that during the preparatory stage family members must work out their different attitudes and motivations regarding migration. The act of migration may be a short period for a family that migrates as a group, or may take several years if the family members migrate separately. In the latter case, the family must cope with the separation of family members as well as the other problems associated with the different stages of the migration experience among different members of the family. The different paces of adjusting to the new cultural system will sometimes seriously affect roles and hierarchy within a family. For instance, when the children are fast in learning the new language while the middle-aged parents are slow, the parents have to depend on their children for social function. This situation unfortunately reverses the roles and status of parent and child (Stagoll, 1981).

There are few investigations which systematically trace the process of cultural adjustment over different generations of a family. Connor (1974) has interviewed Japanese-American families of three generations to examine the extent to which they retained a number of the characteristics which are associated with the family system in Japan. He concluded that even though considerable acculturation has taken place, even the third generation of Japanese-Americans still retain certain characteristics of the more traditional Japanese family system.

Minority

The term minority is used to refer to a group which is proportionally small in size in contrast to the majority group in a society. Although, strictly speaking, a minority can be a privileged group, we are primarily concerned here with minority groups faced with considerable disadvantage and unfavorable treatment by the majority group. When a minority group is less privileged due to factors (associated with deprivation and discrimination) such as less opportunity for education, economic improvement, or psychological well-being, then the group's family life will be significantly affected.

Underprivileged minority status usually occurs in association with differences in ethnicity or race, but may also occur without any relation to these differences. Minority status can develop within a society of uniform ethnic or racial background, created simply by psychological factors in historical perspective. This is exemplified by the existence of *burakumin* in Japan or of the "untouchable" caste in Hindu society. *Burakumin* literally means "people of village" in Japanese. They are a particular group of Japanese who work as butchers or shoemakers. Their work is regarded by the majority of the Japanese as "dirty," perhaps because of the Buddhist prohibition on killing animals. In spite of having the same ethnic-racial background as Japanese nationals and living in close proximity to them, they are identified and labelled as burakumin and discriminated against by the rest of the Japanese (DeVos and Wagatsuma, 1969). No matter how much education young burakumin may receive, they are not allowed to intermarry with other Japanese. Parents of burakumin families thus discourage their children from seeking higher education, in the belief that there is no choice but for their children to become butchers or shoemakers. Their social status causes them to develop this group self-image.

Out of all the psychological ill-effects associated with minority status, it is ethnic identity development that most affects minority families. Like self-identity, ethnic identity is very important for the mental health of the individual and the family. How ethnic identity is encouraged, cultivated, and developed within a family has not yet been well studied (Cross, 1981). There are many issues involving minority families that need investigation with carefully designed research methodology (Staples and Mirande, 1980; Dilworth-Anderson and McAdoo, 1988). One issue that certainly deserves immediate attention is how ethnic identity is developed through parent-child interaction and the process of enculturation.

FAMILY STRESS AND COPING

Family Stress

Family stress refers to any strains, burdens, problems, or conflicts which cause considerable discomfort, tension, or frustration for family members. Family stress usually results in family dysfunction and requires great effort by the family to remove or solve the problems.

The ABCX family crisis model was first proposed by Hill in 1949 as a conceptual foundation for the examination of family stress. According to this model, in addition to the "stressor" (A) itself, "the existing resource" (B) and "perception of the stress" (C) will all integratively affect the nature and severity of the "crisis'' (X). This concept was further expanded in 1983 into the Double ABCX model by McCubbin and Patterson (1983). The model adds post-crisis variables in an effort to describe: (a) the additional life stressors and changes which may influence the family's ability to achieve adaptation; (b) the critical psychological and social factors families call upon and use in managing crisis situations; (c) the process families engage in to achieve a satisfactory resolution; and (d) the outcome of these family efforts.

McCubbin, Joy, Cauble, Comeau, Patterson, and Needle (1980) have reviewed research regarding family stress carried out in the past decade, and have created two major classifications of family stress: normative and non-normative. Non-normative transitions include family stress associated with wars, disasters, or illness; loss of a family member; occupational stress and family life; family conflicts resulting from women participating in the labor force; and long-term chronic stressor events such as unemployment and repeated chronic recession. As for normative transitions over the life span, they include family stress related to the transition to parenthood, child launching, retirement, and widowhood.

Certain types of family stress are more or less culture-related. For example, most African families consider procreation to be one of the major aims of marriage, and thus Nigerian families are extremely concerned with having as many children as possible. Fertility is regarded as a blessing and barrenness as a curse. Barrenness is in fact a potentially serious source of conflicts, quarrels, dissension, and other forms of maladjustment in many Nigerian couples, regardless of their educational or socioeconomic status. Based on this observation, Denga (1982) has conducted an investigation comparing the marital adjustment of mothers with that of involuntarily childless women. He found that, as measured by Spanier's Dyadic Adjustment Scale—which contains the components of consensus, cohesion, satisfaction, and affection—those married women who were unable to bear children due to biological problems were much unhappier than those married women who had children. This illustrated that wives who fail to meet cultural expectations regarding childbearing suffer from marital stress.

Despite recent rapid economic development in Korea, Koreans still strongly believe that it is very important for married women to stay at home to serve as housewives. Most young women, even those who are well-educated and have professional positions, will leave their jobs and become housewives as soon as they are married, in line with their husband's expectations. In fact, most Korean companies will dismiss their women employees once they marry. As a result, less than 15% of married women in contemporary Korea work outside the home.

With this cultural tendency for discouraging Korean women to work outside the home and the modernization of the household environment, with associated improvement of domestic living conditions, the life inside the home is getting easier and more monotonous for the housewife. As a result, many Korean housewives who live in the city area find life at home less challenging and boring and tend to develop neurotic symptoms more often than those who are permitted to work outside the home. Thus, Korean psychiatrists give a label of "housewife syndrome" for those housewives who experience unenjoyable family life and visit the psychiatric clinic with their nonspecific neurotic symptoms (Chang and Kim, 1988).

Family Coping

Coping behavior refers to specific efforts (whether covert or overt) by which an individual or a group attempts to reduce or manage a demand. As pointed out by Patterson (1988), coping most often has been conceptualized at the individual level, but family-coping can also be considered if we think of collective family-group action to eliminate or manage demands, either through coordinated family-group behavior or complimentary efforts of family members.

The function of coping is to maintain or restore the balance between demands and resources. Patterson (1988) has listed different ways this can be accomplished by the family system: direct action to reduce the number and/or intensity of demands; direct action to acquire additional resources not already available to the family; maintaining existing resources so they can be allocated and reallocated to meet changing demands; managing the tension associated with continuing strains; and cognitive appraisal to change the meaning of a situation to make it more manageable. From a family therapist's point of view, an addition can be made to the list: promoting changes in family structure and relations that give the family more strength and skills for dealing with strain and demands effectively.

Although family coping patterns vary for each family, certain patterns of problem-solving can be observed more frequently in families of certain cultural groups. After examining upwardly mobile black families, McAdoo (1982) reported that ties with extended families were a source of emotional and instrumental strength, especially during periods of high stress. The serial reciprocal obligations to kin were not perceived to be excessive, but were felt more strongly by the more recently upwardly mobile. The kin support system was not considered a serious drain on the family's resources, as was the case with black families at the poverty level.

Another study, which compared four ethnic groups in Hawaii (Caucasian, Chinese-American, Hawaiians, and Japanese-American), found that the Hawaiian group, in contrast to the other three groups, tended to utilize the method of seeking spiritual support in times of crisis. In comparison, the Chinese-American group preferred to utilize various coping patterns including mobilizing the resources that exist in the family (Hsu, Tseng, Lum, Lau, Vaccaro, and Brennan, 1988). Thus, there are certain culture-preferred patterns for families to cope with problems.

CLOSING

So far we have tried to examine and understand various aspects of the family – namely, the family system, the family subsystem, the family as a group, family development, and family adjustment. Based on this type of multidimensional approach to comprehending the family (particularly from cultural aspects), and based on such grounds of knowledge, we will move to examine the potential problems and psychopathology of families observed in various cultural groups.

Chapter 6

Marital Problems and Conflict

Moments of unhappiness or dissatisfaction between husband and wife may be expected to occur occasionally as part of day to day life. Some couples, however, experience disharmony or conflict that is frequent or causes serious difficulties between spouses, disturbing their marital life, affecting marital relations, or bringing about distress for either spouse; such couples can be considered as experiencing marital problems. Marital problems will be examined from these aspects: the nature and sources of the problems, the problems associated with different stages of the marital cycle, and marital problems observed in different stages of conflict.

THE NATURE AND SOURCES OF THE PROBLEMS

Based on experience working with married couples within a nuclear family in a society that mainly emphasizes affection between husband and wife, most contemporary family therapists tend to believe that marital problems stem from absence of affection and difficulty with interpersonal relations. For marriages in various cultural settings, however, problems in a marriage may originate from sources outside the marriage itself. For example, difficulties may be related to the cultural aspects of a family system and marriage system, or even due to extra-family factors. Thus, more extensive examination is necessary in order to comprehend the sources of marital problems from cross-cultural perspectives.

The Existence of Cultural Differences
Between Spouses

Basic differences in spouses' value systems, lifestyles, and perspectives (including orientation towards and expectations about marriage) may lead to maladjustment and dissatisfaction. These problems are frequently exemplified by intercultural marriages in which the marriage partners have a wide cultural gap between them.

Discrepancy of Cultural Orientation
Toward Marriage

Based on different orientations, marriage can be seen either as an obligatory union of a man and woman for a lifetime commitment, or as a functional bond primarily based on affection, that will endure as long as intense affection between the marital partners exists. Thus, marital conflict can occur if the partners hold different views on whether marriage should be affection-oriented or commitment-oriented, since they may then have opposite expectations for their relationship. These differences in marriage orientation can be derived from individual expectations but can also be related to different cultural backgrounds.

The Difference in Value, Belief, or Faith

Associated with different cultural backgrounds, people will develop different sets of value systems, beliefs, and faiths, which are rather persistent and have a significant impact on their behavior patterns. If two marriage partners happen to have widely contrasting and incompatible value systems and lifestyles, they may find it relatively difficult to adjust to each other in their marital life, and distressing problems may result.

The Problems Associated with the System
of Marriage or Family

Sometimes the sources of marital tension or conflict are not related to the marital partners themselves but are derived from the particular marital or family systems from which they came. Although patterns of marital and family systems tend to be molded by socioeconomic and cultural factors with a functional purpose, they may also stem from certain strains and problems.

Arranged Marriage versus Love Marriage

After studying marital strains encountered by Japanese women, Lebra (1978) identified two types of marriages: "structured" and "unstructured." According to Lebra, structured marriages refer to those characterized by marital consummation that occurs through the initiative and decision of a third party (either parents, relatives, or a matchmaker). In structured marriages, the marital dyad is not considered autonomous, but rather seen as merely a small unit within a larger family. The husband and wife are expected to perform different tasks; sexual distance is maintained between mates and is further reinforced by the sex-based hierarchical order set up by the society. In contrast, in an unstructured marriage a man and woman meet, interact, and marry by their own initiative and decision, without the interference of a third party. Husband and wife function as an autonomous unit and sexual intimacy is more or less uninhibited.

Based on this distinction between the two marriage patterns that exist in Japan, Lebra reported that the strain of structured marriages is inherent in the structure itself, caused by factors such as regulation of sexual distance. With a group of in-laws as co-residents, greater distance is usually imposed upon the newly-married couple. As husband and wife are dichotomized in their role specialization to an excessive degree, with the husband sometimes devoting his life to his profession without ever joining the domestic sphere and the wife dedicating her existence to the rearing and education of the children, they share nothing in common and end up overly distanced from each other.

As for unstructured marriages, most marital problems originated because the partners were unable to select suitable mates. Since most marriages in Japan were traditionally arranged by the parents, many of the young people were inexperienced in finding suitable mates without their parents' guidance. Furthermore, since the families of origin were not involved in the mate selection and frequently disapproved of the choices made, the new couples were deprived of protection from their families. This was particularly significant in situations where the wife was maltreated by her husband. In extreme cases, as reported by Lebra, the wife was subject to the uninhibited physical or sexual aggression of the anomic behavior of the husband; such shameless actions on the part of the husband were not inhibited by traditional structural constraints. Thus, the genesis and manifestations of strain (i.e., the lack of structural control) are also inherent in the system itself.

Nuclear Family versus Extended Family

The extended family is predominant in cultivating societies. The advantages of such a household structure are economic, since an extended family can provide a larger number of workers than a nuclear family. However, such a household is prone to conflicts in interpersonal relations if it is not well-regulated and controlled. Problems tend to occur between the wives of brothers, who may be jealous of each other or seek a loftier position among family members. Conflicts between the mother-in-law and daughters-in-law arise over issues of household control and obedience to an elder. Such interpersonal conflicts can easily affect relations between the husband and wife and cause marital distress. Most of the young people would prefer to form their own nuclear family if they could.

The nuclear family, however, is not necessarily a better form of household structure. Although the couple may enjoy the autonomy of their married life, they also are deprived of some advantages they might have as part of an extended family. For example, there are no other family members to provide a buffer when there is a conflict. Conflict in the form of a misunderstanding or disagreement can be intensified unless repaired in time. Providing such repairs is often the function of extended family members. When a nuclear family faces a crisis such as the illness of a child, the couple may be placed in a vulnerable, stress-increasing situation if there is no adequate support system available.

Post Marital Residence Choice

The husband usually suffers from greater marital stress within a matrilineal system in which matrilocal residence is practiced, as exemplified by the situation in Truk (Micronesia). After marriage, the husband breaks off almost all relations with his kin and old friends and must form new ties with his wife's kin. He is psychologically placed in a situation wherein his loyalties to his family of origin and his wife's family are tested. This conflict is one factor that contributes greatly to the frequency of marital disruption in Truk (Yamao, 1986).

Polygamous Marriages

Surprisingly, most anthropological literature reports that little conflict or strain exists between co-husbands in polyandrous marriages. For example, Levine (1980) writes that polyandrous marriage in Nyinba (northwestern Nepal) takes place between one woman and several brothers. The marital relationships are usually stabilized by the prevailing Nyinba social principles of equality and unity of brothers, seniority within a sibling group, and respect for individual differences. Since the Nyinba believe that only one man is responsible for the conception of a child, and the attribution of a child's paternity is critical in establishing his rights to inheritance and his social position, a pregnant woman in a polyandrous marriage will try to determine exactly which of her husbands had sexual relations with her at the time of conception. It is rare for all of a woman's husbands to be home simultaneously (some spend most of the year on trading expeditions, while others are away pasturing the herds), so there is seldom any confusion about the rightful allocation of paternity.

In contrast, ample evidence indicates the frequent occurrence of jealousy and conflict among co-wives in polygynous marriages. Competition for affection and benefits and rivalry between the children of different wives are common themes within a marriage of one man to many wives (Ebigbo and Ihezue, 1982).

Adoption Marriage

In societies with patrilineal systems that place emphasis on the continuity of the family clan, like those found in Japan and China, a special arrangement for marriage is necessary if a family has only daughters. Under these circumstances, instead of a woman entering the man's household so that their children will carry the father's name, a man will marry into his wife's household and their children take his wife's family name. In a way, the man becomes the adopted son of his wife's parents and is referred to as the adopted son-in-law. From a cultural viewpoint, a man who accepts such an adoption-marriage faces possible scorn from others for giving up his own family identity (and loyalty). Therefore, not too many men are eager to do so. Several factors may lead a man to enter such a union: he may be deeply in love with the spouse-to-be; he may not care about social attitudes or the reaction from his family of origin; or he could be interested in the benefits attached to such a marriage.

Although (as observed in Taiwan) such marriages carry potential psychological risks, Lebra's study (1978) of Japanese marriages found that adoption-marriages did not necessarily lead to problems. In fact, in comparison to ordinary patterns of patrilocal marriage where the wife went to live with her husband's family, more marital success was reported in matrilocal marriages in which the husband lived with his wife's family. Lebra speculated that there were several reasons for this marital success. Feelings of guilt on the part of the wife and her parents for imposing the socially restrained status of an adopted son-in-law on the husband stimulated their efforts to compensate by providing comfortable living conditions that included dyadic intimacy and privacy. This attitude, in turn, encouraged the husband's reciprocal effort to be integrated into his wife's household.

Influence or Intrusion
from Family of Origin

The boundary between the newly-married couple and their families of origin is defined differently in different cultural systems and marriage forms. At times when there are no problems within the marital dyad itself, influences from the families of origin may become the primary source of disturbance. This situation is more frequently observed in a society in which the cultural boundaries between the new family and the families of origin are not clearly drawn.

Disapproval of the Marriage from Families of Origin

When it is customary for a couple to obtain permission and sanctions from their parents before marriage, failure to seek parental approval may lead to serious disturbances in their marital life, with parental approval sometimes powerful enough to obstruct the marriage. Even couples who elope will still have to face a negative reaction from their families and community unless they move to another society. In some societies, this disapproval is often the main reason why some couples kill themselves by double suicide or love suicide.

Objections from the families of origin may help to bind the couple more firmly together as a reaction to external resistance. Alternatively, they may become more vulnerable and unable to face any dissatisfaction and conflict that occur between them. They may blame each other for problems and feel that perhaps they should not have married. A lack of confidence in their marriage, growing guilt about getting married against their parents' wishes, and deprivation of support from the families of origin can all add to the stress on this marriage.

Influence of Marital Life by In-Laws

In addition to the different marital forms and the previously existing parent-child relationships within the families of origin, the influence of in-laws on marital life can be very serious. When the new couple must live with the parents of either the husband or wife (such as in a stem family) or even with married siblings (in an extended family situation), the impact of co-resident in-laws is always great. Even if the couple chooses neolocal residence, the psychological influence from the families of origin can still be felt. A couple may co-exist satisfactorily on an everyday basis, but go through turmoil whenever faced with the involvement of their in-laws from either side in the form of a visit or a telephone call.

Burden of Obligation Fulfillment
to the Families of Origin

The cultural system also puts pressure on young couples to fulfill the requirements and expectations of their families of origin in various ways, such as through gifts or labor; these expectations may become quite a burden.

Split Loyalties
Between the Families of Origin

If the families of origin from both sides have a strong impact upon the young couple, expect the couple to fulfill many obligations (by providing gifts or favors, etc.) and engage in comparisons and competition on both sides — thus placing themselves in a difficult position. This split loyalty brings about strain and conflict between the husband and wife as it becomes impossible to act fairly and evenly toward both sides and to satisfy all concerned.

The Unhealthy Motive of Marriage

Occasionally a person has motivations or reasons for marrying that are out of the ordinary. When neurotic, unhealthy, or immature motivations are the primary reasons for marriage, they usually lead to eventual failure of the marital union (Lantz and Snyder, 1969). Unhealthy motivations for marriage include:

- marriage as a means of escape from an unhappy family life;
- marriage as a means of escape from feelings of loneliness;
- marriage as a rebound from a previous disappointment in a relationship;
- marriage based on a fantasy of being rescued;
- marriage as a means to gain security or wealth;
- marriage for the purpose of living through another person's accomplishments;
- unintended marriage — one necessitated because of pregnancy;
- marriage as a means of uniting two families of origin.

The Compatibility of the Personality of the Spouse

Marital problems frequently stem mainly from the personalities of the spouses themselves. One or both of the marital partners might have severe personality problems that cause difficulties and result in an unsuccessful marriage. For example, a marriage partner with an antisocial personality disorder who tends to cheat and lie to others, including his/her own spouse, or a spouse with a dependent or inadequate personality who is unable to take basic responsibilities for everyday life, can become troublesome to the marriage.

Sometimes the problems are not a result of an individual personality disorder, but rather are caused by mismatching of the spouses' personalities. As an individual, a partner may be able to adjust reasonably to occupational and social circumstances. Marriage to a spouse with a particular personality-type, however, may result in an undesirable match which creates problems, tension, or conflicts that result in frustration between the partners and a malfunction of the marriage. Patterns of mismatching can be described as follows:

Symmetrical Pattern

a. *Competitive* — Both husband and wife are interested in obtaining power for control and assurance of self-independence. Both are psychologically threatened by the existence and function of the other. When this tendency occurs between a husband and wife, the result is endless competition and a power struggle between them. This mismatching is observed more often in a society where the roles of husband and wife are viewed as equal.

b. *Dependent-dependent* — Both the husband and wife lack the ability to function independently as an individual, and there is a need to depend upon others to perform minimal functions. Although each may be emotionally fulfilled to some extent by the availability of the other, both are dependent and somewhat inadequate and they therefore have difficulty taking initiative as a couple to organize their marital life. This type of matching can exist and function relatively safely and be unnoticed within a large family system where there is support from other family members.

Complementary Pattern

a. *Dominant-submissive* — One of the marital partners is basically dominant while the other is fundamentally submissive so that they match and function complementarily as a pair. Within a patriarchal society, a dominant husband and submissive wife will fit the social norm well and be accepted as an "ideal" couple. Yet if the roles are reversed (the husband is submissive and the wife is dominant), they will be viewed as "deviant" and have difficulty fitting into the expected marital role as it exists in the society. An extremely dominant and submissive pair will be relatively less accepted in a biarchal society in which both husband and wife have to demonstrate certain qualities of autonomy in performing their roles.

b. The *obsessional husband and the hysterical wife* — or the "love sick" wife and the "cold" husband (Martin and Bird, 1959) — is, clinically, the most common mismatched couple observed across all socioeconomic levels and is usually determined by unconscious factors involved in the choice of mates. In this combination, the wife frequently complains that her husband is cold, uninvolved, and does not want to do what she wants him to do. She blames all her problems on his not loving her as she wants to be loved. As pointed out by Martin (1976), she lives a dependent, parasitic life with her husband as the host.

As for the husband, he is often more intellectual, logical, and reasonable in his relationships with other people and with his spouse. He is unable to show feelings of closeness and intimacy. As a result, the husband is a worker and the wife is a talker.

The acceptance and tolerance of this type of matching will vary based upon different contexts of the society in which the couple live. For example, in a society such as contemporary Japan, a man is supposed to concentrate his life primarily on work and expend his energy mostly for the company; his wife is supposed to devote her time to domestic affairs, particularly the care of the children. Such a couple would function relatively well without being labeled as dysfunctional. However, in a society in which affectional expression and communication are considered essential to marital life, the wife will be dissatisfied and the husband will be cold and complaining.

c. *Sadistic-masochistic* is clinically known as a special pathological condition in which one partner obtains pleasure through physically or emotionally hurting the other and the other derives pleasure from being hurt. It is unclear to what extent this combination is observed and tolerated in different cultural settings. Further investigation is indicated.

Interaction or Relational Problems Between Marital Partners

Another angle from which to observe marital maladjustment is to focus on the particular interaction and relational patterns enacted by the marital partners that contribute to the development of problems and subsequent marital failure. This can be analyzed from several different dimensions.

Affection Expression Problem

The husband and wife are not fluent in expressing their feelings for each other and they suffer from a lack of mutual affection. The pattern of expression of affection between spouses is molded to some extent by culture. In some cultures, open expression of private feelings toward one's spouse is encouraged so that these feelings can be easily acknowledged by the partner. In other cultures, such sharing of private affection between a couple is customarily discouraged, particularly in public. Naturally, the latter situation contributes to inadequate expressions of affection between husband and wife, and dissatisfaction develops, particularly on the wife's side.

Communication Problems

Distressed couples very often experience problems in communicating—either they repeatedly engage in ineffectual patterns of communication, or problems of intent versus impact run rampant (Gottman, 1979).

Problems of Role Division

The socially-recognized appropriate roles of husband and wife or father and mother are explicitly or inexplicitly defined by culture. Yet within these cultural definitions there exists a vast range of variations among different individuals based on their personal and family backgrounds. (How to develop and establish suitable roles between husband and wife or father and mother in family development that will fit the psychological needs of each person as well as the function of the family, is a task that should be mastered.) Some couples are torn between the kind of role they want to undertake and the role that is culturally expected of them. Many distressed couples suffer from role complementarity discrepancy; that is, they fail to understand or to conform to the partner's appropriate or inappropriate expectations.

Interaction Pattern Problems

By assuming that each spouse's behavior in an intimate relationship can be viewed as largely a function of the consequences provided for that behavior by the partner, Jacobson and Margolin (1979) have summarized certain behavioral-exchange models frequently observed between distressed spouses. For instance, relatively distressed couples exchange less frequent pleasure-evoking behavior and more frequent displeasing behavior, than do nondistressed couples and also reciprocate punishment to a greater degree. In general, distressed couples are relatively more dependent on immediate rewards and punishments as opposed to delayed ones. By selectively focusing on and tracking negative behavior, distressed spouses often ignore and fail to process their partners' delivery of rewards. Finally, Jacobson and Margolin pointed out that one important antecedent of relationship distress is a deficit in a couple's ability to generate behavior or relationship changes.

Conflict Solution Pattern

A distressed couple exhibits greater difficulty in reaching satisfactory resolutions in their problem-solving attempts (Jacobson and Margolin, 1979). Difficulties in resolving conflicts can be derived from individual factors, such as personality make-up, personal problems, or life experiences and emotional issues related to the partners. Cultural factors can contribute to the restriction and selection of coping patterns to be utilized.

Problems Originate from Relations with Children

A couple may have no difficulty in relating to each other as husband and wife, but encounter problems when children become involved. Marital conflict often begins when the couple has children; the problems disappear when the children are out of the picture. These problems are usually rooted in past experiences the couple has had with their own parents and siblings, and such conflicts are reactivated when they have children of their own. The nature of the problems also varies in association with child development and family life cycle. The conflicts may be observed at specific stages of family development, but not in others. Some examples of problems related to children follow.

Difference in Discipline

Each parent wants to discipline their children a certain way, leading to wide differences in preferred methods of raising children. These methods are frequently rooted in the parents' past experiences; often they wish to carry out the discipline used in their own youth. Discipline also frequently relates heavily to cultural patterns. If the couple comes from widely different cultural backgrounds — particularly in regards to the upbringing and discipline of children — they are likely to have disagreements on this issue. For example, a husband with a Hawaiian heritage may feel strongly that children "should be seen but not heard" at dinnertime and prefer to use physical punishment to discipline children who do not follow his (Hawaiian) cultural teachings. The Caucasian wife who believes that children talking to parents at the dinner table is desirable behavior may strongly disagree with her husband's view. She would be greatly upset to see her husband using his fist to punish their children when they tried to carry on a conversation with parents during mealtime.

Difference in Involvement

The different emotional investment made by a father and mother in a child may create distress between parents and child. How the cultural factor contributes to the splitting of parent-child involvement is exemplified by a situation encountered by a Chinese family in Taiwan. When the husband accepted the culturally prescribed arrangement to become an adopted son-in-law to his wife's family in order to continue the family clan (as the wife is an only child), he insisted on a condition wherein all the children born would carry the family name of both sides, alternatively, according to birth order. This was an effort to ensure that half of his offspring would carry the paternal surname, instead of it being lost completely as the custom of adopted son-in-law dictates. As a result, all his sons and daughters inherited different surnames. The parents became discriminately involved with their children, becoming more emotionally involved with the children who carried the surname of their own family. The situation was intensified and aggravated further since the grandparents on both sides also tend to heavily favor those grandchildren with their own surname. Thus, the family was practically split into two groups (Tseng, 1970).

Triangular Conflict

This particular parent-child relation results when the parents hold opposite positions concerning a particular child so as to create emotional tension and conflict among the three individuals involved. The triangular relationship is characterized by favoritism and jealousy, by taking sides against one another. It has been hypothesized by cultural anthropologists that, within a larger family, the triangular complex between parents and children is reduced by the presence of other adult family members such as uncles, aunts, and grandparents. However, clinical experience has revealed that the presence of other adults sometimes may complicate and intensify the triangular conflict rather than minimize it. Therefore, there is a need for further investigation and clarification about this type of conflict.

Involvement in Extramarital Affairs

Marital distress may be complicated by the involvement of one partner in a sexual affair with a lover. Such circumstances are usually colored by the occurrence of mistrust, anger, jealousy, and resentment between the couple, making the marital relationship stressful and much more complicated. Yet, it needs to be kept in mind that the acceptance and tolerance of extramarital affairs varies greatly among different societies. Affairs may be considered absolutely disgraceful in many conservative cultures; they may be viewed as a part of life in others. For example, in the Philippines, there is a double standard for this issue. Extramarital affairs are not tolerated for a wife, but it is culturally considered "macho" behavior for a man to have as many lovers as possible (Ponce, 1988). In Belau, Micronesia, under the old postpartum practice of sexual abstinence, the wife would return to her natal family as soon as she found she was pregnant, staying until after the baby was born and had grown up. Under these conditions, unfaithful behavior on the husband's part was frequent. Detection and prevention of such affairs fell to the wife's brothers. Concerns about unfaithfulness were frequent themes in folklore (Polloi, 1986).

Primary Sexual Problems

Even though sexual difficulty is usually associated with, and secondary to, marital (emotional) problems, there are times when the couple is distressed by primary sexual problems that are physiological or organic in nature. It is important to keep in mind that in different sociocultural backgrounds, there are different understandings and expectations about sexual activities. Various attitudes of how people feel comfortable in dealing with the sexual issue and presenting sexual problems to the outsider exist.

Other Factors Concerning Stress in Marriage and the Family

There are many external factors beyond marriage and family that may directly and seriously affect the function of marital life and bring distress, burdens, and unhappiness to a marriage. Such factors may not be of concern in some societies, but may be frequently encountered problems in others. Following are some examples:

a. Availability of spouse — Because of social conditions (such as war), political movements, or for occupational reasons, husbands and wives may have to face separation periodically or for a single extended period. Such separations may influence the relationship and adjustment between spouses. A typical example is the military husband who is involved in strategic defense work (e.g., aboard a nuclear submarine) and has to go to sea periodically for several months at a time with a total communication blackout, who then returns home for a few months, then leaves again. Such repeated separations and reunions as a part of marital life cause difficulty in adjusting to husband-wife relations and role division.

b. Medical/mental problems of the spouse — When one spouse has severe medical or mental problems, particularly of a chronic nature, the presence of such problems may understandably bring about distress and seriously affect their marital relations.

c. Financial problems — Although money cannot necessarily buy happiness, severe financial problems often add problems to a marriage and affect marital adjustment. Even though financial difficulties may not occur frequently in some societies, they can be serious problems for other societies and become the primary cause of the marital distress.

PROBLEMS OBSERVED IN DIFFERENT STAGES OF THE MARITAL CYCLE

Associated with marital development in the life cycle, the spouses have to perform different tasks, overcome challenges, and at the same time deal with new problems.

Marriage-Establishment Phase

When a couple is formally wed and starts to live together, they begin the formation of a bond relationship and the development and refinement of role division as husband and wife. This is an important stage of adjustment for those couples who do not know each other very well. Some couples — whose marriage was arranged by others — may have met for the first time at the wedding; they must begin their relationship as strangers.

This can be a honeymoon stage for many couples, but can be a time of frustration for others. It is a time to leave fantasy behind and face the realities of married life, to shift from emotional romance to the responsibilities of daily life, and to determine quickly the division of labor roles between husband and wife. This stage will be more complicated if the marital life is undertaken within a large family system. The spouses not only have to learn how to relate to each other, but also how to adjust to the larger and complicated family-kin system. Such adjustments can be especially hard for the wife if she has married into a patrilocal and extended family system in which she must adjust to living with parents-in-law and siblings-in-law. If her husband does not extend adequate support, she may be the recipient of stress from all sides, particularly from her mother-in-law and sisters-in-law. There is no shortage of tales that describe the hardships endured by a young bride upon entering her husband's family home.

Although there may be culturally regulated rituals regarding the step by step separation of young couples from their families of origin, such socially recognized customs do not necessarily coincide with the psychological needs of the spouses and families involved. Some couples may try to separate too abruptly from the family of origin of one spouse and thus become subject to criticism. An intense attachment to the family of origin by either spouse may elicit complaints from either the spouse-partner or from the family of origin of the other side. How to maintain and withdraw ties to families of origin in a culturally appropriate way must be learned by the young couple in societies where family relationships are of concern and heavily emphasized. Otherwise, family relationships may develop into a frequent cause of trouble for the young couple.

Childbearing Phase

Although it is universally true that having children of their own is a great joy and fulfills the cultural expectation for mature adults to carry on the family line, stepping into the childbearing phase can be a time of stress for some couples. Stress is especially prevalent if there is strong cultural meaning attached to childbearing and if there are specific social expectations associated with bearing a child. For example, in a society in which having children is very important, infertility can cause anxiety and be a source of unhappiness and strife between husband and wife. If the gender of a child is very important, pregnancy can be an anxiety-prone experience for the woman as she increasingly worries about the sex of her unborn child.

After the birth of the child, the parents must learn to adjust to their newly-acquired parenthood, and learn how to extend relations from a dyad to a triad. It is difficult for some couples to undertake the new responsibilities of parenthood. Parenthood then becomes the reason for dysfunctioning of the family.

Child-Growing Phase

Proper and successful rearing and disciplining of the child becomes an essential duty of the parents when their baby begins to grow. All parents have certain ideas and expectations of how a child should be raised and disciplined based on their own experiences; such ideas and expectations are naturally molded by the culture as well.

It is common for a mother and father to have different ideas about the best way to raise and discipline a child. Parents must share a basic philosophy of how to raise their children and know how to exercise their differences in such a way that they are complementary to each other as parents. Sometimes the differences between parents can be so wide and opposite in nature that they become a source of tension and conflict. For example, one parent, based on cultural background, may firmly believe that it is desirable for even young children to experience hardship for learning purposes. If the other parent strongly insists that children should enjoy life as much as possible while they are young, their strong oppositional views will seriously affect their method of raising their children, and these conflicting views could become a source of unhappiness in the family unless they can reach a compromise.

Triangulation with the child is another phenomenon that frequently causes tension and conflict between spouses at this stage of

family development. Although the dynamics for forming an intensified triangular conflict between the parents and a child is a complicated process, it is usually related to several psychological factors.
It may be a reactivation of conflicts experienced when the parent
was a child, or deeply rooted in personal experiences associated
with sibling rivalry experiences. Alternately, the parent may feel
psychologically insecure and perceive the existence of a child as a
threat, or there may be long-standing conflict and competition between the husband and wife that is aggravated by an addition to the
family.

Based on different cultural backgrounds, the intensity of triangular conflict varies and the solution pattern for such conflicts will be
sanctioned differently (Hsu and Tseng, 1974).

Child-Leaving Phase

After the children have grown up, the time for them to leave their
parents and home varies greatly among different societies. In some
societies, leaving home is encouraged quite early, as soon as the
child reaches puberty, so that it seems wrong if the child remains
with the parents by the age of twenty. On the other hand, in some
societies, the physical separation of the child from the parents is
never even considered; children are expected to live with their parents throughout their lives.

Marital problems can occur between the husband and wife on the
issue of a child leaving the parents' home if parents have different
views and needs concerning the child. The most frequently observed phenomenon is that for various reasons (such as the husband
is not always available and close to his wife, or it is considered
essential the child stay, as in the case of the eldest son) the mother is
intensely attached to her children or to a particular child so that
separation becomes a troublesome issue for the family.

The Empty Nest Phase

After the children have grown up and left the family, the husband
and wife are alone together and may now enter an enjoyable stage
of life and an opportunity to start a second honeymoon stage. In
reality this period can be critical for the husband and wife as they

now have to reestablish a close relationship, which could be a difficult task for them.

This is particularly true for couples in a country such as Japan, where the husband has been working hard and may have devoted his life to his work, socializing mainly with colleagues in his company and leaving his wife to devote her life entirely to raising her children, socializing primarily with female friends in her own network. The time when the children leave home coincides with the husband's retirement from his job. For the first time since their marriage they are together all day and sometimes begin to experience marital problems. The wife complains that her husband interferes in domestic life, which she has had completely under her control for the past several decades.

The husband feels lost in his new life, separated from his work-related (male-dominated) social network, and finds it impossible to join the predominantly female social network enjoyed by his wife. As a result, they enter a problematic stage of marital adjustment. Actually, some wives in their fifties who have been dissatisfied with their husbands but have stayed married for the sake of their children suddenly demand a divorce from their husbands during this stage of their lives.

Widowing Phase

Associated with the increase in aging, many spouses begin to face the loss of their marital partners. Statistically, females live longer and there is more chance that the woman will be widowed.

Traditionally embedded in the patrilineal and patriarchal family system, the Hindu culture subscribes strict rules for widows. A widow must abstain from any social life except for encounters with immediate family members such as her children. She is not allowed to interact with any man, including her brothers-in-law. No matter how young she is, a widow is expected to observe a life of total social seclusion and remarriage is out of the question. This cultural custom is set up to protect the man-oriented family system. Many widows suffer from such a deprived life. This custom is still observed among some Hindu groups residing in Fiji; it is the main reason contributing to depression for many widows.

In contrast, many widowers suffer from depression, not only because they have lost their lifelong partners, but for other reasons. In societies such as Korea or Japan where men have never been expected to do any domestic work (such as cooking), the husbands encounter great difficulty in adjusting to their lives as widowers. Even though his children may try to be supportive and helpful, the widower who never did any domestic work may have a hard time even preparing a simple meal for himself. Frustration and depression are increased as a result of these difficulties.

MARITAL PROBLEMS OBSERVED AT DIFFERENT STAGES OF CONFLICT

Associated with the length of time involved in marital problems, the nature and manifestation of marital conflicts will differ. Therefore, it will be useful to recognize and differentiate between marital problems observed at different stages of conflict in time perspectives. Such recognition will assist the clinician in developing different therapeutic approaches as well as making relevant prognostic predictions (Guerin, Fay, Burden, and Kautto 1987).

Early (Acute) Stage

At the early stage, even though the problem may burst out suddenly and dramatically, in general the onset is insidious and the level of conflict is still low. In spite of the existence of problems, communication between the spouses remains open, criticism is transient and limited, and the tendency to polarize power is minimal. The disturbance can still be eliminated relatively easily as long as a basic healthy relationship exists between the spouses.

Middle (Intermittent) Stage

After repeated recurrence of conflicts, tension becomes high. Criticism increases, and even though communication between spouses may still be open, the affectional climate is either getting cooler or full of tension and anger. Marital relations are characterized as "conflict habituated" as described by Cuber (1965), a marital configuration in which verbal conflict between spouses is a continuing, almost incessant condition. Eventually, the relationship becomes considerably more distant and engagement ceases. The spouses' ability to communicate begins to deteriorate as well (Guerin et al., 1987).

Terminal (Chronic) Stage

If the problems last for many years and termination of the marriage in the form of separation or divorce is not sanctioned by society, the marital problems become chronic. They are manifested in the "devitalized" configuration (Cuber, 1965); the partners lose interest in having close sharing and tend to act with distance and in parallel without interaction. If society permits the termination of marital relations, the partners may seek divorce.

SUMMARY

In summary, the issues of marital problems need to be approached and understood from various perspectives within the context of different cultural backgrounds. The sources and the nature of the problems need to be considered broadly; this is particularly true in societies where the function of marriage is seen as more than affection between husband and wife. There are many factors, within and outside the marriage, that affect the functioning and success of the marriage and also cause problems and unhappiness.

The nature of marital problems needs to be understood from the perspectives of the family cycle as well as from the point-of-time factor that molds the manifestation of marital problems in different stages of conflict.

Chapter 7

Parent-Child Problems

Research into parent-child relationships has promoted the recent development of several new ideas (Walters and Walters, 1980). There has been a move away from the unidirectional model of causality (from parent to child) towards a reciprocal model concerning parent-child relationships. According to this model, children are important determinants of their parents' (as well as their own) behavior. In order to understand concurrent contributions of parents to each other and their children in the parent-child relationship, studies should focus on the mother-father-child relationship, rather than on the father-child or mother-child relationship.

It is quite clear that the nature of parent-child relations varies between families and cultures, depending on how parents and children view each other's existence and how relations between them develop based on their views (Arnold, Bulatao, Buripakdi et al., 1975; Callan, 1982). For instance, a child can be seen by parents as a symbol of their love, a proud product of their marriage, a family treasure to continue their lineage, an additional source of manpower, a source of security in their old age, or a burden to raise and care for. Conversely, a child may view a parent as a benevolent and protective figure, a person to depend on, a source of support in times of crisis, a source of guidance, an adult who sets limits on the child's behavior and life, or someone who pushes the child to work for him/her. The relationship between parent and child varies accordingly, as does the specific type of parent-child problems that arise.

Cross-cultural differences in the parent-adolescent relationship are exemplified in Kandel and Lesser's (1969) study in the United States and Denmark. Results revealed that adolescents in both countries were close to their parents, especially their mothers. However, American adolescents viewed their parents as considerably more authoritarian than the Danish youths did. American parents set more rules and offered fewer explanations for their rules and decisions than did their Danish counterparts. Danish adolescents had a stronger feeling of independence from parental domination than American adolescents, who were less likely to feel as though they were treated as adults and given sufficient freedom by their parents.

A common belief held by the majority of global mental health workers is that the parent-child relationship has great impact on the child's mental health. Past examinations of the emotional and psychological impact of parent-child relations, however, have been far from satisfactory, particularly where cross-cultural studies of parent-child problems have been concerned. Nevertheless, the limited information and knowledge available on this subject will be elaborated in three different levels: common parent-child relational problems observed, specific parent-child interactional problems, and specific child psychopathology associated with parent-child relations.

COMMON PARENT-CHILD RELATIONAL PROBLEMS

Before discussing some commonly observed parent-child problems, it is first necessary to examine some of the child developmental issues and parent-child relational issues.

According to Offer (1982), the concept of "adolescent turmoil" was introduced at the beginning of the century by G. Stanley Hall, one of the first American psychologists. Anna Freud expanded considerably on the topic, stating that the biological changes that occur during puberty wield tremendous powers which lead to chaos in the adolescent psyche. The notion that an adolescent needs to go through emotional turmoil in order to grow into a mentally healthy adult became widely accepted by mental health workers. Only later did anthropologist Margaret Mead (1928), based on her observation of Samoan society in the Pacific, point out that adolescents do not necessarily go through emotional turmoil if their society and culture provide a smooth transition from adolescence to adulthood.

Offer (1982) recently examined a large sample population of normal adolescent students by questionnaire survey, and found that only a small portion of the subgroup (about 15 percent) attested to feeling empty emotionally and being confused most of the time, indicating that they were experiencing the emotional turmoil of adolescence as defined clinically. It would be interesting to learn through an empirical study how much of this subgroup would experience emotional turmoil in different societies, and to test whether their adolescent turmoil is related to parent-child relations molded by cultural factors. According to Mead's (1928) speculation, adolescents in complex societies face difficulties due to "the presence of conflicting standards and the belief that every individual should make his or her own choice, coupled with the feeling that choice is an important matter." In contrast, adolescents in simple societies do not usually face such difficulties.

Regarding the perceptions of intergenerational continuity Thompson, Clark, and Gunn (1985) have conducted a survey of families (predominantly white Protestant upper-middle class) in the United States to examine the attitudes and values of two generations. Selected areas including familism, foreign involvement, drug use, equal partnership in marriage, maternal employment, sexual permissiveness, fundamental religiosity, and the work ethic were evaluated. The results confirmed that youths tend to overestimate actual differences in attitude between the generations, while parents tend to underestimate actual intergenerational differences. It would be extremely interesting to expand this type of survey cross-culturally to reveal to what extent the degree of discontinuity is demonstrated between parents and children among different cultural groups.

Relationship Problems

Although the relationship between parents and children is ideally a warm and intimate one, it may instead be a cold and distant one in some families. This may stem from problems of the individual parent or child. For instance, a parent may have basic personality disorders which prevent positive relations with the children, or a child may have a specific mental condition — such as autism — which significantly limits meaningful human relations with his/her parents.

Beyond individual psychopathology, parent-child problems can be indirectly molded by sociocultural background: how the parents value the existence and function of the children and vice-versa.

The pattern of availability and degree of involvement of parents are commonly observed to vary among different cultures. In some cultures both the father and mother are equally available to the children, while in others, child care is left almost entirely to the mother. Popplewell and Sheikh (1979) have examined the role of the father in child development, extensively reviewing literature in various areas, including general personality functioning, cognitive development, and sex-role development. They pointed out the common belief in a relationship between male children's perception of their father's masculinity and the degree of male sex-role preferences they exhibit. They also noted that boys who are deprived of a father model clearly seem more seriously disadvantaged than girls who face this same deprivation. They echoed Bigner's (1970) conclusion that the father should take a more active role in child-rearing in order to partially offset the cultural mother-centeredness of American families.

Although there are innumerable sources of childhood disturbances and parent-child conflicts, Wimberger (1965) viewed three factors as especially important in contemporary American culture: lack of emotional contact between parents and the child, devaluating attitudes of the parents, and lack of defined limits by which the child can evaluate his behavior.

An analysis of parent-child relations among black families in the United States was done by Willie (1988). Contrary to popular belief, Willie argued that there is more harmony than conflict between older and younger generations in black families. He attributes this to the following: older blacks do not esteem their culture as a model for the young, older blacks respect the aspirations of younger family members and identify with their new way of life, and older blacks of all social class levels expect and want family members of the next generation to surpass their elders in achievement. Thus, the adaptational patterns of older blacks differ from those of many older whites, who tend to view their own way of life as the model to which younger generations should conform.

Quakers traditionally take pacifist positions in times of war and practice nonviolence in other types of conflicts. This suggests that nonviolence is an integral part of the Quaker value system and leads to an expectation that family conflicts among Quakers will be dealt with accordingly. However, a survey conducted by Brutz and Ingoldsby (1984) indicated quite the contrary. Comparisons between the results of their questionnaire survey of Quaker families and findings from a national study on family violence indicated that in addition to relatively frequent incidents of spouse violence and sibling violence, Quaker fathers reported more acts of overall violence toward their children than did fathers nationally. Methodological issues, including the possibility that the Quaker respondents may have been more scrupulously truthful in reporting their violence than the respondents in the national survey, led the investigators to interpret the data cautiously. Nevertheless, one hypothesis given by the investigators was that it may be more difficult and require greater interpersonal skills to apply pacifism to one's personal life than to advocate pacifism as a solution at international or social justice levels.

The psychological self-portrait of the adolescent has been extensively examined by Offer, Ostrov, and Howard (1981) in samples from the United States and three other countries—Australia, Israel, and Ireland. The feelings and attitudes teenagers had towards their families were surveyed as part of the self-reported questionnaire. Overall, the teenagers were found to have positive feelings toward their parents. The investigators claimed that no significant cross-cultural differences existed regarding the parent-child relationships described, although there was a tendency on the part of teenagers in the three non-American cultures to describe their relationships with their families even more positively than American teenagers.

However, when the normal teenagers were compared with the physically ill adolescents and the deviant (emotionally disturbed or delinquent) teenagers, they found that the physically ill adolescents were similar to their healthy peers, but the deviant group showed obvious differences. The disturbed and delinquent teenagers did not share their parents' standards as often as did either the physically ill or the healthy teenagers. The disturbed and delinquent adolescents were more likely to believe that their parents were ashamed of them, shared their parents' values less often and less completely, and did not see themselves as being an integral part of a cohesive family structure. This suggests a close relationship between perceived family image and adolescent behavior.

Problems of Communication

In many families, problems are most commonly encountered in parent-child communication. This is particularly true in societies in which the relationship between parents and children tends to be distant and serious in nature, making meaningful exchanges of ideas and feelings difficult.

Comparison of the family backgrounds of non-delinquent adolescents (from regular schools) and delinquent adolescents (from reform schools) in China led Li, Fang, Tseng, and Hsu (1988) to some interesting findings regarding parent-adolescent communication. In contrast to the non-delinquent group, the delinquent group was characterized by relatively low scores in parent-adolescent communication; specifically, there were more communication problems between male delinquents and their fathers and female delinquents and their mothers. The study indicates that Chinese adolescents' behavior problems are closely related to a lack of adequate communication between the adolescents and their same-sex parents. The extent to which this phenomenon is true for adolescents in other societies needs future investigation.

The difficulties and communication problems between parents and children of immigrant families have been pointed out by some investigators — Izutsu, Furukawa, and Hayashida (1989) concerning Japanese-Americans in Hawaii, and Kinzie, Tran, Breckinridge, and Bloom (1980) concerning South-Asian refugees to the United States. These phenomena usually occur in situations where a family migrates to a host society with a different primary language. While the parents are usually slow in learning the new language in the new setting, the youngsters shift quite quickly to the new language and forget their home language. In addition to the different value systems they begin to adopt, serious communication problems between the generations develop due to language factors. The parents and children both find it difficult and frustrating to be unable to communicate adequately in either language. In the Japanese-American situation, the communication between grandparents and grandchildren becomes almost impossible as they share almost no common words between them and are almost foreigners to each other.

Problems of Discipline

Concerning the effects of social class upon parent-child relationships, Kohn (1963) has discussed class differences in parents' values in relation to child discipline. Kohn indicated that in the United States, working-class parents (from the lower social class) reacted more to the consequences of their children's actions, while middle-class parents reacted more to the intent of their children's actions. Similarly, class differences in values led middle-class and working class parents to perceive their children's behavior quite differently; misbehavior which prompts middle-class parents to action does not seem as important to working-class parents, and vice versa. As reported by Bronfenbrenner (1958), middle-class parent-child relationships are more egalitarian and focused on acceptance, while those in the working-class are oriented toward maintaining order and obedience. Furthermore, as indicated by Kohn, most middle-class fathers agree with their wives and play a role close to what their wives would have them play. However, many working-class fathers do not see any reason why they should have to shoulder the responsibility.

Problems of Generational Gaps

Due to their different life backgrounds and experiences, parents and their children commonly have different value systems and different perspectives. A relatively rapid change in society and its cultural system, however, can lead to these differences being so great they form a wide gap between the two generations referred to as a generation gap. This gap can be the major source of problems between parents and children growing up. Often, the children will complain that their parents are stubborn and outdated, while the parents will be uncomfortable seeing their children behaving untraditionally, causing mutual distress and tension.

It is not merely the difference in value systems, but the uncertainty and confusion which usually weaken parental authority and make the situation worse. If a basic emotional bond and fluent and adequate communication do not exist between parents and children, the generation gap can bring tension and conflict.

El-Islam (1983) has described the serious generational gaps and conflicts arising in families in Arabian Gulf communities. Traditional Arabian culture emphasizes a hierarchical family order in which dominance of male over female and older over younger is observed. Respect for and obedience to elders are at the top of the list of family traditions. The discovery of oil, however, has brought major socioeconomic changes, including substantial rises in educational, informational, and material opportunities spurred by the increase in national income. Saudi Arabia progressed from eighteenth-century conditions to twentieth-century conditions over a time span of only two decades. The number of educated females, for example, is rising so rapidly that younger daughters in a family are getting the education which was denied to their older sisters. Educated women challenge the traditional limitations of their roles in marriage and mothering. The gaps between parents and children are becoming wide and the conflict between them is rising. As a result, parents blame themselves for providing their children with the education that led to their departure from time-honored traditions.

SPECIFIC PARENT-CHILD INTERACTIONAL PROBLEMS

When problems between parents and children are serious, they may be manifested in specific dysfunctional ways under different cultural circumstances, including child abuse, incest, or parental abuse.

Child Abuse

Child abuse refers to a situation in which one or more children are maltreated by the parent or parents in a way that seriously affects the physical and mental conditions of the children. Maltreatment of a child can take the form of negligence, overindulgence, or emotional or physical abuse.

Family studies of child abuse have been carried out by numerous investigators, and patterns of family interactions frequently observed in cases of child abuse have been extensively reported. For instance, Terr (1970) has indicated that important factors leading to abuse were fantasies of the abuser about the child (i.e., fear of the child), exaggerated dominant-submissive patterns in the parents' marriage, and contributions of the child to the battering. Green, Gaines, and Sandgrund (1974) have explained that the maltreatment syndrome is usually the end result of three potentiating factors: the abuse-prone personality of the parent; characteristics of the child that make him vulnerable as a scapegoat; and current environmental stresses. They furthermore noted that role reversal was a prominent feature in the psychodynamic makeup of these families; the parents relied on the child to gratify dependency needs that were unsatisfied in their relationships with their spouses and families. In other words, child abuse has been seen as a dysfunction of parenting.

Korbin (1981) has clearly pointed out the factors in cultural context which affect the occurrence of child abuse and neglect. One factor is the cultural value of childen — if a culture values its children, they are likely to be treated well. Another is beliefs about specific categories of children — some children may be considered inadequate or unacceptable by cultural standards and thus, fail to receive the same standards of care usually accorded to children. Another factor is beliefs about age capabilities and developmental stages of children — cultures vary in terms of the age at which children are expected to behave in certain ways. The last factor is the embeddedness of child-rearing in kin and community networks — a network of concerned individuals beyond the biological parents is a powerful deterrent to child abuse and neglect.

According to Levinson's (1988) holocultural study of family violence in 90 small-scale and peasant societies as included in the Human Relations Area Files data archives, physical punishment of children (including spanking, slapping, beating, scalding, burning, pinching, etc.) occurred in 74.4% of the societies analyzed. Further examination in terms of the degree of frequency of physical punishment of children revealed that 13.3% of societies "regularly" used physical punishment, 21.1% "frequently" used it, 40% "infrequently" used it, and 26.5% "never" used it. This information provides a general idea of how physical punishment is practiced among different societies around the world.

Levinson (1988) also points out that from a cross-cultural viewpoint, it is quite obvious that children are more likely to be punished physically in societies where people believe that supernatural spirits are malevolent and punishing. This cultural patterning of child abuse has also been reported by independent holocultural studies carried out by Lambert, Triandis, and Wolf (1959), Whiting (1967), Otterbein and Otterbein (1973), and others.

Child abuse in various cultural groups is studied infrequently, and it is difficult to compare systematically the data reported. However, some findings will be described here to indicate the nature of cultural variations of child abuse and to illustrate Korbin's (1981) viewpoint that in various ways cultural factors will shape the occurrence of child abuse. For instance, LeVine and LeVine (1981) described that in Sub-Saharan Africa, the use of child labor, which like many other aspects of African child-rearing practices have evolved in response to the exigencies of an agricultural economy, might seem harsh or neglectful by Western standards. The sexual molestation of girls is a known phenomenon in tropical Africa; in addition to father-daughter incest, seductions of pubescent girls by male schoolteachers are the occasion for recurrent scandals in Nigeria and Kenya.

As for rural India, Poffenberger (1981) found that abusive parental behaviors that deviate from the norm and result from the adult's emotional disturbances may not find widespread expression. He speculates that there is probably less of the extreme, irrational abuse that is common in other societies including Western ones. This is due to the strong family support system available to Indian parents and the restraining influence of extended family members when parent tempers get out of control. In India, however, infants may suffer deprivation of food, usually because there is simply not enough of it to go around. Also, the differential treatment of male and female infants in traditional Hindu society leads to a higher death rate among female infants. A sample survey of a village revealed that almost two-thirds of the children in the village studied were boys (Minturn and Hitchcock, 1963). When the mothers in the villages were questioned, they reported that nearly twice as many girls as boys had died in childhood. The investigators attributed the shortage of girls in the village to the benign neglect of daughters by their parents and better medical treatment for boys.

Ekeda (1987) from Japan reported that the Japanese people generally associated the phenomena of child abuse with stepmothers. Many Japanese folk stories have this theme; incidents of child abuse reported in the daily newspaper frequently have the headline, *"Again* a stepmother was found abusing her stepchild!" illustrating that this is a common association and understanding in Japanese society. Ekeda investigated the actual prevalence of child abuse by biological parents and stepparents and found that young children were more often abused by their biological parents rather than by stepparents — since they were generally raised and cared for by the former. The abusers of older children, however, were more often stepparents than biological parents. She interpreted that by noting remarriage in Japan usually occurs when the child is older, and the stepmother generally has difficulty relating to the preschool-age stepchild who has reached the developmental stage of first rebellion. This phenomenon is further aggravated by two more factors which have cultural roots. The first is the common belief that "blood is thicker than water" — the stepparent is not to relate with the stepchild with the genuine care and privilege of intimacy which usually exists between biological parent and child. The second factor is that the Japanese father is generally busy in work and social activities outside the home, and thus often is unavailable for the family. This leaves stepmother and stepchild without a buffer for their conflictual relationship.

From a cross-cultural point of view, the phenomena of child abuse can thus be influenced by cultural factors at many different levels. These factors are: the parents' culturally embedded basic and general attitude towards children, or any special attitude towards or treatment of a particular child due to the child's gender, age, sibling position, or physical/mental condition; the nature of culturally sanctioned parent-child relations commonly practiced; the culturally permitted methods of disciplining children; and the cultural definition of and attitude towards child abuse. Although the maltreatment of children can potentially occur in any corner of the world, the nature, style, and severity of the child abuse varies greatly among cultures.

Child Overprotection

The matter of child overprotection (otherwise known as maternal overprotection) as a phenomenon of parent-child relational problems rarely has been a concern of child mental health workers in most contemporary Western societies. There are two reasons for this: first, there is a basic assumption that overprotection (in the form of indulgence or protection) would cause less harm to a child than negligence or abuse. Second, in most contemporary Western societies, the parents value the early independence of the child and emphasize his/her autonomy, leading to less frequent observation of maternal overprotection. As for medical literature, descriptions and concern about excessive maternal care of children can be found several decades back (Levy, 1943). In many non-Western societies in which the close mother-child relationship is tolerated and accepted culturally, the problems of excessive parental overprotection and indulgence still can be observed as needing mental health concern.

As described by Levy (1943), maternal overprotection is characterized by excessive contact between mother and child, infantilization of the child, and prevention of independent behavior. As a result, the child is delayed in emotional development and tends to manifest a psychological tendency towards self-centeredness, low threshold for stress and frustration, and demanding attitude. Male children are likely to have delayed psychosexual development including gender identity and sex-role performance problems.

In contemporary China, the government policy of "one-couple-one-child" leads to a tendency for Chinese parents to overprotect their single child. Preschool teachers frequently comment that their students are more spoiled than a decade ago. A questionnaire survey of only children and multisibling children suggested that only children tend to exhibit negative behavior, including preference and refusal of food, obstinancy, temper outbursts, and nail-biting (Tao and Chiu, 1985).

The phenomenon of maternal overprotection occurs in Japan for different reasons. Many Japanese mothers are housewives whose primary mission and role is to stay at home and take care of the children, while the fathers are usually busy in their work and return home late. In this situation, the mother is likely to devote her energy and attention to her children, forming strong and intimate bonds with them, particularly with her son(s). As a result, sons may become rebellious and violent towards their overprotecting mothers after reaching adolescence, resulting in the parent abuse phenomena which will be described later.

Incest

Anthropologist Hoebel (1972) described mating with any person who is culturally defined as a member of one's kinship group as commonly forbidden. Any such prohibited mating is considered incestuous and is prohibited by incest taboos which are universal among all peoples. Specification of the boundaries of a kinship group varies considerably among different cultures, however, as do attitudes and reactions to the breaking of the incest taboo.

From a clinical point of view, any form of sexual contact between an adult and child is viewed as inappropriate and referred to as sexual abuse of a child, which is distinct from other forms of child abuse. The premise is that a dependent, developmentally immature child should not be involved in sexual activities that he/she does not fully comprehend (Becker and Coleman, 1988). Sexual abuses of children are customarily subdivided into cases of intrafamilial abuse, incest in the strictest sense, and extrafamilial child sexual abuse.

As reviewed by Finkelhor (1987), current research shows that the number of cases of sexual abuse reported to child protection agencies in the United States has grown dramatically in the last decade; however, this does not necessarily reflect an actual rise in incidents. Many studies of communities in the United States have failed to find differences in child abuse rates among social classes or racial subdivisions.

The dysfunctional family system has been pointed to by many researchers as causal in the occurrence of incestuous behavior. For instance, Thorman (1983) has indicated that the deficiencies in specific areas are: lack of strong relation between the parents; mothers who are physically or psychologically absent; reversed mother-daughter roles; unequally distributed power between husband and wife; lack of autonomy among family members; socially isolated family members who are unable to cope with stress; and so on. Finkelhor's (1979) survey identified the family features most significantly associated with sexual abuse as: the presence of a stepfather, the separation of the child from his or her natural mother, the mother's punishment of the child's sexual curiosity, the father's lack of physical affection toward the child, the child's limited friendships, and others.

These findings of family background all relate to the situation in the United States. How and if they apply to other societies is not certain, and studies of sexual abuse in other cultural societies are very scant. One exception is Ekeda's (1987) review of her clinical cases of Japanese parent-child incest and description of family features associated with the occurrence of such problems. These features include: being a nuclear family which migrated to the city; being cut off from family of origin and kin with limited resources of support; being isolated from the neighbors; financial insecurity; the absence of the mother due to death, separation, or hospitalization; the father's behavior problems as manifested by drinking, a criminal record, or a peculiar personality.

Maltreatment of Parent by Child — "Parental Abuse"

Maltreatment of a parent by a child refers to a situation which, by definition, occurs only after the child has grown-up.

The term "parental abuse" currently is used by mental health workers in Japan to describe situations in which children, usually teenagers, undertake physical violence towards their parents — mainly towards their mothers. This culture-related type of violence is a new but rapidly growing phenomenon which first surfaced in contemporary Japanese society during the last decade (Yoshimatsu, 1984). It generated great social concern and has since been labeled parental abuse by the mental health workers, in contrast to child abuse.

As reviewed by Inamura (1980), most of the children who become violent towards their parents are high school students (44.3%) or junior high students (24.3%), and more frequently male than female (5 to 2 ratio). Most of them (82.9%) are the first child, and one-third of them (31.4%) are the only child. The parental victims are mostly mothers (82.0%) but occasionally fathers (7.9%). The violence occurs frequently in association with the absence of fathers (25.7%). Review of their past history disclosed that among the teenagers who showed violent behavior toward their parents, many (66.6%) of them had difficulty making friends at school, and most of them (87.1%) already had the problems of not attending school regularly.

Further analysis of family relations indicates that most of the mothers are characterized by being perfectionistic, competitive, sensitive, and nervous. They tend to be overprotective toward their sons, yet simultaneously have unrealistically high expectations and are overintrusive. As mothers, they tend to care intensely for their children and attempt to control their lives. The fathers, meanwhile are commonly quiet, over-involved in their work, and out-of-touch with matters at home, including relations with the children. In general, the fathers tend to shy away from the children or become unavailable for them, especially after they reach the teenage years. This is coupled with the fact that the authority of the fathers is generally questioned and weakened; after the war, the generation of presently middle-aged fathers lost their confidence in providing discipline for their teenaged sons (Yoshimatsu, 1984).

It is therefore better to understand the phenomenon dynamically from the point of the parent-child relationship and child development: a teenage child who has been overprotected and indulged when younger, reacts to the overintrusive and over-demanding mother through rebellious behavior in its extreme form — violence towards her. Thus, this phenomenon reflects the particular parent-child relationship frequently observed in contemporary Japan, and, as pointed out by Inamura (1980) and Yoshimatsu (1984), is culture-related.

Another form of maltreatment of parents is observed in the latter part of the life cycle, when the parents are aged and incapacitated and are ignored, neglected, or even abused by their adult children.

Due to remarkable increases in life expectancy in most modern societies, the proportion of senior citizens in the total population is
increasing. It has been estimated that in many developed Western
societies, one-fifth of the total population is above the age of 65,
and this will also become the case in many developing societies.
Associated with the move towards modernization, urbanization,
and industrialization, the trend has been for the nuclear family to
become the basic household. When parents become aged and func-
tionally incapacitated—either mentally or physically—providing
care for them becomes a serious family and social problem. It certainly poses a dilemma for their middle-aged children, who are usually busy with their own lives. In the past in many societies, the
aged-parents expected to be cared for by their children, but the situation is changing for several reasons. The life span of aged-parents
is lengthening, the number of adult-children to provide care for
their aged-parents has proportionally declined greatly due to the
decrease in average family size, and the aged-parents are usually
not living in the same household as their children due to the rise of
the nuclear household. Further, most of the adult-children are working outside their homes and are not available to take care of the aged
and incapacitated parent(s) at home. Based on these social circumstances, the phenomenon of maltreatment of aged-parents is growing in many societies. This includes societies in which filial piety
has traditionally been greatly emphasized and the care of the elderly
by the young was expected culturally.

SPECIFIC CHILD PATHOLOGY
ASSOCIATED WITH PARENT-CHILD RELATIONS

Runaway from Home

It is generally understood that pathological child runaway behavior—running away from home habitually—is very closely related to
the family environment, and particularly the parent-child relationship.

By utilizing its multi-ethnic society, Mathews and Ilon (1980)
have studied chronic runaways from different ethnic groups in Hawaii. Data were collected from the runaway youth facility and the

subjects were divided by ethnic background: Caucasian, Asian, Hawaiian/part-Hawaiian, Cosmopolitan (individuals whose ancestry included three or more racial ethnic groups), and miscellaneous. They found that while Caucasian runaways were least likely to become chronic runaways, the opposite was true of Hawaiian or part-Hawaiian runaways. Several explanations can be offered for the relatively high occurrence of chronic runaways among the Hawaiian group. Traditionally, the custom of *Hanai* (adoption) of children between families and relatives is commonly practiced so that children feel free to come and go between related families. This is coupled with the fact that Hawaiian parents' use of physical violence towards children as a way to express frustration or react to some crisis in the family is relatively frequent. Thus, some of the children learn to hide, seeking protection from the families of kin or friends, who usually offer an attractive refuge for the runaway.

Juvenile Delinquency

Youth conduct problems and their relationship to family background are another area that has been thoroughly investigated by various disciplines. By comparing families of schizophrenics, delinquents, and normal youths (as revealed from tests on differences), Stabenau, Tupin, Werner, and Pollin (1965) have found that the family interactions of the delinquent group (in contrast to the schizophrenic and normal groups) are characterized by unstable family organization and absence of clear role differentiation, undercontrolled affect with depressive mood, open conflicts among members, and shifts of focus on communication. These findings show that there are unique family interaction patterns associated with the delinquent group.

Dividing child discipline into three sequential dimensions — policy making, policing, and punishing — Singer (1974) reported that the disciplinary configurations in American families with antisocial offspring were very restrictive in policy making, had loose policing, and lenient punishments.

Similarly, DeVos and Wagatsuma (1972) carried out a study of family life and delinquency in Japan. They reported that their findings tended to confirm a number of conclusions previously reported

from the United States about the influences of family life on delinquency. Specifically, they found social deviancy in youths is apt to
occur among those suffering neglect or deprivation during their for-
mative years. The interesting point of their investigation was that
they paid attention to specific features of the family, most notably
sibling position. As it is a common observation in Japan that the
eldest son is treated differently from other children in the family,
and middle children are relatively neglected, DeVos and Wagatsuma examined the sibling positions of the parents as well as those
of the youths. By contrasting these observations with families without delinquency, they found that there were relatively more first
sons among *parents* of the nondelinquent families, while there were
more second sons among *parents* of the delinquent families. A similar situation was observed for the *youths*, that is, more first sons
among non-delinquent groups and more second sons among delinquent groups.

As for the mothers, it was revealed that there were more mothers
in the first- and second-sibling positions among the non-delinquent
group, while there were more mothers among the delinquent group
with third- or later-born daughters in their own families. Based on
these findings, they suggested that a position of relative neglect of
the parents of delinquent subjects may contribute to the relative
neglect of one or more of their own children, and in a sense, to the
continuation of a pattern that contributes to delinquency. Unfortunately, the factor of sibling position in relation to delinquency has
not been investigated in other societies and it is difficult to ascertain
to what extent this is a universal phenomenon, or whether it is a
unique phenomenon observed only in societies (such as Japan) in
which sibling order has a significant implication in terms of treatment received from the parents.

It is becoming obvious that parent-child relations are crucially
related to the mental health problems and various parent-child relational problems existing among different cultural backgrounds.
There is a growing need to develop more systematic, empirical
cross-cultural research in the areas of child-rearing patterns, parent-
child relations (both functional and dysfunctional), and children's
relations with the family. Based on such findings, we can better
clarify the ways in which culture contributes to parent-child rela-

tional patterns and to the occurrence of parent-child interactional problems. Such findings will certainly guide us towards developing intervention and prevention of parent-child relational problems within the context of cultural background.

Chapter 8

Families with Specific Problems

In the fields of clinical psychiatry and abnormal psychology, many psychopathologies have traditionally been described and understood as abnormal problems or psychiatric disorders for individuals. In order to comprehend the nature of such problems or disorders, a number of approaches, including biological, psychological, and sociocultural, have been explored. As one such approach, family therapists and researchers have joined the field and tried to make contributions by comprehending problems or disorders within the context of the family.

FORMULATIONS OF FAMILY AND PSYCHOPATHOLOGY

Theoretically, there are several ways to conceptualize individual pathology related to the family (Block, 1974; Tseng and McDermott, 1979). These formulations are elaborated as follows:

The Family as the System of Pathology

The manifested individual abnormality or disorder is a part of the display of the total family psychopathology. Although individual psychopathology may initially receive clinical attention, individual psychopathology is merely an expression of the pathological function of the whole family. Closer examination generally reveals a particular set of dysfunctional family relationships that deserve therapeutic intervention.

For example, a person with a psychosomatic disorder is associated with a family characterized by enmeshed subsystem boundaries, overprotectiveness, rigidity, and lack of conflict solution; therefore, the family represents a potent therapeutic resource (Minuchin, Rosman, and Baker, 1978; Russell, Olson, Sprenkle, and Atlano, 1983).

The Family as the Cradle of Pathology

The family dynamic and environment serve as the source for an individual to develop certain vulnerabilities, particularly throughout his/her early life. Based on these developmental predispositions rooted in the family, the pathology of an individual is manifested after reaching adulthood, particularly when the individual is exposed to certain stressful situations.

For instance, Beiber, Dain, Dince, Drellich, Grand, Grundlack, Kremer, Rifkin, Wilbur, and Bieber (1962) based on the findings of analysis of male homosexuality, have hypothesized that particular father-son, mother-son, and interparental power-affect parameters exist in early development that contribute to the formation of male homosexuality. When a boy is exposed to a characteristic triangular pattern wherein his mother, who is close-binding intimate, is dominant and minimizing towards her husband—who is a detached father, particularly a hostile-detached one—there is a high chance that the boy will become homosexual. Although such speculation is no longer readily accepted, it does reflect one way to view the family's environment as contributing to the development of certain pathologies later in the life of an individual.

Family Pathology as a Concomitant Manifestation of Individual Pathology

This formulation takes the position that the expressions of certain observed family behavior patterns are the manifestations of subclinical pathologies of parents or family members who have genetic predispositions of the same spectrum. Thus, the irrational thoughts and communication patterns manifested by a schizophrenic family may be viewed as the concomitant, but subclinical, individual manifestations of the same schizophrenic disorder (Wender, Rosenthal, Kety, Schulsinger, and Welner, 1974).

The Family as the Catalyst of Pathology

Pathology problems or disorders are primarily related to an individual predisposition, yet the unique environment and dynamic of the family provoke, maintain, or aggravate the individual psychopathology. Therefore, the modification or removal of the specific family situation is desirable for improvement of the condition of an individual disorder.

This position is supported by experiments conducted by Purcel et al. (1969) on children with asthma. In these experiments the children remained in their own homes; all parental and sibling figures were removed and substitute parents were provided. The results showed that children with a history of emotionally precipitated asthmatic attacks had fewer attacks when people were removed from the house, even though the allergenic situation was not changed.

Family Reacting to the Pathology

This type of pathology occurs when manifested family problems or dysfunctions are a secondary reaction to the presence of the disorder or malfunction of a family member. This possibility is illustrated by a situation in which the family reacts dysfunctionally to the medical or neuropsychiatric problems of a family member. The family needs assistance to cope with the individual's problems.

As pointed out by Russell et al. (1983), early theory and research were oriented towards identifying given symptoms with specific family patterns. For instance, there was an earnest search for the characteristics of the "schizophrenogenic family" and the "alcoholic marriage." This simple one-to-one correspondence between a particular style of family interaction and a specific individual symptom can no longer be assumed. Many studies have suggested that there is no one type of family system associated with a given symptom. For example, according to Olson, McCubbin, Barnes, Larsen, Muxen, and Wilson (1983), Killorin and Olson have collected data on 200 family systems that include an alcoholic member. These 200 families reported their own styles of interaction as falling within every type of family functioning pattern as categorized and measured by the Circumplex Model of Family System.

Although we are still far from knowing for certain the exact nature of the relations that exist between family members and various identified individual psychopathologies, it is useful to explore and clarify possible relationships which may exist. Various specific kinds of problems, disorders, or situations will be reviewed here with their relations to the family, with particular elaboration from cross-cultural perspectives.

SPECIFIC PSYCHIATRIC DISORDERS IDENTIFIED

Schizophrenia

In research on family theories of specific psychiatric disorders, schizophrenia was focused on first and has received the most attention. Clinical and theoretical interest in familial roots of schizophrenia were stimulated by From-Reichman (1948), who described the schizophrenogenic mother. Almost a decade later, Bateson, Jackson, Haley, and Weakland (1956) advanced the concept of the "double bind." Then, Lidz, Cornelison, Terry, and Fleck (1958) described schizophrenic families in terms of the "transmission of irrationality"; later, Wynne, Ryckoff, Day, and Hirsch (1958) described them in terms of "pseudomutuality" involving transactional thought disorders. The work of these three groups directed further research into three areas: parental thought disorders, deviant family communication style or patterns, and double-bind parent-child relationships.

As indicated by Dell (1980), family theories of schizophrenia can be divided according to epistemological viewpoints. (1) The *etiological explanation* takes the view that interaction patterns observed in families of schizophrenics are understood to exist prior to the onset of schizophrenia and are direct causes of the patients' illness. (2) The *responsive explanation* contends that the distinctive patterns in schizophrenic families developed in direct response to the onset of schizophrenia. (3) The *transactional explanation* considers that causality must be understood in terms of complex feedback models and sets of interdependent forces. (4) The *genetic explanation* considers attributes designated as schizophrenogenic to be concomitant, not causal. According to this view, personality characteristics associated with the parents are in the schizophrenic spectrum, i.e., the biological parents carry some of the same genetic load as their offspring and as one manifestation of this load they are cold, rejecting, ambivalent, and double-binding (Wender et al., 1974).

Due to increased knowledge that schizophrenic disorders are found in various sociocultural settings with a limited range of difference in prevalence, as well as the high prevalence of disorders associated with genetic relations in family and the response to psychopharmacology, psychiatrists now strongly consider schizophrenic disorders to be predominantly related to biological factors. The existence of empirical evidence on the family's role in schizophrenia has been critically reviewed by Goldstein and Strachan (1987). They pointed out that there is a paucity of theoretical frameworks guiding research on this subject. This view is echoed by Dell (1980) who indicates that there is epistemological confusion in researching family theories of schizophrenia. He shows that there is a need to distinguish between several different epistemological approaches—the etiological explanation, the responsive explanation, the situational explanation, and the transactional explanation—as well as the genetic explanation.

Instead of searching for the family's role in causing schizophrenic disorders, most contemporary family therapists have been concerned about whether or not family therapy is needed for schizophrenic patients, and if required, what kind of family therapy is needed in such circumstances. As indicated by Goldstein (1981), both medication and a form of family therapy play significant roles in decreasing relapse in acute, young schizophrenics after discharge into the community. The most notable effects of treatment are in the improvement of emotional blunting and withdrawal. Goldstein speculated that there may be two levels of therapy effects, nonspecific and specific. A family support system appears to reduce the affective symptoms associated with the postacute phase of a schizophrenic episode, such as emotional withdrawal and blunt affect. Falloon (1981) further emphasized that studies of schizophrenic patients and their families revealed that not only did the schizophrenic patients demonstrate ineffective coping behavior, but members of the patients' households appeared similarly deficient in the communication and problem-solving skills needed to prevent a fully developed relapse of symptoms. Thus, an effective family therapy intervention program should incorporate education of the family (about the nature and management of schizophrenia), teaching more effective nonverbal and verbal communication to all family members, and teaching more effective problem-solving skills to help identify and cope with stressful life events.

Very few investigations have been carried out to test family theories of schizophrenia cross-culturally. Nevertheless, several findings have indicated how sociocultural factors may affect schizophrenia through the family system. The World Health Organization's world study of schizophrenia (Satorius, Jablensky, and Shapiro, 1977) revealed that schizophrenic disorders that occurred in less-developed societies tended to have a better prognosis than those found in developed societies. One reason offered is that family support available in less-developed societies may contribute to the rehabilitation and recovery of patients suffering from schizophrenic disorders. An experimental program carried out in Beijing, China (Shen, 1985), illustrated that schizophrenic patients who stayed in their home setting in the community, participating in regular social-occupational activities, fared better than those who were placed in a hospital setting for therapy. Similarly, a follow-up study of schizophrenic patients in Qatar (in the Persian Gulf) by El-Islam (1979) reported that the schizophrenics who were living in extended families had a better prognosis than those who were living in nuclear families. He speculated that additional family members contribute by taking an interest in the patient and attempting to combat the patient's social withdrawal.

Neurotic Disorders

In contrast to psychoses, such as schizophrenia, neurotic disorders refer to a group of minor psychiatric disorders predominantly associated with psychological factors. Therefore, there is more room for elaboration of the psychological, familial, and cultural aspects of the nature of such problems. Following are discussions of several kinds of unique neurotic disorders which are considered culturally-related.

Social Phobias

Social phobias refer to psychological conditions characterized by persistent, irrational fear of situations in which the individual may be exposed to scrutiny by others, and compelling desire to avoid such situations. Such disorders are observed more frequently in some societies, such as Japan (Kitanish and Tseng, 1989) and Korea (Lee, 1987). In Japan, such disorders are professionally labeled as *taijin-kyofushio* — literally, "disorder of fearing people (human)." A special way of treating such disorders, called Morita therapy, has been developed.

In Japan, such disorders are usually observed among young people around the time of adolescence, when they become concerned about how they appear to others — especially their peers. They become extremely preoccupied with their behavior in front of others and believe they are being judged. Clinically, the patients develop a fear of eye-to-eye contact with others, become easily flushed in front of others, and hesitate to interact or communicate with others. The resulting behavior is avoidance of social contact.

Psychological examination always reveals that such disorders occur among children who are oversensitive, self-conscious, and lack self-confidence. Family histories reveal that discrimination and favoritism among the children by their parents are frequently observed and the patients feel that they are unwanted, unfavorable, or disgraceful in their parents' eyes. Sometimes, there is a history that something "disgraceful" has happened in the family, i.e., the parents are divorced or are socially unsuccessful, and these incidents cause the patient to feel embarrassed and disgraced. In other words, the family provides a situation that lowers a child's self-esteem and makes the child extremely sensitive towards others' views of him/her.

Such family backgrounds are coupled with social-cultural situations in which appropriate social relations are demanded and emphasized. Intensive interpersonal relations have been maintained and are of concern. Above all, interactions and communications are usually subtle and nonverbal, which complicate the interrelationships with others in the social situation.

Sexual Neuroses

One group of male patients manifest their psychosexual problems in the form of intensive concern over excessive discharge of semen, professionally addressed as spermatorrhea, or a fear that the penis will shrink into the abdomen and cause death (clinically called *koro*, or penile contraction panic disorder). Spermatorrhea has been described among Hindu patients in India (Carstairs, 1956) and koro has been reported sporadically among Southern Chinese and other South Asian people.

The common psychological feature among these unique sexual neurotic cases — manifested as spermatorrhea or koro — are problems with gender identity development and feelings of insecurity in psychosexual function. Researchers have indicated that the fathers of these patients are either distant from their sons, seldom available due to frequent absences, or are weak and do not provide an adequate male figure for identification. On the other hand, the male patients, as boys or adolescents, have been extremely close to or attached to their mothers and have had difficulty growing as independent youngsters with masculinity (Rin, 1965). This situation is very similar to the triad-family background, which has been described by Beiber et al. (1962) for Western male patients with disorders of gender identity (e.g., homosexuality). For Eastern male patients, such symptoms are diagnosed as sex-related neurotic disorders.

Neurasthenia, Anxiety, and Depression

Although there are few studies which focus primarily on the study of the family dynamic and background associated disorders of anxiety and depression, one investigation that took place in Beijing compared the family background of three kinds of neurotic disorders observed among Chinese in Beijing (Xu, Cui, Tseng, and Hsu, 1988). The family was examined regarding family functioning, satisfaction, and strains among three neurotic subgroups of neurasthenia, anxiety, and depression. As a result, it was revealed that the depressive group, particularly female patients, perceived their families as less cohesive and adaptable and they were less satisfied with their families. Regarding family strains, anxiety groups reported less strain in areas related to basic family conditions and operations. The study indicated that for the Chinese, family as a stressor contributes more toward depression, less toward anxiety, with contribution toward neurasthenia falling in between.

Eating Disorders

Eating problems in the form of overeating or refusing to eat have become a common concern among people in well-developed societies, particularly in the West. Clinically, such disorders are manifested either as obesity associated with bulimia and overeating, or conversely, as anorexia nervosa. Considerable attention has been given by family therapists to the treatment of such disorders, and the effectiveness of family therapy has been asserted for such family-related problems (Minuchin, Baker, Rosman, Liebman, Milman, and Todd, 1975; Minuchin et al., 1978; Palazzoli, 1974).

Investigation of the family background associated with such disorders has revealed that the families tend to be characterized by enmeshed subsystem boundaries, overprotectiveness, rigidity, lack of conflict solution, and child involvement in parental conflict (Russell et al., 1983). After examining 105 patients with bulimia, Johnson and Flach (1985) reported that the bulimic patients' perceptions of their families included low cohesiveness, a lack of emphasis on independent and assertive behavior, and a high level of conflict coupled with a low emphasis on open expression of feelings.

From cross-cultural aspects, it should be noted that the prevalence of eating disorders, in the form of either overeating (and obesity) or undereating (as in anorexia nervosa), may vary considerably among different societies. In general, the phenomenon is more prevalent among well-developed and affluent societies and less so among underdeveloped and deprived societies. In societies where there is a shortage of food, people are less likely to overeat, and also unlikely to undereat. Thus, there is good reason to believe that the phenomenon of eating problems has something to do with the socioeconomic situation. An illustration is given by findings from Singapore, Taiwan, and Japan, where obesity among adolescents was seldom heard of before World War II. After the war, when socioeconomic conditions improved, there was an increase in obesity among adolescents, particularly males. With improvements in nutrition and decreased opportunities for physical exercise in the newly industrialized environment, particularly for male adolescents, problems of obesity began. Thus, socioeconomic environmental change can influence weight significantly.

Furthermore, there are some cultural factors that apparently affect attitudes and concerns about weight. In the multi-ethnic society of Hawaii, Hawaiians, in contrast to Japanese-, Chinese-, or Filipino-Americans, tend to have weight-problems and obesity-related health problems. It is clear that in addition to genetic factors, the phenomenon is closely related to traditional cultural attitudes among Hawaiians, who value heavy weight and consider the gaining of body weight a sign of affluence and success (for males) and beauty (for females). Thus, genetic and cultural factors override the family factor. This leaves the theoretical question of whether or not, among the Hawaiians who are overweight, there still can be observed unique family characteristics that have been described for overweight persons in other ethnic groups. This deserves further investigation.

When behavior problems were examined in Chinese children, who were mostly only-children (as a result of the one-child-per-couple national family planning policy), it was found that "the matter of picking at food" is considered one of the most common child behavior problems, as perceived and reported by Chinese parents. This can be interpreted by keeping in mind that within the Chinese culture, great emphasis has always been placed on both the giving and receiving of foodstuffs. Thus, areas related to food also naturally become the areas where children are most likely to manifest behavior problems and where parents will perceive and react to child behavior problems (Tao and Chiu, 1985).

Eating behavior problems therefore need to be evaluated from different levels: genetic background of the individuals, the socioeconomic background of the society, cultural attitudes toward eating, as well as the family's contribution toward such eating-related behavior disorders.

Alcohol Problems

Clinical interest in researching family-related aspects of alcoholism began in the middle of this century. Early family studies have focused on the pathology of the nondrinking spouse, concerning the personality and role of the wife of the alcoholic in relation to the inception and maintenance of her husband's excessive drinking. Most clinically-oriented studies (Price, 1945; Futterman, 1954) portrayed the wife as a disturbed personality with dependency conflicts and complex needs that directed her to choose an alcoholic as a husband. She dominated the marriage by taking over the roles her husband could not fulfill because of his drinking, and then castigated him for his insufficiency (Ablon, 1980).

Skeptical of the stereotyped clinical description of typologies of alcoholic wives, Jackson (1954) reviewed a natural history of the alcoholic process. She presented a contrasting point of view, emphasizing that particular so-called pathological behavior constellations of wives represent their particular way of coping with stress during the various stages of alcoholism. These behaviors reflect how the family, as a unit, adjusted to the alcoholism of one of its members. Another trend among researchers is to regard the total family unit as the necessary functional context for an understanding of the individual alcoholic's drinking patterns. Consequently, there is increasing interest among family researchers in studying family structure and behavior in alcoholism (Steinglass, Benett, Wolin, and Reiss, 1987; Jacob and Seilhamer, 1987). For instance, Steinglass (1979) has examined families containing one alcoholic and one nonalcoholic spouse in the family interaction laboratory using the Reiss Pattern Recognition Card Sort, a procedure with high predictive validity in the study of family interaction patterns and psychopathology. As a result, he found that if families were subdivided into "wet" versus "dry" groups based on the current drinking status of the identified alcoholic, individuals in wet families tended to act independently, while individuals in dry families were highly coordinated, displaying a rigid adherence to a family level pattern of problem-solving. This indicated that behavioral styles in alcoholic families differ depending on whether the identified alcoholic is currently drinking or not. It supports the position that the major perpetuator of drinking patterns is the overriding need for the maintenance of the status quo or family homeostasis that has developed within the family system.

Although it is well-known that the prevalence of alcoholism differs significantly among different ethnic/cultural groups, the significance of cultural patterning for family roles and behavior has been given scant attention. Ablon (1980) recently studied a population of middle-class Catholic families, primarily American-born Irish, German, and Italian second or third generations, living in a metropolitan area of Southern California. Through interviews and observations over a four-year period, Ablon found that problematic drinking patterns occurred with greatest severity in families of cultural groups exhibiting the highest levels of expressed and accepted family and subgroup societal controls concerning family life. Thus, Irish Catholics, who traditionally display the greatest control in all facets of life, also exhibited more problem drinking behavior than other Catholics.

Through such case material, Ablon indicated that Irish Catholic normative life career themes involve critical elements of control that often appeared to be injurious to the marital relationship. Among these elements were domineering mothers, religious sanctions related to sex, strictures against birth control, husbands' irregular work hours, the importance of men's peer groups, and failure to separate from the family of origin. Through this study, an attempt has been made to illustrate the importance of looking at the behavior of family members as they relate to each other in a complex of social and cultural expectations, rather than focusing only on individuals as interacting bundles of pathological needs.

Kaufman's 1985 examination of the psychodynamic environment of the family echoed the view that Irish-American alcoholic family patterns are substantially influenced by ethnic factors. According to Kaufman, the Irish often drink for reassurance and to escape from burdens of guilt and the need to repress sexuality and aggression. Irish families are frequently ruled by domineering, matriarchal mothers, who continue their dominance of the family even when the children are middle-aged. Many Irish fathers in inner cities work extra jobs and evening hours and thus spend little time with the family. An absentee father accentuates the tendency for the mother to be responsible for and over-involved with family functions and tasks.

Examining alcoholism and the Hispanic family, Panitz, McConchie, Sauber, and Fonseca (1983) have elaborated the role of machismo in the development of alcoholism in Hispanic-American males. They pointed out that widespread acceptance of the machismo ethos and its determining role in the structure dynamics and value systems of the traditional Hispanic family encourage alcohol abuse by men.

In contrast, and despite traditional attitudes in modern Japan making it socially disgraceful for women to indulge in drinking, there has been a remarkable upswing in alcohol consumption among women during the past ten years that has increased national alcohol consumption sevenfold (Yoshida, 1985). It was concluded that with the rapid socioeconomic improvement, most housewives were relieved of their daily, heavy household chores, yet were not encouraged to engage in professional fields. Their empty home life contributed to their indulgence in drinking as a way of passing time. In other words, this is closely related to the life pattern of housewives within the social context.

It is well-known that there are serious drinking problems among native American Indian men (Westermeyer and Neider, 1985), described as the results of cultural deprivation. Most of the older men have lost their dignity as fathers or husbands, and the younger men have lost their ethnic and personal identities. Thus, drinking problems are attributed to the dysfunction of the family in a rapidly changing and culturally deprived society. Such phenomena are echoed in many island societies in the Pacific (Rubinstein, 1986), where young men in particular are experiencing serious alcohol problems which are also having a devastating effect on the family.

Thus, a cross-cultural review of alcoholism and the family illustrates that the nature of the family dynamic and system that contributes to or is associated with drinking problems varies tremendously from culture to culture. Instead of merely looking at the family system, there is a need to examine the sociocultural system beyond the family that affects the family's life and behavior, which, in turn, influences drinking problems among family members.

SPECIFIC FAMILY PROBLEMS RECOGNIZED

Several family problems have been manifested in specific forms that deserve special attention and discussion, particularly from the viewpoint of culture perspectives.

Family Violence — Spouse Abuse

Aggressive physical abuse of a spouse is a special marital problem which requires special attention and intervention. According to Levinson's (1988) holocultural study of family violence in small scale and peasant societies (included in the Human Relations Area Files data archive), wife-beating is the most common form of family violence, occurring in 84.5% of the 90 societies examined. By studying primitive cultures, Lester (1981) found that wife-beating was more common in societies characterized by high divorce rates and in which women were perceived as inferior. Societies that not only experienced high rates of alcohol abuse, but also high rates of alcohol-related aggression, also had higher rates of wife-beating.

As for the situation among developed societies, the occurrence of wife-beating tends to be underreported, making it difficult to obtain the actual figures of prevalence. O'Leary and Curley (1986) predict that at least half of all married adults in the United States, male and female, will experience one or more acts of physical aggression by their marriage partner. Furthermore, Straus, Gelles, and Steinmetz (1980) estimated that approximately 10% to 15% of women in the United States will be victims of repeated and serious physical aggression by their partners.

After comparisons of six societies — the United States, Canada, Finland, Israel, Puerto Rico, and Belize, Steinmetz (1981) revealed preliminary findings that the percentage of husbands and wives who use violence apparently was not an accurate predictor of the severity and frequency of violent acts. For instance, Finland, in which over 60% of husbands and wives reported using violence, has the lowest mean frequency scores of actual violent acts. On the other hand, the kibbutz sample from Israel had the fewest number of husbands and wives using violence, but those who did use violence were extremely violent.

Gelles (1980) points out that several theoretical approaches have been used by various researchers to explain and understand the violence occurring in a family. These approaches include the psychiatric model, the social-psychological model, and the sociocultural model. Merely from a cultural point of view, there are several factors that may account for the varying prevalence of wife-beating among different ethnic and cultural groups. These include the basic attitude and relations between men and women, the role status of husbands and wives, attitudes toward physical violence as a way of coping with frustration, and the social reaction to the occurrence of violence between spouses within the family setting.

Family Suicide

Family suicide refers to situations in which suicidal behavior involves multiple members of a family. In a strict sense, these occur as a double suicide of parents coupled with the murder of their children. Family suicide is frequently observed in Japan (Ohara, 1963). This special form of suicide usually occurs when one of the parents encounters an unbearable situation, such as severe debt or an incurable disease, or becomes involved in socially disgraceful events, and decides to solve the problem by ending his/her life. The spouse who learns of the contemplated suicide consents to die with his/her mate. Eventually the parents kill their young children and finally kill themselves—that is, homicide and suicide are combined, or they make plans so the whole family can die together, perhaps by taking poison. Recently, a more modernized method of family suicide is through drowning after driving the automobile into the sea.

There are several motivations behind family suicide. One is the cultural assumption that no one will care for the orphaned children, that they are best cared for by their parents. Family suicide occurs in a society that greatly values the tie between parent and child; it is believed that it is better to die together as a family than to leave behind a member of a broken family. Although it has long been forbidden legally in Japan for parents to kill their children and to carry out family suicide, this phenomenon is still observed. Reactions by society are usually sympathetic rather than critical.

Collective Family Mental Disorder

Occasionally more than one member of a family becomes psychiatrically ill through a process of contagion — the psychiatric condition of one person in the form of dissociation, conversion, delusion, or other abnormal behaviors, is transmitted to another family member. If two family members are affected, it is addressed as *folie à deu* (double insanity); if more than two persons in a family are involved, the condition is referred to as *folie à famille* (family insanity).

Although this phenomenon is considered rare, sporadic occurrences have been reported. In reviewing the English literature, Gralnick (1942) found 103 cases of folie à deu reported between 1879 and 1942. The majority of these cases occurred between sister and sister, and mother and child. Ten cases belonged to the category of folie à famille or collective family psychoses. Since 1942, case reports have continuously appeared in the literature. For example, Gregory (1959) and Kreitman (1962) both have reviewed situations wherein both husbands and wives were mentally ill; Waltzer (1963) reported a psychotic family involving a dozen members; and Goduco-Angular and Wintrob (1964) described a case of folie à famille that occurred in the Philippines.

Tseng (1969) reported a paranoid family in Taiwan in which a man transmitted his persecutory delusion to his sister and then to his sister's husband, and later to five of their children. This unique phenomenon occurred at the time Taiwan was threatened by the possible invasion by communists from Mainland China. The man developed a delusion that he was persecuted by underground communists. While facing a series of real stresses — unemployment, theft, and sickness — the family reacted by adopting and sharing the political delusion that they were persecuted by the communists. They became a cohesive family and isolated themselves from the surrounding community in an effort to combat the underground enemy.

Woon (1976) described a Chinese-Malaysian family in which two brothers and one sister simultaneously developed a dissociated condition, creating a sensational turmoil in a village in a rural area of Malaysia. The situation occurred after their aged father, a village shaman, suffered a stroke, making it necessary to choose a successor from among his children. Affected by intense feelings of competition and unable to handle such emotions, the siblings developed dissociated conditions one after another.

After reviewing these reported cases, it becomes apparent that in addition to the existing premorbid personality of the family members, a strong emotional bond between family members facilitated the occurrence of a collective psychiatric condition in the family, particularly when they faced a stressful situation together. To share and to be involved in a similar psychiatric condition appeared to be an alternative way for them to deal with the common crisis they encountered.

SPECIFIC STRESSES ENCOUNTERED BY THE FAMILY

Hill (1958) has indicated that a family's vulnerability to crisis depends on the interaction of their stress with both existing resources and the family's perception of the crisis. The spectrum of stress, as perceived by families, varies among different ethnic-cultural groups (Hsu, Tseng, Lum, Lau, Vaccaro, and Brennan, 1988).

There are many kinds of catastrophes or stresses that a family may encounter; some of these will be reviewed and elaborated upon from cultural perspectives.

Illness of a Family Member

The serious illness of a family member usually has a tremendous impact on the lives of other people in the family. Several factors contribute to the response patterns of the family unit to the serious illness of a relative.

The family may never have had any prior intensive interactions with physicians, nurses, or other health care providers. They may not know how to structure their relations with them and how to articulate their needs to medical personnel on whom they must now depend. Thus, there is a need to help the family relate to the health care providers (Wellisch, 1985). This is particularly true for those immigrant families who do not know how to relate to and adjust to the health care system in a new cultural setting. At the same time, the doctors and nurses may not understand how to relate appropriately to families of different cultural backgrounds.

Obtaining relevant personal medical histories and sharing and interpreting the results of the findings to the patient and to family members must be handled sensitively with a regard for cultural differences. The health worker must endeavor to facilitate interaction and communication within the family when dealing with such situations. When sharing information, the family must be helped through different stages of reaction to regain some sense of control in order to cope with the situation to their maximum capacity.

Suicide of Family Members

The behavior of a suicide varies widely among different sociocultural environments in terms of frequency, method, and motivation. It appears to be universally true that men tend to commit suicide by more aggressive methods, while women attempt suicide through less aggressive, less certainly fatal methods (Tseng and McDermott, 1981).

In terms of age, several patterns have been described regarding the age distribution of the frequency of suicide (World Health Organization, 1976). In the Hungarian pattern, the frequency of suicide increases continuously with the increase of age, particularly after the middle years. This pattern is also most frequently observed in the United States. In the Japanese pattern there are two peaks in the curve of age distribution—one around the age of twenty, and another after middle age. The Micronesian pattern has only one sharp peak between the ages of 20-30 and a decline after the 30s (Rubinstein, 1986).

These patterns of age distribution reflect the different life stresses experienced and reacted to by people of various societies. In Micronesia, as well as in many other parts of the Pacific, and to some extent for native Americans, some young people experience extreme confusion and frustration when faced with rapid social change and cultural uprooting, and tend to engage in impulsive, self-destructive behavior as a way of coping with the situation.

In Japan, Taiwan, Singapore, and some other South Asian countries, as well as some South American countries such as Argentina or Peru, the strain and pressures of life are greatest for the young, who are expected to abide by the restrictions and expectations of the society and culture. The situation improves somewhat when they become middle-aged and begin to enjoy privileges, power, and success. In the latter part of the life cycle they gradually lose what they acquired in middle age.

In contrast, for many Western societies, including the United States and typified by Hungary, life is most glorious for youths who enjoy all the autonomy and excitement in life. Responsibilities and burdens begin to increase after middle age, and privileges, enjoyment, and hope tend to decline with the increase of age. Thus, different patterns of personal life cycles and the different nature of family development in different societies contribute to various patterns of age distribution in suicide.

In examining family background with regard to suicidal behavior, Rosenbaum and Richman (1970) found that the families of suicidal patients expressed more hostility and offered less support than families of nonsuicidal patients. By interviewing a clinical population consisting of suicidal and nonsuicidal patients and their families, they found that mutual feelings of discontent exist between the suicidal patients and their families. The theme of family meetings was most often that of maintaining the suicidal patients as blameworthy individuals who had no right to complain about anyone else. The majority of the families expressed feelings of being fed up with the suicidal patients, of considering them a burden, and of believing that the family would be better off if the patients were dead or would go away. In general, the suicidal patient was typically either self-blaming or quiet, while the others were critical and reproachful. The authors concluded that suicidal behavior is particularly likely to occur when there is increased stress accompanied by hostility and death wishes from the family and significant others when the suicidal person is unable to retaliate, and external support is unavailable or withdrawn.

Regarding family therapy of an attempted suicide, Richman (1979) emphasized that the basic goal of therapy is to help initiate and catalyze a healing process that will enable the family to accept changes in both the individual's and family's existence; to decrease the amount of destructive family interaction; to make contact with and among the family members; and to provide hope.

Dying and Death of a Family Member

While the death of a loved one is usually the most catastrophic event for an individual or family (Frantz, 1984), the degree of stress experienced is dependent upon several interacting variables, as pointed out by Crosby and Jose (1983). For example, many families experience extreme stress when the death of a family member is unexpected, in contrast to a situation involving prolonged illness and anticipated death. If the family is simultaneously experiencing other crises, the death of a family member will naturally increase stress to an almost intolerable level as there are few personal or interpersonal resources left to cope with the death. The family undergoes the formation of new role realignments and structures, the need to establish new patterns of authority and decision-making, the loss of economic security, and the loss of emotional support.

The stages through which the dying person passes have been postulated by Kubler-Ross (1969): denial, anger, bargaining, depression, and acceptance. Various mechanisms for coping with death have been listed by Crosby and Jose (1983), and include a strategy to keep busy, a get-away strategy, and so on. In spite of these universal patterns, the reactions to death experienced by the dying person as well as members of the family vary according to the prevalent cultural attitudes towards death and the process of mourning, and the culturally patterned behavioral response to a death.

By examining individual grief and mourning processes across cultures through a review of the ethnographic literature, Rosenblatt, Walsh, and Jackson (1976) found that societies that performed final ceremonies some time after a person's death lacked prolonged expressions of grief, whereas grief is prolonged (and often disturbed) in societies that lack final post-burial ceremonies. Reid (1979) has reported the elaborate and extended mortuary rites of the Murngin (the people of northeastern Arnhem Land, Australia) that promote and structure the mourning process and facilitate the full reintegration of the bereaved into the social life of the community.

In comparing bereavement in Samoan and American communities, Ablon (1971) brought up the issue that Samoans view death as a natural event in the experience of living. In contrast, death in the United States is a subject that is generally hidden, or at least ignored as much as possible. Furthermore, the effective and available support in the family- and community-oriented society of Samoa contrasts with the larger American society in which many persons must rely on impersonal community aid to deal with instances of death and misfortune.

Different experiences of widowhood have been described cross-culturally by Mathison (1970) as follows. India is a strong patrilineal social organization in which women are devalued. The Hindu religion has decreed that a widow shall not remarry, although a widower is urged to remarry as soon as possible. The situation is worsened by another Hindu custom in which girls are frequently betrothed while still very young to much older boys or even to men. With the age differential and the death rate in India, it is not uncommon for a girl to become a widow before the marriage is even consummated. Throughout history, the life of a widow in India has been dismal. She can stay with her husband's family, but is then regarded as the menial of all the other persons in the household. She cannot attend ceremonies of rejoicing as her presence is considered a bad omen. As pointed out by Mathison (1970), at least part of the rationale behind the dehumanizing treatment of widows lies in the Hindu belief that the husband's death has in some way resulted from sins the wife has committed in a past life.

In contrast, the fate of widows among the Trobriand Islanders is consistent with a matrilineal social organization in which women occupy a more prestigious position than in other societies. The widow is provided with highly structured rituals to observe during her bereavement. During the several days of funeral rites, the widow is required to mourn ostentatiously and dramatically, and must shave her head and howl loudly with grief. After this, she enters a small cage built into her home, and remains in the dark for a period of six months to two years. This is said to keep the husband's ghost from finding her. Kinsmen are with her at all times. Once the period of mourning is terminated, she is ceremonially washed and dressed in a gaily decorated grass skirt. She is then considered to be available for remarriage. Since women in this culture control material goods through the matrilineal descent system, and are thus an economic asset to men, remarriage is highly likely (Mathison, 1970). This system serves as a contrast to different family systems associated with different views toward death, widowhood, and remarriage. The lives of women after the loss of their husbands vary tremendously, with different psychological and family mental health implications.

REMARKS

Attention has been paid to various specific psychiatric disorders and mental health problems associated with family life, background, or functioning. This chapter has attempted to compare and clarify findings that indicate the family's contribution to such disorders or problems. More importantly, we have tried to examine the findings from various sociocultural settings and to illustrate that there is a great need to expand our study of family pathology into cross-cultural perspectives. In this way we can better understand to what extent the findings and conclusions obtained for one society are specific and society-limited or broadly applicable and generalizable transculturally. By seeking cross-cultural examination and validation, current knowledge and theories can be challenged for broader applications.

Chapter 9

Culture and Family Assessment

CULTURAL CONSIDERATIONS
IN FAMILY ASSESSMENT

Expansion of the Understanding
of Family Dimensions

If we are dealing clinically with families of different ethnic/cultural groups, we must extend our orientation and understanding of dimensions of the family. In addition to the conventional dimensions with which family researchers and therapists are concerned (i.e., family development, family subsystem, and family group), it is necessary to expand our knowledge and understanding of the cultural aspects of family systems as focused upon by cultural anthropologists. These cultural aspects include anthropological aspects of marriage forms, kinship relations, marital residential choice, family authority, and family values (Tseng, 1986). Otherwise, our knowledge of the family will be limited for transcultural applications, and "cultural myopia" will leave us shortsighted in underwriting the family.

Clarification of the Concepts
of Normality and Dysfunction

When an evaluator is assessing a person with a cultural background different from his/her own, the concepts and definitions of normality and pathology must be considered cautiously (Westermeyer, 1985). Such caution should also be exercised when examining a family. The definitions of "functioning," "dysfunctional," "healthy," and "pathological" vary among families of different cultural backgrounds.

Various definitions of normality have been applied when dealing with individuals, e.g., normality construed as "health," "utopia," "average," "process," or "coping and adaptation" (Offer and Sabshin, 1974). In a similar way, family functioning could be approached in different ways, such as "asymptomatic," "optional," "average," "transactional," or "adaptive" family functioning (Walsh, 1982).

As clinicians, we tend to utilize our professional knowledge and conceptions to judge the health of a family. For example, individualism is healthier than enmeshment, mutuality is more mature than isolation, flexibility is more adaptive than rigidity (Barnhill, 1979). Some Western family therapists (Lewis, Beavers, Gossett, and Phillips, 1976) also believe that certain family attributes, such as being "open in the expression of affection," having "respect for subjective views," and "encouragement of personal autonomy" are desirable for psychological health in family systems. These views, however, may not be applicable to families of other cultures. In an Asian family, for example, "collectiveness and sharing" are always valued and "concealing of private affection" is more or less emphasized. Thus, what is healthy and desirable functional family behavior may be subject to cultural variations and therefore require careful definition (Schwartzman, 1982).

Recognition of Cultural Variations of Family

For various reasons, including social, economic, ecological, psychological, and cultural factors, family systems have developed and differentiated into various forms. Some are similar in certain respects while others lack all but the slightest parallels. As clinicians, it is better to not only recognize these differences but to understand also the implications of such variations from functional perspectives. For example, in some cultures there are relatively few basic kinship terms used. Any adult male in the clan is addressed as "father," and young men are called "brother." No distinction is made between blood-relatives and non-family members in kinship terminology. This has been observed in Polynesian families, including Hawaiian ones, and is referred to by anthropologists as a Hawaiian-type kinship system. This phenomenon does not stem from an unde-veloped cognitive concept of family relationships, nor does it reflect an enmeshed relationship. Rather, it is the result of emphasis on the cohesiveness and belonging of members of a large clan. Under such kinship terms, the family boundary is greatly expanded. In fact, in island societies where the population is limited and people are quite dependent on each other, efforts to clearly distinguish between nuclear family members and extended family members are not sanctioned.

In contrast, kinship terms are greatly elaborated and differenti-ated in families of other cultures, such as in the Chinese family system. In Chinese families the uncles, aunts, nephews, and nieces on the paternal and maternal sides are all addressed differently; the older and younger uncles, brothers, and sisters also all have differ-ent terms of address. This reflects the need to distinguish clearly between the paternal and maternal sides of the family in a society that places great emphasis on the patrilineal system. Also, siblings in a traditional Chinese family system occupy different roles since an authoritative hierarchy based on ordinal position is stressed. Recognition of such variations in kinship terms will help us to un-derstand the implications of behavior in each system.

Adjustment of Culture-Influenced Perceptional Bias

The practice of clinical diagnosis relies heavily on the evaluator's subjective observation and judgement. Such observations are usu-ally based on the evaluator's professional perception, but are also influenced by personal sensitivity and experience. In the case of transcultural evaluation, clinical assessment will be further subject to the influence of the cultural backgrounds of both the evaluator and his/her clients. To some extent, culture-related perceptional bias will always exist and will require adjustment and correction.

For example, in a cross-cultural research project, a Japanese fam-ily interaction videotape was shown to both Japanese and American psychiatrists for their assessment of parent-child interactional patterns. The videotape depicted a family of four which consisted of the mother and father and two teenagers, a son and a daughter. The family was asked to invent a story based on a cartoon shown to them. In response to the request, this family performed as follows. With permission from the father, the mother spoke with her teenage daughter (the identified patient), who refused to respond despite the mother's repeated attempts to persuade or coerce the girl to tell a story about the picture. The father, meanwhile, talked privately with his teenage son, but did not interact directly with the mother or daughter. From this vignette interaction, most American evaluators perceived and interpreted the father to be "passive" and "not involved" in the family interaction. Interestingly however, the Japanese evaluators disagreed with such comments. They viewed the father as being "all right" in his behavior and "involved" with the family members. The Japanese evaluators made such remarks based on the fact that in a Japanese family, the father normally will not interact directly with a grown-up daughter, since it is considered the mother's job to relate to the daughter. Thus, the Japanese evaluators did not view the father in this case as unconcerned about his daughter, but rather as behaving in an adequate and appropriate fashion. These findings clearly illustrated that the perception of a family's interaction pattern is subject to and influenced by the evaluators' own cultural background, and is in need of cautious adjustment in the actual transcultural practice of family assessment (Tseng, McDermott, Ogino, and Ebata, 1982).

Awareness of the Existence of Cultural Blind Spot

No matter how much we try to learn about the cultural background of the client, we may still have a blind spot which prevents our complete understanding of the cultural meanings of such behavior. We may even miss the point completely; such a condition is called "cultural scotoma" — an area to which we are blind.

For instance, in the process of interviewing Hawaiian parents who were complaining about the misbehavior of their children, the father kept saying that "children are to be seen but not to be heard" at the dinner table at home. Without knowing that this is a cultural custom expected by the interviewees, the evaluator almost ignored the issue until the mother explained to the evaluator that, according to their Hawaiian customs, children are supposed to eat quietly at dinner time without speaking and are to listen carefully to the conversation of the adults. This is different from, for example, the American culture in which mutual conversation among family members at the dinner table is considered desirable family behavior.

An evaluator should keep in mind that such blind areas could surface at any time. Both the evaluator and the clients should be aware of this possibility and actively inquire into and explore meanings within the cultural context so that misunderstandings can be minimized.

PROCESS OF CULTURE-ADJUSTED FAMILY ASSESSMENT

Basic procedure needs to be observed in the initial assessment of any family. This includes making social greetings, identifying present problems, taking a history of the problems, making an observation of family patterns, making a preliminary family diagnosis, and defining and contracting the goals of intervention. However, there are several issues that need to be considered when approaching families with cultural backgrounds different from those of the evaluators.

Cultural Engagement

In a family session it is essential that the evaluator or therapist be able to engage the family in accordance with the background of the family members, which includes their personal style, educational level, and social class. Along the same lines, it is desirable for the evaluator or therapist to make a cultural engagement with the family. By simply learning how to extend social greetings or demonstrate etiquette in accordance with the family's ethnic or cultural background, the evaluator or therapist will show respect and understanding of the ethnic or cultural backgrounds of the family. Such actions usually will assist the evaluator or therapist in establishing rapport with the family more rapidly.

Gearing to Existing Authority Hierarchy

A family of a different cultural background may observe and practice different patterns of authority hierarchy. It is very important and useful to recognize quickly such hierarchical patterns in the assessment session and to try to comply with and utilize these existing systems of hierarchy, although they may be subtle or almost invisible.

For example, in dealing with Asian families which traditionally greatly respect the father's authority, it is important to begin by paying respects to the father and addressing questions to him, inviting him to start the conversation or asking his permission to begin dialogue with the other family members. Such rituals are necessary even if the father does not appear to be authoritative. Furthermore, it may be therapeutic to repeatedly support the family's authority figure if they emphasize the importance of such family authority.

In many Pacific families, which are traditionally characterized by a maternal hierarchy, the therapist should show respect to the grandmother of the family, no matter how quiet she may appear and even if she does not exercise her culturally-inherited authority in front of the other family members. After all, she is the person behind the scenes who ultimately makes the final decisions regarding the family. If the therapist does not handle her correctly, the cooperation of the entire family could be lost.

Culture-Appropriate Communication

It is common knowledge that communication patterns are molded by cultural systems in terms of the channel of communication to be used, the language of expression, and the way in which the meanings are transmitted. Culturally-appropriate communication patterns should therefore be observed and respected within transcultural settings (Hsu and Tseng, 1972; Putsch, 1985).

The existence of a culturally-molded communication channel is well illustrated by the following incident which occurred in Truk (Micronesia). A professional nurse who spoke fluent English requested an English-speaking foreign doctor-consultant for marital counseling. An appointment was made and the nurse and her husband met with the consultant for a family session. The consultant soon discovered that the husband spoke only broken English and despite the language difficulty, was the only one who answered the consultant's questions. The wife, who had spoken to the consultant prior to the session, was quiet most of the time, never spoke directly to the consultant, and replied to her husband in their local dialect of Trukese when she had to do so. Thus, throughout the session, the dialogue was carried out directly between the husband and the consultant. The wife responded to the consultant only indirectly through her husband (and in the local language)! After the session, the wife returned to see the consultant, who was curious enough to ask her about what had happened. He was told that according to their cultural custom, wives were not supposed to have any direct dialogue with men outside of the family. Therefore, in the presence of her husband, she was acting properly as a wife. However, when talking as a professional nurse to the consultant, she could carry on a conversation in English with the doctor-consultant. It was vital that the consultant respect and observe this culturally-defined communication etiquette and not break a cultural taboo by communicating directly with the woman, even though family assessment and intervention under such circumstances would be difficult.

Culture-Relevant Exposure of Private Matters

The kind of subjects that can be revealed to outsiders and the way disclosures are made are closely related to cultural practices. In the process of exploring family life, certain rules need to be observed in dealing with some private matters. For instance, when examining family history in Micronesian families, direct inquiries about the death of parents or grandparents must never be made, as it is taboo for them to mention the death of an ancestor. Micronesians have indirect and subtle ways of mentioning the demise of their ancestors. A direct question about the death of an ancestor places the respondent in an embarrassing and difficult situation; one must learn subtle ways of inquiring about such matters.

In dealing with a family that customarily respects parental authority, it is very important not to let the parents disclose their shortcomings or faults in front of their children; these disclosures will hurt their image as authoritative parents. It is also undesirable to force them to reveal their private feelings toward each other in the presence of their children, as it may embarrass them.

Establishment of an Appropriate Therapist's Role

Based on the various cultural systems, the role of the therapist is viewed differently by people of various cultural groups. For some, it is essential that the therapist maintain an image of authority and power as a leader who meets their cultural expectations; for others, it is preferable to demonstrate egalitarian and democratic leadership in dealing with the family situation. As an evaluator or therapist, it is better to learn beforehand the ordinary cultural expectations of authoritative figures of the family concerned and attempt to carry out the culturally appropriate role as a therapist from the start.

Clarification of Approach, Procedure, and Goal

Families from different cultural backgrounds may not have the same orientation and understanding a therapist/evaluator may have concerning family assessment and intervention. For some, it is a first-time experience; others may be biased by misinformation. It is usually necessary and helpful to discuss and clarify understandings and expectations and explain intentions of carrying out family assessment and intervention.

THE SCOPE OF COMPREHENSIVE FAMILY ASSESSMENT

In order to conduct culturally-relevant and clinically comprehensive family assessments the following areas need to be carefully evaluated:

I. BASIC INFORMATION

Genogram —
> Description of the relations among three generations including: spouses, parents, children, grandparents; indication of the household composition; ordinal position of siblings; any changes including death, separation.

Background of each family member —
> Age, sex, education, occupation, religion.

Medical/psychiatric/legal history of family members —
> Major psychiatric disorders, depression, suicide, alcohol or substance abuse, accidents, legal involvement.

II. PRESENTING PROBLEMS

> Identification of current problems that primarily concern the family;
> Description of any precipitating factors or circumstances, and the development of the problems;
> The understanding of the nature of the problem by the family;
> The family's past attempts to solve the problem;
> The family's goals and expectations for treatment.

III. ETHNIC/CULTURAL BACKGROUND

Marriage Form — Refers to the number of spouses in a marriage:
> Monogamy — composed of one man and woman (heterosexual);
> Polygamy — polygyny, polyandry;
> Group marriage — composed of multiple men and women.

Descent System — Rule which defines how descent is affiliated with sets of kin:
> Patrilineal — through men's kin;
> Matrilineal — through women's kin;
> Bilineal — through both men and women's kin;
> Ambilateral — through either men or women's kin.

Rule of Marital Choice—
    Exogamous—partner to be chosen from outside the group;
    Endogamous—partner to be chosen from inside the group.

Method of Mate Selection—
    Arranged—by family or clan;
    Self-Choice—by partners themselves.

Post-Marital Residence—Refers to the place where the newly-
    wed couple establishes their home:
    Matrilocal—with or near the wife's parents' place;
    Patrilocal—with or near the husband's parents' place;
    Bilocal—with or near either the wife's or the husband's
        parents' place;
    Neolocal—at a new place of their own.

Households—Concerns all the persons who live in one house:
    Nuclear—only the couple and their unmarried children;
    Stem—the couple, their parents and the couple's unmar-
        ried children;
    Joint—the couple and their children, their parents, and
        the couple's unmarried siblings;
    Extended—the couple, their parents, the couple's mar-
        ried siblings and their children.

Family Authority—Refers to the family figure to whom au-
    thority is designated for making major family decisions:
    Patriarchal—father (or grandfather);
    Matriarchal—mother (or grandmother);
    Egalitarian—both father and mother;
    Democratic—all the members of the household.

Primary Axis (Dyad)—prominent dyad on which the loyalty,
    affection, or bond exists:
    Conjugal (horizontal)—between husband and wife;
    Consanguinal (vertical)—between parent and child of
        one gender, such as father-son, mother-daughter, or
        mother-son, etc.;
    Sibling—such as between brother-sister.

Family Values/Beliefs/Attitudes — a particular set of value systems or beliefs jointly shared and firmly held by a family. It may cover many areas such as:

Moral issues

Religion

Life philosophy

Sexual attitudes

Attitudes toward family planning, abortion, size of family, ordinal position of children;

Child-rearing practices

Concept of Marriage — seeing marriage as primarily based on either customary commitment or mutual affection;

Familism — believing that a family should behave as a collective group or as a member of autonomous individuals;

Role expectations for spouses, parents, siblings, children;

Generational gap

Attitude toward aging

Family Rituals — symbolic forms of communication that are repeatedly acted out in a systematic fashion over time:

Family celebrations — those holidays and occasions that are widely practiced throughout the culture, and which are special in the minds of the family members;

Family traditions — less culture-specific and more idiosyncratic for each family;

Patterned family interactions — the ones most frequently enacted but least consciously planned by the family.

IV. FAMILY DEVELOPMENT HISTORY

It is important to make a longitudinal and chronological review of family development from the establishment of the marriage until the present. Particular highlights should be noted at critical periods of family growth, which can be described by the milestones of the family cycle. Any disruptions, changes or complications in the course of development of family life should also be noted.

Family Development Stages —
    Marital formation
    Childbearing
    Childrearing
    Family maturing
    Family contracting

Developmental Variations —
    Separation/Divorce
    Single parent family
    Remarriage

V. CURRENT FAMILY FUNCTIONING

The cross-sectional aspects of the family concerning the current daily life of the family, should refer to information provided by the family and may include these areas:
    Financial situation
    Social network: kin and non-kin networks
    Family socialization, recreation/common hobbies
    Family task allocation
    Family function: Decision making
                     Communication
                     Expression of Affection

VI. FAMILY INTERACTIONAL FUNCTION (FAMILY MENTAL STATUS)

The family's interactional pattern as observed by the evaluator may be referred to as the "family mental status." For the sake of convenience, it may be described and addressed in terms of:

Boundaries — The borders, territories, and limits maintained between individual family members, between subgroups (such as intergenerational boundaries), or with extrafamily groups.

The nature of the boundaries can be:

Clear vs. ambiguous

Closed vs. open

Permeability—the degree to which members are open, receptive and permeable to others' ideas

Invasive—the members speak for one another, or indulge in "mind reading"

Alignment—A prominent line or lines formed among members by alliance.

Coalition—union between parents (husband-wife), parent-child, or siblings

Triangulation—oppositional relations involving three party members, such as father-mother-son

Cross-generational coalition

Cohesion—the degree to which family members are separated from or connected to their family. It can be described in the spectrum of:

Disengaged—separated—connected—enmeshed

Power/control—the power relations within the family can be analyzed in terms of:

Power distribution:

Authoritative (monopolized), egalitarian, or democratic

Execution consistency:

Rigid—flexible

Power area:

General (extensive), specific (selective)

Power expression:

Implicitly vs. explicitly

Power strength:

Strong—weak—lack of power

Communication—Expression and exchange of ideas among family members. The overall pattern of communication can be described by the spectrum of:

Clear/open—confused—lack of communication

Channel: who speaks to whom, through whom, central switchboard

Style (mode): verbal, nonverbal
Special patterns of communication: Accusations
                                         Interruptions
                                         Lecturing
                                         Mind-reading/
                                             intrusions
                                         Incongruencies
Clarity: clear vs. unclear
        tangential — change topics into something else
        amorphous — dissolve into nothing
Congruence: affect-verbal discrepancy
               statement-context discrepancy
Responsiveness (how the message is received by others):
    Empathetic — nonempathetic
Responsibility (how persons take responsibility for their
  own actions):
    Responsible — irresponsible
Goal-directed negotiated: efficient — inefficient

(Subsystem) Relationships —
    Marital relations: Complementary
                    Symmetrical
                    Conflicting
                    Dependent
                    Incompatible
                    Disengaged
    Parent-child relations: Permissive
                       Indulgent
                       Rejected
                       Ignored
                       Punitive
    Sibling relations: Competitive — cooperative
                 Intimate — distant

Affection —
    Expressiveness: Open/direct — Restrictive/indirect
    Mood and Tone: Intimate — distant
                  Warm/pleasant — angry/hostile/cynical
                  Optimistic/humorous — pessimistic

Role Division —
    Clear — Confused — Unclear
    Fixed — Fluctuating
    Symmetrical — Complementary
    Appropriate — Inappropriate
Organization — the organizational structure of the family as a
    whole in performing its function and task:
    Overstructured
    Pathologically integrated
    Emotionally detached
    Disorganized/chaotic

VII. FAMILY STRESS/PROBLEMS

Stress/problems refers to the life events, changes, or situations
that may cause significant psychological distress in a family.
Such problems include: situations for which the family has had
little or no prior preparation, any sharp or decisive changes for
which old patterns of adjustment are not adequate, any emotional tension, anxiety or dysphoria related to intrafamily matters, and daily life patterns that bring burdens or deprive the
family of the pleasures of life.

Spectrum of Problems — can be identified in numerous areas:
    Living arrangements
    Daily household functions
    Financial
    Pregnancy/childbearing
    Child-rearing
    Parent-teenage interaction
    Dating/marriage
    Marital
    Extended-family
    Family transition
    Work
    Education
    Undesirable events/situation
    Sociocultural

Nature of Stress — Can be comprehended by:
  Dynamic development of the problems
  Perception of the stress/problems by the family
  Crisis meeting resources

VIII. PROBLEM SOLVING PATTERN

Types of coping that can be utilized to solve family problems:
  Negotiation
  Compromise
  Active problem solving
  Acquiring social support
  Seeking spiritual support
  Reframing
  Passive appraisal

Dysfunctional Coping patterns:
  Conflict avoidance
  Scapegoating
  Paralysis by ambivalence
  Extreme permissiveness
  Extreme authoritarianism

Adaptability — the extent to which the family is flexible and able to change to resolve the problem:
  Chaotic — flexible — structure — rigid/stereotyped — effective
  Efficient — good — poor — inefficient

IX. FAMILY STRENGTH

Family strength can be defined as those qualities that contribute to a successful marriage and successful family relationships. Family strength also refers to resources and variations which a family is able to use to prevent and resolve stress and crisis situations in the family system. Some examples of strength are:
Cohesion
Concern for each other
Commitment to the family
Pride and loyalty to the family
Positive values and beliefs
Utilization of external resources

X. FAMILY SATISFACTION

Family satisfaction is measured by the level of satisfaction family members have toward their marriages or family life.

XI. FAMILY DIAGNOSIS AND DYNAMIC FORMULATION OF PROBLEMS

Family diagnosis and a dynamic formulation of problems are a comprehensive and integrated manner of describing the nature of the family problems and summarizing the way in which the problems are dynamically developed by the effects of contributing factors.

XII. SUGGESTED INTERVENTION PLAN

A suggested intervention plan describes the plan and strategies needed to carry out intervention for the family.

CROSS-CULTURAL ASPECTS OF MEASUREMENT OF FAMILY FUNCTIONING

General Consideration of Transcultural Measurement

In order to conduct relevant assessments of cross-cultural psychopathology by utilizing standardized instruments, several issues first need to be considered from a methodological point of view (Good and Kleinman, 1985).

First of all, it is important to be aware that the range of the variable to be measured — expression of symptoms, personality, behavioral pattern, or stress — may vary among different cultural groups so that the instruments used need to encompass adequately this range of expression. Secondly, the transcultural applicability and validity of the items, content, and questions of the instrument need careful evaluation during the process of translation. Thirdly, culturally-sensitive and relevant interpretation of the data obtained by both insiders (emic perspective) and outsiders (etic perspective) of the cultural groups being assessed is desirable.

Regarding the translation of an instrument for transcultural application, Brislin, Lonner, and Thorndike (1973), as cross-cultural re-searchers, have made suggestions for several approaches. These include translation by expert-bilinguistics, followed by back-trans-lation; trial on bilingual subjects to cross-examine the equivalence of the translation; and pretesting of the instrument on a sample of target subjects to check its practical application.

Concerning the conceptualization of problems encountered in cross-cultural comparative study, Straus (1969) elaborated the is-sues in the matters of "phenomenal identity" and "conceptual equivalence." Straus has pointed out that use of identical proce-dures in different cultural societies for eliciting and quantifying data (phenomenal identity) does not necessarily result in measurement of the same variable (conceptual equivalence), since the stimuli (ques-tions, tasks, or items) used to elicit responses may have different meanings in different cultural societies. Similarly, the same mani-fest response may have different meanings in different cultures.

Based on the stimuli presented for measurement and the re-sponses manifested, Straus listed four possible types of taxonomy of measurement equivalence. The first type, "culturally universal measurement," refers to measurements which use identical stimu-lus materials in each society and obtain responses in identical ways. The second type, "culturally ipsatized measurement," refers to in-stances in which the identical instrument is used in several societies under study, but the results are judged relative to others in that society, rather than relative to some universal standard of interpre-tation or scoring. The third type, "culturally modified measure-ment," refers to measurements in which the indicators are altered to make them culturally appropriate but the original scoring is re-tained. The last type, "culturally specific measurement," repre-sents maximum phenomenal variability in order to achieve maximal conceptual uniformity. In order to attain better conceptual equiva-lence, it has been suggested that several techniques can be applied. For examples, use of expert judges to evaluate the appropriateness of the indicators, revalidation and restandardization of the test for the culture in which it will be employed, semantic differential of the proposed interview questions or test items, and construct valida-tion.

Cross-Cultural Application
of Family Measurement

All the measurements for marriage and family frequently used by contemporary (Western) investigators and clinicians have been reviewed by Grotevant and Carlson (1989) and Fredman and Sherman (1987). The reviews are sufficiently comprehensive and inclusive for the readers to understand most of the family measurements frequently used. Grotevant and Carlson subdivided the family measurements into the categories of (1) observational measures—by (a) family interaction coding schemes, and (b) rating scales of family functioning; and (2) self-report measures—which includes (a) whole-family functioning, (b) family stress and coping, and (c) parent-child relationships. In Fredman and Sherman's review, there are measurements for (a) marital satisfaction and adjustment scales, and (b) marital communication and intimacy scales.

In the above reviews, the nature of the instruments, including the purpose, indication, reliability, and validity of the measurements has been extensively elaborated. Unfortunately, the aspect of cross-ethnic/cultural application is barely discussed at all. This reflects the level of art in the field of family measurement and assessment.

Examination of manuals or books concerning individual measurements for family assessment produced several findings in regards to the cross-ethnic/culture application.

For instance, the FACES III (Family Adaptability & Cohesion Evaluation Scales) designed by Olson, Portner, and Lavee (1985) for self-report of whole family functioning has taken into consideration cross-ethnic and culture applications for the instrument. As stated by Olson et al., in order to make the Circumplex Model culturally relevant to a variety of families with different ethnic and cultural backgrounds, a hypothesis was developed to reflect this diversity. The hypothesis states that "if normative expectations of families support behavior extremes on one or both of the dimensions, families will function well as long as all family members are satisfied with these expectations." In this way, the family serves as its own norm base. The only criticism of FACES is that, as pointed out by Grotevant and Carlson (1989), the instrument attempts to measure complex family-level variables with 20 simple items within two dimensions of family functioning — cohesion and adaptability. Thus, the instrument may not adequately capture the richness or complexity of family life for clinical or research assessment, particularly from the viewpoint of cross-cultural application.

Concerning the observational measurement, Lewis' group has used rating scales of family functioning (the Beavers-Timberlawn Family Evaluation Scales) for the assessment of normal Caucasian families (Lewis et al., 1976) and black families in Texas (Lewis and Looney, 1983). They claim that, in spite of the fact that

> the socioeconomic circumstances of these two groups of families are very different, the families look much alike when their relationship processes are studied in family interactional testing . . . Although there are some modest differences between the scores for the two samples, there are no differences in the scores for the families seen as most competent. The working-class black families demonstrate interactional processes that are similar to those of the earlier studied, more affluent (Caucasian) families. (p. 87)

These findings deserve careful interpretation from the point of cross-ethnic family assessment. The definition of a "competent" family given by the instrument designer and then used by raters to assess the competency of families may involve methodological error; this is one of the errors which commonly occurs in cross-ethnic or cross-cultural assessment.

Furthermore, the effect of the rater's cultural background has not been carefully considered and assessed. Clinical and research experience has shown that the ethnic-cultural background of the evaluator can significantly affect the process of transcultural assessment — namely the assessment of subjects whose ethnic/cultural backgrounds are remarkably different from that of the evaluator. The effects are derived from several sources; the *definition* and *criteria* of desirable behavior expected as well as the *sensitivity* and *perception* of observations carried out by the raters will definitely be influenced by the cultural background of the rater and the subject assessed (Tseng et al., 1982; Hsu, Tseng, Ashton, McDermott, and Char, 1985).

Finally, the degree of diversity of cultural backgrounds needs to be taken into consideration in any process of assessment. For example, the cultural differences between Caucasian families and black families from the southern United States may not be so great when compared to differences between Caucasian families and black families from the African continent. Similarly, the difference between the Caucasian-American and the Japanese-American is less obvious culturally when it is compared with the differences between the Caucasian-American and the Japanese national. It is not the different ethnic backgrounds that are of concern, but rather the degree of diversity of cultural backgrounds that affects the behavior of the family.

In summary, the focus on the cultural aspects of family assessment among clinicians and investigators has just begun. Clinical experience has indicated that cultural factors do obviously influence the process and result of family assessment. They affect the measurement design itself, the method of application, the process of assessment made by the family or the evaluator, and the interpretation of the results obtained.

Chapter 10

Culture and Family Therapy

CULTURAL CONSIDERATIONS OF FAMILY THERAPY

It is now becoming commonly accepted that cultural considerations are necessary in carrying out any form of psychological treatment, with family therapy being no exception. Such considerations
are actually even more essential in family therapy, since the family
life and behavior of family members are heavily subject to cultural
impact (DiNicola, 1985). From both a theoretical and practical
point of view, it is useful and necessary to examine how the therapy
of families should be modified and conducted in a culturally-relevant way that is more meaningful and effective in terms of the cultural background of the family and the social setting within which
the family is going to live and function (Falicov, 1983; McGoldrick, Pearce, and Giordano, 1982).

Applicability of Family Therapy

Family therapy should be considered and applied whenever it is
indicated and necessary, as long as the problems are dynamic or
closely related to family relations, or there is a need to mobilize
family resources and make good use of the input of family members
to cope and adjust to the problems.

It has been suggested that family therapy is particularly appropriate and indicated for ethnic-cultural groups that emphasize family
structure in their life pattern, such as the Italians, Portuguese, or
Chinese. Clinical experience, however, has shown that an emphasis
on family and close family interrelations does not directly favor the
family therapy approach. As pointed out by Moitoza (1982), Portu-

guese families' closed family system prevents them from actively seeking family therapy; instead, they attempt to solve their problems via their own family resources and support system. This is true for many other ethnic groups characterized by close family relations. When a close family seeks therapy, the family's values and tight intermember relations can be utilized; it will usually take considerable effort, however, for a therapist to work on the intense and complicated family dynamics. Such families usually stress compliance and have learned to avoid dealing with negative feelings openly so that harmony can be maintained. Thus, it will take much work for this family type to unlearn its way of dealing with psychological issues. It is a surmountable challenge, as long as the therapist does not assume that families from cultural groups that emphasize and value family functions and systems will automatically be simple targets for family-oriented therapy.

Alternatively, it cannot be assumed that family-oriented therapy is unsuitable for families of cultural groups that de-emphasize the family system and place more relative value on an individual system. Family therapy may actually prove to be particularly useful to such unlikely candidates by providing an opportunity for self-examination of the relatively neglected aspects of their life (i.e., the family system) as well as by encouraging them to place more value on the function of the family.

When we consider the global community, it is quite apparent that different portions of the globe present a wide range in levels of stress and problems with which families must cope. For some families, the primary problem is daily survival—how to cope with the material and physical environment; other families direct the majority of their energy towards improving their emotional life. Families in the first situation need assistance in practical issues such as finding employment, obtaining rice or bread for daily sustenance, or getting decent housing. Helping them deal with their emotions, affection, communication, and role performance is relegated to a secondary position. The goal of therapy therefore needs to be focused on immediately helping the families adapt to the mundane and adjunctive improvement of their psychological life.

Families in the second situation, meanwhile, do not regularly face the practical problems of daily life, but instead are concerned with the psychological and behavioral aspects of their family life. Family therapy can therefore be focused from the outset on matters such as affection, communication, boundaries, and role division. This is the basic orientation needed in approaching families in different socio-cultural settings.

Therapist-Family Relationship

When the family to be treated is of a different cultural background from that of the therapist, cultural effects on the therapist-family relationship need to be closely examined from the very beginning of contact.

1. *Cultural transference of therapist-client relationship on family therapy.*

Interpersonal relationships are always subconsciously influenced and shaped by cultural factors, and the relationship between therapist and family is no exception. Our views, attitude, and expectations toward another group are usually influenced by any preexisting cultural views, attitudes, or expectations, whether right or wrong, towards that particular group. This phenomenon, called cultural transference (Tseng and Hsu, 1972), needs to be specifically evaluated and addressed when we are involved with a family who has a different ethnic-cultural background from our own.

An illustration is given by McGoldrick and Pearce (1981). They point out that the Irish cultural attitude towards authority figures will often lead members of an Irish family to show extreme loyalty and willingness to follow through on therapeutic suggestions. This type of cultural transference can be utilized in the therapeutic situation to direct the family to move towards desirable change and improvement, but carries with it the risk of producing compliance without real motivation for change. Under these circumstances, the therapist must help the family members develop a genuine investment in the process of change and not rely on their culture-molded politeness, sense of responsibility, and obligation to duty.

With the Asian family, Hsu (1983) has indicated that the therapist should be flexible, establishing a professional relationship with the family that fits their cultural expectations instead of maintaining a rigid and pure professional role and relationship as emphasized by analytic therapists. For example, based on the concept of family-extended social relationships, the members of a Chinese family may often feel more comfortable if allowed to familiarize their relationship with the therapist by addressing the therapist as an Uncle X or Auntie Y rather than Doctor X or Y. In this case, the therapist needs to feel comfortable accepting a pseudo-kin relationship rather than the strictly professional one. This flexibility will certainly enhance culturally sanctioned ways to establish and maintain rapport with clients. Meanwhile, the therapist should manage not to lose the expected position as a knowledgeable expert who can actively make wise suggestions for solving problems.

The age and gender of the therapist is of considerable concern in situations dealing with families of certain ethnic-cultural backgrounds. As pointed out by Moitoza (1982), strong sexual stereotyping in Portuguese culture makes it extremely difficult for a woman therapist, especially a young one, to do family therapy with a Portuguese-American family. Although a solo female therapist may initially be accorded a certain measure of politeness, she will eventually meet tremendous resistance from both the husband and wife for different reasons. The husband, based on his cultural expectation that only a man can take a superior role, will show great resistance to being "treated" by a female. Meanwhile, the wife may feel threatened by the woman therapist and regard her as a potential rival for her husband. This phenomenon can be observed in many other ethnic-cultural groups which have strong sexual stereotypes. There is almost no need to point out that for an Islamic family, a male therapist will be the only acceptable possibility and it would be nearly impossible for a woman to function as a therapist with any family which has a dominant male figure.

In contrast, the grandmother is regarded as the head of the household and the final decision-maker in Hawaiian families, and female therapists (particularly those with seniority) are thus considered preferable.

2. *Respect and utilize the culturally-defined and sanctioned family hierarchy and relations already existing within the family.*

For a cultural group which emphasizes a certain respected role for the family leader, it is essential to recognize and respect this role of the family head in therapy sessions. For instance, the father is regarded as the head of the household in Japanese families. During the initial stages of therapy it is very important to acknowledge and reinforce the status of the family head. This can be accomplished by simply addressing any initial inquiries, explanations, or requests to the father. This is particularly needed because the father already feels ashamed and defeated in turning to outsiders for help with a family problem. The therapist's failure to pay respect to the unspoken lead figure may lead to frustration and resentment of the father and result in the family's premature termination of therapy under the father's influence. This view is supported by Welts (1982) concerning the Greek family in which there is a rigid family role definition of the father as the leader of the household. The therapist should show deference to the respect for the father who will need to feel in control of the therapy.

In families of different cultural systems, the defined and recognized family leader is sometimes someone other than the father. For instance, the Hawaiian family is rooted in a traditional matrilineal system in which the grandmother is the person who has the final say. No matter how she might behave, often quietly and unnoticeably in a situation such as family sessions, she is the person who needs to be recognized and dealt with as the key person in family matters, particularly involving major decisions for the family. If this person is not addressed by the therapist, the therapist will certainly miss a lot of the show.

3. *The effect of the therapist's cultural background and value system.*

The therapist's cultural value system, as well as his/her individual and gender background (Hare-Mustin, 1978) and personal beliefs must also be considered. The therapist will consciously or subconsciously hold certain values and opinions towards various life issues, directly or indirectly influencing the course of therapy. Basic orientation towards marriage, divorce, and abortion are examples of value- and belief-laden attitudes which relate closely to family life and which will inevitably mold the direction of marital or family therapy. A therapist who is culturally oriented towards separation or divorce as reasonable ways to solve marital problems will certainly encourage these possibilities among other alternatives. However, a therapist who believes that a marriage is sacred and needs to be maintained for a lifetime will tend to counsel against breaking up a marriage and will rarely suggest that a couple discuss termination of the marriage as a means of solving the marital problem. A family therapist needs constantly to examine and evaluate how his/her own cultural and personal belief system may affect his/her treatment of the family. Therapists need to consider whether they are biased, restricted, or liberal in helping the family in selecting the direction for solving the problem. As a rule of thumb, it is best to explore the value system held by the family and the cultural background within which the family is going to live and function. Based on these considerations, transactions between the values of the therapist and of the family will occur in the course of the family therapy, and an appropriate therapeutic direction will emerge (Falicov, 1982).

Selection of Treatment Models

Many different schools or modalities of therapy have been described and emphasized by various groups of therapists (Kaslow, 1982; Crespi, 1988). There has been a recent tendency to integrate these diverse modalities into a set of unified and comprehensive systematic models. Sluzki (1983) has tried to view various modes of family therapy centered in interpersonal process, in structural phenomena, and in reality construction. This definition does not attempt to blur the distinctions among various models but seeks instead to show their common denominator and thus expand the conceptual and clinical repertoire of the system-oriented family therapist. In the area of culture-oriented family therapy, the therapist should not be preoccupied on any particular modes of family therapy, but rather should learn how to select a culturally-relevant approach in treating certain types of family-cultural groups.

1. *Matching of Treatment Models.*

Is there any particular fitness between the family types and the choice of treatment? This is a theoretically as well as practically interesting question for us to ask and try to answer. Unfortunately, this issue has not yet been thoroughly examined, particularly from cross-cultural perspectives. However, there are some suggestions derived from clinical experience. For example, Falicov (1982), investigating Mexican families, or Minuchin, Montalvo, Guerney, Rosman, and Schumer (1967), working with Chicano families, have proposed that the cultural emphasis on hierarchies within these families lends itself to a structural family therapy approach. In contrast to this, Herz and Rosen (1982) mention that the Jewish family closely relates to a cultural tendency of treasuring suffering as a shared value. By emphasizing the verbal expression of feelings in family therapy, the focus of therapy on this process and interaction can motivate Jewish families to see talking and insight as a relevant solution. Zuk (1978) has pointed out that Jews generally do well in family therapy. The favorable response of Jewish families stems from the cultural emphasis placed on high familism, high egalitarianism, high secularism, maternal intrusiveness, verbal rather than physical aggressiveness, an assertive stance toward problem-solving, and the maintenance of a scapegoat theme. It has been suggested by Zuk that in treating Jewish families, it is important to keep this entire set of values in mind rather than any one particular value.

McGoldrick and Pearce (1981) have suggested that the Irish family will probably respond more readily to a fairly structured, problem-focused (especially child-focused) family therapy approach. The Irish are apt to be threatened by therapy directed at uncovering hostile or erotic feelings and may respond better to a positive reframing of the strategic brief therapy model. Similarly, Hsu (1985) emphasizes that with traditional Chinese families it is desirable for the therapy to be problem-oriented and focus on external factors in the initial stages of treatment. This mode of treatment is more easily understood and accepted by the family because it accords with their cultural expectations for therapy, and is also considered a relevant way to deal with many other ethnic-cultural groups, including Mexican-American families.

2. Priority Focus of the Treatment.

For the Japanese family, which emphasizes parent-child relations as the primary axis and the spouse subsystem as the secondary one, it is more desirable, as suggested by Suzuki (1987), to deal with family matters according to cultural priorities, i.e., to work on parent-child relations before beginning work on husband-wife issues. For example, within a Japanese family in which the mother is excessively attached to her child and less involved with her husband, it is more natural to help first the mother and the child to let go of each other. Once the mother can allow her child to be independent, she will be able to attend to the needs of her husband more effectively. In other words, the importance of the husband-wife axis should not be emphasized too soon. It needs to be worked out towards the end, not the beginning, of the therapeutic process. Otherwise, it will frighten both the husband and wife into thinking that they have a problem as a couple. This point of view has been echoed by an American family therapist (Colman, 1987) who has experienced therapy with Japanese families in Tokyo. She comments that taking consideration of the vertical ties of parent to child is of foremost importance in Japan; it is culturally proper for the marital subsystem to be addressed only after there has been a positive resolution of the parent-child relationships. This runs contrary to the approach of most American family therapists, who usually see the marital subsystem as the fundamental target for therapy since American families emphasize the husband-wife axis as the primary one.

Similarly, when dealing with families from cultural groups in which the parents are very much respected and not supposed to be challenged (exemplified by Mexican or Latin families), it is very important that family therapy primarily focus on treating one targeted *child* rather than treating the *whole family* and refrain from mentioning treating the *parents*. It is easier for the parents to think that a therapist is meeting with them to work on the problems of the identified child and that they are involved merely to learn how to help and guide the disturbed child. In the course of learning how to help their child, the parents will naturally discover how to change themselves. It is wise not to mention that parents and children need to be treated as a whole family in order to solve family problems including the problems of the parents.

Choice of Intervention Techniques

1. *Basic Family Therapy Strategies Utilized by Family Therapists*.

There are numerous therapeutic techniques described by contemporary family therapists in treating the family (Barker, 1986). Such therapeutic techniques are geared toward the underlying family pathology and the manifested family problems (Gurman and Kniskern, 1981). Before discussing how cultural considerations are necessary in choosing appropriate therapeutic techniques, some therapeutic foci and techniques utilized clinically for certain family pathology are listed in Table 1 for review.

2. *Cultural Considerations in Applying Certain Therapeutic Methods.*

In addition to basic clinical considerations of underlying family pathology and manifested family problems, further discussion is necessary from the cultural point of view as a basis for selecting and applying the strategies listed above.

Special caution must be exercised with families of cultural groups that are not accustomed to direct confrontation. As elabo-

TABLE 1

FAMILY PATHOLOGY AND THERAPY STRATEGIES

MANIFESTED PROBLEMS	UNDERLYING PATHOLOGY	THERAPEUTIC FOCUS	THERAPEUTIC TECHNIQUE
FAILURE TO PERFORM BASIC LIVING TASKS	Inadequate family fuction for performance	Work with supra-system	Utilize external supporting system
STRUCTURAL PROBLEMS, such as: Enmeshment	Ambiguous subsystm boundaries	Helping erect subsystem barriers	Family sculpturing
Disengagement	Distant relationship	Promoting commumication Promoting emotional involvement	Role playing
IDIOSYNCRATIC ROLE, such as: Scapegoating Family angel	Role allocation	Reallocation of role	Role programming
STABLE COALITION, such as: Detouring coalition Triangulation	Alignment problems	Reallocate parent-child role	Assign tasks Boundary making

rated by Costello (1977), young children in an Anglo setting might actively voice their opinions to contribute to therapeutic intervention. Children in Chicano families, however, are unlikely to be allowed to participate in the parents' business. If a child were to disagree openly with his/her father (particularly in front of others — including the therapist), the father's shame would be translated into physical discipline of the child as soon as they got home. Thus, the therapist should take pains *not* to shame the father in the presence of the children in order to avoid endangering the therapeutic alliance.

Role playing is one therapeutic technique which can be utilized to induce practical and concrete changes in behavior among family members. It is thus one of many powerful therapeutic maneuvers available to the family therapist. However, when such a maneuver is intended for application, it is necessary to consider how family members will interpret and react to this therapeutic procedure. With a family from a culture which emphasizes hierarchy and formality, it is rather difficult for the parents and children to act out "informal" and "strange" behavior roles which do not respect hierarchy. This is true for both parents and children who are not used to such things. Furthermore, family members may not understand the meaning and intentions behind doing such silly things in front of a therapist. Therefore, when applying any therapeutic exercise which may produce strong "cultural resistance," careful thought must be given beforehand to issues such as whether or not such a therapeutic maneuver is suitable for application, whether the maneuver's meaning has been carefully explained to the family members, and whether they understand its significance.

3. *Making Use of Existing Family System.*

Within families of different cultural systems, there are always unique aspects that can be used to advantage in therapy. For instance, as Suzuki (1987) illustrated, different sets of kin terms may be used in daily life within a Japanese family. The parents, for example, may be addressed as *oto-san* (father) and *oka-san* (mother) by their children, as "your husband" or "your wife" by a third party, or as *dan-na-san* (literally meaning "house-head" and used by the wife to refer to her husband) and *oku-san* (literally meaning "inner-person" and used by an outsider to refer to the housewife), as well as simply *anohito* (literally meaning "that person''). Every change in naming implies a corresponding change in relationship and circumstances. The family therapist can selectively utilize specific kin terms in family sessions to signify the different roles and relationships which exist or ought to be changed within a family.

4. *Utilization of Culturally Sanctioned Family Coping Pattern.*
The family strengths and coping mechanisms which already exist in the function of a family can often be successfully utilized in family therapy. Within a Chinese family for example, family life is geared towards the children, and it is considered virtuous for the parents to act benevolently to give their children a better life. Due to this cultural orientation, if there is a need to mobilize the parents in the course of treatment, to change their behavior or improve their interaction with their children, the therapist can appeal to parental benevolence, reinforcing the parents' intentions ''to do the best for the sake of (their) children'' in contrast to the couple's sake or parents' sake, as pointed out by Hsu (1983).

After working with American Indian families, Attneave (1982) suggested that the therapist should not hesitate to share the interest that families usually have in keeping alive their own native language, folkways, crafts, and values associated with their tribal identities. Restoration of a sense of innate worth and goodness, of feelings of adequacy and of the integration of person, place, and family is essential to American Indian families who must constantly work to rebuild their cultural identity.

Utilization of the power of myth, magic, and family ritual for families who are accustomed to this orientation has been proposed by Seltzer and Seltzer (1983). This view has been supported by the experience of working with families of certain cultural groups. For the Hawaiian family, which is oriented to the existence of supernatural beings and which highly values the influence of gods, praying by the participating family members as a part of the therapy session has been adopted in the traditional family group healing practice called *Ho'oponopono*. In such folk family therapy, certain essential rules and rituals are observed in contrast to contemporary family therapy. Folk family therapy does not hesitate to make use of the family member's orientation to supernatural powers. As a part of this therapeutic process, at the beginning and end of each session all the participating members are asked to pray together to god for enhancing their family strength to face and deal with the problems.

TREATING CULTURE-RELATED FAMILY PROBLEMS

Some family issues are particularly affected by charged cultural factors and deserve special attention in order to achieve their resolution.

Cultural Differences Between Spouses (Intercultural Marriage)

When a man and a woman from very divergent cultural backgrounds get married, they have to deal with their widely different value systems, life patterns, and ways of dealing with marital and family matters. This is particularly true during the initial stages of their marital development, when the two partners need to learn to adjust to each other and live as a unit — as a married couple. After this initial adaptation, intercultural adjustments need to be made at each stage of family development. During the stage of child-rearing for instance, the parents must learn to work out different ways of disciplining their children as well as how to perform their expected parental roles. At the stage of family contracting, they must decide how soon and in which ways they will let their children go and let them lead their own lives. Towards the latter part of their marital life, the aged parents must again decide how they will live. Although the cultural differences between spouses can be a positive challenge and stimulate adjustments (Tseng, 1977), it can also be a source of stress and problems.

When a couple has problems which primarily relate to differences in their cultural backgrounds, the therapy needs to focus on several perspectives. First of all, the couple needs help to acknowledge the existence of their different cultural backgrounds. They have to learn that their behavior towards each other and the source of their dissatisfaction or unhappiness is not so much related to the affection and feelings they have towards each other, but rather is associated with their upbringing. Consequently, they will not feel frustrated or angered by the behavior demonstrated by each other.

For instance, Soon-Hyong (Korean husband) not wanting to step into the kitchen to help Nancy (Caucasian wife) with cooking is not because Soon-Hyong does not like being alongside Nancy or does not enjoy doing tasks together as husband and wife, but rather it is because his behavior is greatly influenced by his Korean culture which holds that a man should not step into the kitchen. This represents an intrusion into female territory, and also means that he will be ridiculed by his male friends. On the other hand, Nancy desiring a car of her own and wishing to work outside as a career woman does not mean she does not want to respect her husband by staying at home as a housewife — as a married Korean housewife is expected to do — but rather simply means that according to her contemporary American values, a woman should aim for self-development. In other words, it will be therapeutic to assist the couple by explaining and elaborating on the nature of their behavior which is rooted in their cultural heritage, so that their behavior will not be regarded simply as a reflection of their feelings or attitudes towards each other.

After an understanding of the nature of their cultural behavior is achieved, the second step is to help them discover ways to resolve the situation and bridge the gap between what they believe or value in life and unwanted effects in their marital life. There are certain basic rules to apply to the cultural differences which may exist between spouses; these include negotiation and compromise between opposing beliefs, taking turns between alternate ways, or finding and working on a third option (Tseng, 1977). An example is Kamehame (a Hawaiian husband) who became quite upset when his children talked at the dinner time, since according to Hawaiian custom children should "be seen but not heard" at meal time. Meanwhile, his Caucasian wife, Mary, felt strongly that it would be desirable for their children to join the conversation during meals. This couple could be helped by trying different approaches, such as trying Kamehame's Hawaiian way and Mary's American way on alternate weeks, or if this does not suit the children's development then perhaps trying to observe the Hawaiian way during the main dish and the American way while having dessert. The specific method to be tried and adopted is not as important as encouraging the couple to value each other's respective cultures, to respect each other's needs, and to learn to negotiate and compromise between themselves in such a way that both will feel comfortable in functioning as husband and wife — simply stated, these are basic rules for a viable couple to observe and follow.

It will sometimes become extremely uncomfortable for a person to change his/her accustomed way of life and to adjust to an "alien" way of behaving, even if it is potentially helpful to the marriage. In such cases, it can be helpful for the husband and wife to have the opportunity to return temporarily to their own, original and traditional way of behaving, often referred to as a "cultural time-out" or "cultural holiday." For example, an Italian wife can join her Italian relatives and eat Italian foods such as spaghetti or ravioli, while a Japanese husband can eat *sashimi* (raw fish) and sing Japanese songs. This will provide either spouse an opportunity to regress (culturally) and reexperience and enjoy their old ways of life physically, physiologically, and psychologically. This type of "time-out" will continue to benefit them even after they return to their normal routine after the "cultural vacation."

Cultural Differences Between Generations (Generation Gaps)

It is common for certain differences in viewpoint and opinion between parents and children to be brought about by age, developmental factors, and the different environments in which each generation has grown up. However, when a family faces a rapidly changing cultural environment in their own society or encounters a different sociocultural environment after migrating to an alien culture, the differences between parents and children can create a large schism between generations resulting in serious family problems.

For this problematic generation gap, the strategy in family therapy is similar to what has been described for conflicts in the intercultural marriage. Namely, the goals are to promote communication between generations so they can understand the nature and source of their cultural differences; to encourage the family to seek a compromise and solution for both generations and to recognize the principle of it being acceptable to all; and to place the ultimate emphasis on *mutual* understanding, empathy, and willingness throughout the dialectic.

Culturally Up-rooted Family

When the socio-cultural system of a group of people has been rapidly destroyed, families within that system will suffer from loss of their cultural roots, resulting in deterioration of the family as a whole. This is usually manifested by parents losing their cultural methods for organizing the family and subsequently experiencing confusion over how to perform properly their parental function. The children, meanwhile, often dissociate themselves from their parents both cognitively and emotionally and are unsure of their identity and direction in life. Such families have not only lost their own identity, but have also lost their cultural goals for functioning. This cultural up-rooted phenomenon is frequently observed among families of many ethnic groups, including Native Americans, Afro-Americans, Micronesians, and South-Asian refugees.

For families who have suffered the loss of their traditional cultural system, treatment needs to focus on the restoration of their culture system by recognizing the importance of their original cultural roots. Therapy also should emphasize restoration of the parents' basic confidence and ability to organize and lead the family, as well as enhance the establishment of a restored family identity secured within the ethnic/cultural identity of their own group.

GOALS OF FAMILY THERAPY

The goals of family therapy and the strategies for reaching these goals have been viewed in various ways by family therapists; these views have been reviewed by Glick, Clarkin, and Kessler (1987). Based on their summary, the goals of family therapy have been modified and expanded to meet cultural applications. (See Table 2.)

TABLE 2

GOALS OF THERAPY AND THERAPEUTIC STRATEGIES

Goals of Therapy	*Therapeutic Strategies*
1. Supporting adaptive mechanisms	Increased use of existing adaptive coping patterns
2. Expanding emotional experience	Promote communication Reinforce appropriate emotional expression
3. Development of interpersonal skill	Improve communication
4. Reorganizing the family structure	Clarification of boundaries
5. Increase insight	Increase awareness of behavior patterns and the nature of problems
6. Appropriate mastery of development tasks	Stimulate development progress
7. Cultivate "family culture"	Reestablish set of beliefs and rules to be observed in the family
8. Enhance sociocultural function of family	Build adequate social extra-family network
9. Reestablish cultural identity for family	Search for and establish sense of belonging to and identification with a particular group

CULTURAL IMPLICATIONS OF FAMILY THERAPY

Although there are numerous ways to conceptualize the nature of therapy, such as (from the point-of-view of nonspecific healing) cultivation of hope for the client, or (from the analytic point-of-view) as working on the resistance or (from existential perspectives) as working on the change of life attitude, the nature of therapy can also be examined from a cultural orientation. This is the point-of-view applied to family therapy below.

1. *To Restore the Cultural Norm of Family Function.*

In each society, there is a setting-dependent culturally-sanctioned way for a family to function, interact, and adapt. If for some reason a family is unable to perform in this way, the purpose of therapy is to help the family restore these culturally appropriate functions. For instance, within polygamous societies, harmony among the wives of the same husband needs to be kept if the function of the household is to be maintained. The primary goal of family therapy under these circumstances is to help the wives avoid open conflict and rivalry among themselves. On the other hand, in a primarily monogamous society, the emphasis of marital therapy is on helping the couple involve themselves in a one-to-one relationship without seeking involvement with others beyond the monogamous system.

Some families (such as contemporary American ones) are culturally expected to allow their offspring significant autonomy and independence after they reach puberty. If for some reason the parents have not helped their children master this developmental task according to a culturally expected pace, then the focus of family therapy should be on assisting the children to become more independent after puberty. This fulfills the therapy's goal of assisting the family to perform culturally expected functions. However, in societies in which it is important for the offspring to stay with their parents as long as possible — even after marriage — so that long-term continuity between generations is protected, family therapy should be directed towards the adult offspring learning how to stay in the family of origin and how to adjust to parental generations besides their own generations which include married siblings and their children. Autonomy and independence of the children will necessarily be underplayed.

2. *To Establish a Cultural System in a Family.*

It is necessary to have certain common rules and principles observed within a family; these are essential to the value system and in some ways can be referred to as the culture of the family. If for any reason this family culture is lacking or only vaguely present, family members may not be sure how to behave. The object of the therapy should be to help the family establish commonly shared values (Trotzer, 1981), ideology, beliefs, customs and rituals (Palazzoli, Boscolo, Cecchin, and Prata, 1977) so that each family member may know and observe them. The disorganized family and culturally up-rooted family are examples of families which need this type of focus in therapy.

3. To Promote Cultural Exchange Within a Family.

When there is a great gap between opinions, beliefs, and attitudes of family members (either between parents and children or between spouses), the goal of family therapy is to promote the exchange of different points of view and to enhance cultural empathy and cultural translation (DiNicola, 1986). This point has been elaborated specifically for the unique situations in which there are wide cultural gaps between spouses (intercultural marriage) and between parents and children (generational gap). In addition to these specific examples, it should be stated that the overall goal of therapy for most family circumstances is to promote communication and enhance mutual understanding.

4. To Permit a Cultural Time-Out for a Family (Or Some Members of a Family).

For some families, the nature of stress and subsequent problems is directly related to family members (at least some members) experiencing exhaustion from constant and long-term compliance to a particular set of rules and ways of life which are too restrictive or alien. In such cases, the goal of therapy will be to provide periodic cultural time-outs or to reserve a place for cultural islands so they can take a retreat or vacation.

5. To Supply a Counter-Culture System to a Family.

Family life is sometimes greatly restricted by rules, concepts, and patterns of life which leave only limited ways to cope with situations. Under these circumstances, it is therapeutic to help family members recognize the existence of alternatives and widen their access to other resources. Occasionally, we can be so trapped in our own tunnel vision of life and value system that we are unable to receive different attitudes or views. In this situation, bringing in opposite but functional ways for consideration will not only neutralize the family's extreme position and attitudes, but will provide an opportunity for them to reexamine their orientation and belief system (Hare-Mustin, 1978).

Thus, the purpose of family therapy can be described from a cultural perspective as working on the cultural system of the family in various ways with the aim of promoting the function of the family.

CULTURE-DEFINED FUNCTIONING FAMILY

In the treatment of an individual, it is necessary to define what is considered a healthy functional person as a standard to guide the course of therapy. Analogously, in family therapy it is necessary to visualize a well functioning normal family as the final goal towards which treatment is directed. The concept of a functional or healthy family needs to be defined carefully and elaborated further in therapy for families of different cultural groups so that the idea of a functional family is consistent with the relevant cultural background.

The universal concept of family has been defined anthropologically (Hoebel, 1972) as the institutionalization of mating and the channeling of sexual outlets; the nurture and enculturation of the young; the organization of a complementary division of labor between spouses; and the establishment of relations of descent and affinity within the network of kinship. Thus, these are the basic functions a family needs to fulfill.

From a psychological point of view, there are several tasks that the family needs to master. It must maintain stable cohesion among members for family identity and emotional support while keeping certain boundaries between members for individual autonomy (Olson, McCubbin, and Associates, 1983; Lewis, Beavers, Gossett, and Phillips, 1976); move and go through progressively different stages of family development and meet and perform various tasks required for each stage of development (Duvall, 1971); and adjust and cope with various stressors or problems encountered in family life with a certain degree of flexibility and with appropriate coping mechanisms (Olson et al., 1983).

When this view is applied to families of various cultural backgrounds with different family systems and social settings, it becomes a matter of which components of family function ought to be emphasized to a greater or lesser extent on the basis of being "relevant," "appropriate," or "desirable." This is essential so that a set of desirable functional family goals can be visualized.

As summarized by Barnhill (1979), many contemporary American family researchers and therapists have described and emphasized various aspects of important functions that a family needs to perform (mainly regarding the American family): clear communication (Bateson, Jackson, Haley, and Weakland, 1956; Satir, 1967), clear role reciprocity (Lidz, Fleck and Cornelison, 1965; Spiegel, 1957), mutuality (Wynne, Ryckoll, Day and Hirsch, 1958), clear generational boundaries (Haley, 1967; Minuchin, 1974), clear perception (Bowen, 1960; Boszormenyi-Nagy, 1965), individualization (Bowen, 1960; Whitaker, Felder and Warkentin, 1965), flexibility (Ackerman, 1966) and stability (Jackson, 1968). These important aspects of family function bring to mind the proverb in which many blind persons describe various parts of an elephant — depending upon the part they touched. All of these aspects are perhaps correct in their own way and all are very important for the (American) family. At another level, however, if viewed by outsiders from a different cultural background or who work with families of diverse origins, the elephant described by these family clinicians and researchers is *merely* one kind of elephant. It is an American elephant — the psychologically healthy family desired in contemporary American society! It does not sufficiently and relevantly describe another kind of elephant, specifically, the functioning family of different cultures (Vogel and Vogel, 1961). There are many varieties of elephants that exist in this world which can be described (by other groups of "blind" persons) in different ways.

For instance, additional important factors are: maintaining the sense of family and emphasizing family loyalty (rather than individualization or self-autonomy); keeping and fulfilling the obligation between husband and wife (rather than affection); providing for the continuation of multiple generations of family (rather than the family of your own generation); and stressing hierarchical structure of family and valuing harmony among family members (rather than the psychological needs of the individual). These aspects can be described and emphasized by different groups of family therapists and researchers (another group of "blind" persons) for another kind of elephant which may be the components of the desirable healthy family for another culture.

In summary, the profile of the normal and healthy family for each sociocultural setting needs to be defined not only to meet the universal ideals for the psychological life of the family but also conceptualized and modified in culturally-relevant ways. Based on these culturally-adjusted profiles of the functioning family, therapy can be directed and developed toward culturally-appropriate ultimate conditions for the family.

CLOSING

We are living in a society where the family pattern is constantly undergoing rapid change. Within this evolution is an associated improvement of transportation providing increased access to encounters with people from all parts of the globe and resulting in novel exposure to families of diverse cultural origins. From a practical point of view, we are required to treat many families from different subcultures and cultures. Theoretically, we have been given an opportunity to examine how our own concepts of family functioning and strategies for intervention can be applied transculturally, mandating that we develop a clinical knowledge base and skills for broader usage and culturally-relevant application.

It is essential for the competent family therapist to recognize the cultural dimensions of a family system and possess rudimentary cultural knowledge of the family, so that a culturally relevant family assessment can be performed based on a culturally appropriate understanding of family pathology and problems. Culturally suitable therapy can then be performed to work toward the psychologically and socio-culturally functioning family. This is a new task for family researchers and therapists around the world in the coming decade, and we hope this book will be useful for this purpose.

References

Ablon, J. (1971) Bereavement in a Samoan Community. *British Journal of Medical Psychology*, 44:329-337.

Ablon, J. (1980) The Significance of Cultural Patterning for the "Alcoholic Family". *Family Process*, 19:127-144.

Ackerman, N.W. (1966) *Treating the Troubled Family*, Basic Books, New York.

Adamek, R.J. (1982) Testing the Family Role Complementarity Model. *Journal of Comparative Family Studies*, 13:1-11.

Albrecht, S.L. (1980) Reactions and Adjustment to Divorce: Differences in the Experiences of Males and Females. *Family Relations*, 29:59-68.

Arling, G. (1976) The Elderly Widow and Her Family, Neighbors, and Friends. *Journal of Marriage and the Family*, 38:757-768.

Arnold, F., Bulatao, R.A., Buripakdi, C., et al. (1975) *The Value of Children: A Cross-National Study*. Vol. 1, Introduction and Comparative Analysis. East-West Center, Honolulu.

Attneave, C. (1982) American Indians and Alaska Native Families: Emigrants in Their Own Homeland. In: McGoldrick, M., Pearce, J.K., and Giordano, J. (Eds): *Ethnicity and Family Therapy*, The Guilford Press, New York.

Back, K.W. (1971) Transition to Aging and the Self-Image. *Aging and Human Development*, 2:296-304.

Balkwell, C. (1981) Transition to Widowhood: A Review of the Literature. *Family Relations*, 30:117-127.

Balswick, J.O., and Peek, C.W. (1971) The Inexpressive Male: A Tragedy of American Society. *The Family Coordinator*, 20:363-368.

Bank, S. and Khan, M.D. (1975) Sisterhood-Brotherhood is Powerful: Sibling Sub-systems and Family Therapy. In: Chess, S. and Thomas, A. (Eds): *Annual Progress in Child Psychiatry and Development*, Brunner/Mazel, New York.

Barnhill, L. (1979) Healthy Family System. *Family Coordinator*, 28:94-100.

Barker, P. (1986) *Basic Family Therapy*, 2nd Ed., Oxford University Press, New York.

Bateson, G., Jackson, D.D., Haley, J., and Weakland, J.H. (1956) Toward a Theory of Schizophrenia. *Behavior Science*, 1:251-264.

Bean, F.D., Curtis, R.L. Jr., and Marcum, J.P. (1977) Familism and Marital Satisfaction Among Mexican Americans: The Effects of Family Size, Wife's Labor Force Participation, and Conjugal Power. *Journal of Marriage and the Family*, 39:759-767.

Becker, J.V. and Coleman, E.M. (1988) Incest. In: Hasselt, V.B.V., Morrison, R.L., Bellack, A.S., and Hersen, M. (eds); *Handbook of Violence*. Plenum Press, New York.

Beiber, I., Dain, H.J., Dince, O.R., Drellich, M.G., Grand, H.G., Grundlack, R.H., Kremer, M.W., Rifkin, A.H., Wilbur, C.B. and Bieber, T.B. (1962) *Homosexuality: A Psychoanalytic Study*. Basic Books, New York.

Bell, N.J. and Avery, A.W. (1985) Family Structure and Parent-Adolescent Relationships: Does Family Structure Really Make a Difference? *Journal of Marriage and the Family*, 47:501-508.

Benedek, T. (1974) The Psychobiology of Parenthood. In: Arieti, S. (Ed): *American Handbook of Psychiatry*, 2nd Ed. Vol. I, The Foundations of Psychiatry. Basic Books, New York.

Berkner, L.K. (1972) The Stem Family and the Developmental Cycle of the Peasant Household: An Eighteenth-Century Austrian Example. *American History Review*, 77:398-418.

Berreman, G.D. (1980) Polyandry: Exotic Custom Vs. Analytic Concept. Special Issue: Women with Many Husbands: Polyandrous Alliance and Marital Flexibility in Africa and Asia. *Journal of Comparative Family Studies*, 11:377-383.

Berrien, F.K., Arkoff, A., and Iwahara, S. (1967) Generation Differences in Values: Americans, Japanese-Americans, and Japanese. *Journal of Social Psychology*, 71:169-175.

Bigner, J. (1970) Fathering: Research and Practice Implications. *Family Coordinator*, 19:357-362.

Bilge, B. and Kaufman, G. (1983) Children of Divorce and One-

Parent Families: Cross-cultural Perspectives. *Family Relations*, 32:59-71.

Blake, J. (1979) Is Zero Preferred?—American Attitudes Toward Childlessness in the 1970s. *Journal of Marriage and the Family*, 41:245-257.

Blanchard, W. (1958) Thailand: Its People, Its Society, Its Culture. Human Relations Area File Press, New Haven.

Block, D.A. (1974) The Family of the Psychiatric Patient. In: Arieti, S. (Ed): *American Handbook of Psychiatry*, 2nd Ed, Vol. 1, Basic Books, New York.

Blood, R.O. and Wolf, D.M. (1960) *Husbands and Wives*, The Free Press, Glencoe.

Booth, A. (1977) Wife's Employment and Husband's Stress: A Replication and Refutation. *Journal of Marriage and the Family*, 39:645-650.

Borland, D.C. (1982) A Cohort Analysis Approach to the Empty-nest Syndrome Among Three Ethnic Groups of Women: A Theoretical Position. *Journal of Marriage and the Family*, 44:117-129.

Bossard, J.H.S. and Boll, E.S. (1950) *Ritual in Family Living*. University of Pennsylvania Press, Philadelphia.

Boszormenyi-Nagy, I. (1965) A Theory of Relationships: Experience and Transaction. In: Boszormenyi-Nagy, I. and Framo, J. (Eds): *Intensive Family Therapy*. Harper, New York.

Bourguignon, E., and Greenbaum, L. (1968) *Diversity and Homogeneity: A Comparative Analysis of Societal Characteristics Based on Data from the Ethnographic Atlas*. Columbus.

Bowen, M.A. (1960) A Family Concept of Schizophrenia. In: Jackson, D. (Ed): *Etiology of Schizophrenia*. Basic Books, New York.

Brandwein, R.A., Brown, C.A., and Fox, E.M. (1974) Women and Children Lost: The Social Situation of Divorced Mothers and Their Families. *Journal of Marriage and the Family*, 36:498-514.

Brislin, R.W., Lonner, W.J., and Thorndike, R.M. (1973) *Cross-Cultural Research Methods*. John Wiley & Sons, New York.

Bronfenbrenner, U. (1958) Socialization and Social Class Through Time and Space. In: Maccoby, E.E., Newcomb, T.M., and

Hartley, E.I. (Eds): *Readings in Social Psychology.* Holt, New York.

Brown, J.K. (1963) A Cross-Cultural Study of Female Initiation Rites. *American Anthropologists,* 65:837-853.

Brutz, J.L. and Ingoldsby, B.B. (1984) Conflict Resolution in Quaker Families. *Journal of Marriage and the Family,* 46:21-26.

Buric, O., and Zecevic, A. (1967) Family Authority, Marital Satisfaction, and the Social Network in Yugoslavia. *Journal of Marriage and the Family,* 29:325-336.

Burke, R.J. and Weir, T. (1976) Relationship of Wives' Employment Status to Husband, Wife and Pair Satisfaction and Performance. *Journal of Marriage and the Family,* 38:279-287.

Callan, V.J. (1982) Australian, Greek and Italian Parents: Differentials in the Value and Cost of Children. *Journal of Comparative Family Studies,* 13:49-61.

Caplan, G. (1953) Problems of Infancy and Childhood. In: *Transactions 7th Conference.* Josiah Macy, Jr. Foundation, New York.

Caplow, T. (1968) Two Against One: Coalition in Triads. Englewood Cliffs, Prentice-Hall, New Jersey.

Carstairs, G.M. (1956) Hinjra and Jiryan: Two Derivatives of Hindu Attitudes to Sexuality. *British Journal of Medical Psychiatry,* 29:128-138.

Carter, E.A. and McGoldrick, M. (Eds) (1980) *The Family Life Cycle: A Framework for Therapy.* Gardner Press, New York.

Caudill, W. and Weinstein, H. (1969) Maternal Care and Infant Behavior in Japan and America. *Psychiatry,* 32:12-43.

Caudill, W. (1963) Sibling Rank and Style of Life Among Japanese Psychiatric Patients. *The Proceeding of the Joint Meeting of the Japanese Society of Psychiatry and Neurology and the American Psychiatric Association,* May 13-17, Tokyo, Japan.

Caudill, W.A. and Schooler, C. (1973) Child Behavior and Child Rearing in Japan and the United States: An Interim Report. *Journal of Nervous and Mental Disease.* 157:323-328.

Chalifoux, J.J. (1980) Secondary Marriage and Levels of Seniority Among the Abisi (PITI), Nigeria. *Journal of Comparative Family Studies,* 11:325-334.

Chang, H.I., and Kim, H.W. (1988) The Study of "House-Wife

Syndrome'' in Korea. In: Yoshimatsu, K., and Tseng, W.S. (Eds): *Asian Family Mental Health*. Psychiatric Research Institute of Tokyo, Tokyo.

Chen, K.C., and Rai, C.H. (1979) The Change of Chinese Family System: The Investigation of the History and Size of the Household. (In Chinese). The Selected Monograph (26), The Institute of the Central Research, Taipai.

Cherlin, A. (1983) Changing Family and Household: Contemporary Lessons from Historical Research. *Annual Review of Sociology*, 9:51-66.

Chin, A.S. (1970) Family Relations in Modern Chinese Fiction. In: Freedman, M. (Ed): *Family and Kinship in Chinese Society*, Stanford University Press, Stanford.

Chiriboda, D.A., Roberts, J., and Stein, J.A. (1978) Psychological Well-being During Marital Separation. *Journal of Divorce*. 2:21-36.

Cohen, M.L. (1976) *House United, House Divided: The Chinese Family in Taiwan*. Columbia University Press, New York.

Cohler, B.J., and Lieberman, M.A. (1980) Social Relations and Mental Health: Middle-Aged and Older Men and Women from Three European Ethnic Groups. *Research on Aging*, 2:445-469.

Collver, A. (1963) The Family Cycle in India and the United States. *American Sociological Review*, 28:86-96.

Colman, C. (1987) A Commentary (For ''Family Therapy in Japan'' by Suzuki, Koji). *AFTA Newsletter* 27:18.

Connor, J.W. (1974) Acculturation and Family Continuities in Three Generations of Japanese Americans. *Journal of Marriage and the Family*, 26:159-165.

Cooney, R.S., Rogler, L.H., Hurrell, R., Ortiz, V. (1982) Decision Making in Intergenerational Puerto Rican Families. *Journal of Marriage and the Family*, 44:621-632.

Costello, R.M. (1977) ''Chicano Liberation'' and the Mexican-American Marriage. *Psychiatric Annals*, 7:64-73.

Crespi, T.D. (1988) Specifications and Guidelines for Specialization in Family Therapy: Implications for Practicum Supervisors. *International Journal of Family Psychiatry*, 9:181-191.

Cromwell, R.E. and Olson, D.H. (1975) *Power in Families*. Halstead Press, New York.

Cromwell, V.L. and Cromwell, R.E. (1978) Perceived Dominance in Decision-Making and Conflict Resolution Among Anglo, Black and Chicano Couples. *Journal of Marriage and the Family*, 40:749-759.

Crosby, J.F., and Jose, N.L. (1983) Death: Family Adjustment to Loss. In: Figley, C.R., and McCubbin, H.I. (Eds): *Stress and the Family*, Vol. II: Coping With Catastrophe. Brunner/Mazel, New York.

Cross, W.E. (1981) Black Families and Black Identity Development: Rediscovering the Distinction Between Self-esteem and Reference Group Orientation. *Journal of Comparative Family Studies*, Special Issue: The Child and the Family, 12:19-49.

Cuber, J.F. (1965) Three Prerequisite Considerations to Diagnosis and Treatment in Marriage Counseling. In: Klemer, R.H. (Ed): *Counseling in Marital and Sexual Problems: A Physician's Handbook*. The Williams & Wilkins, Baltimore.

Dell, P.F. (1980) Researching the Family Theories of Schizophrenia: An Exercise in Epistemological Confusion. *Family Process*, 19:321-335.

Denfeld, D. (1974) Dropouts from Swinging: The Marriage Counselor as Informant. In: Smith, J.R., and Smith, L.B. (Eds): *Beyond Monogamy*. The Johns Hopkins University Press, Baltimore.

Denfeld, D., and Gordon, M. (1974) The Sociology of Mate Swapping: Or the Family that Swings Together Clings Together. In: Smith, J.R. and Smith, L.G. (Eds): *Beyond Monogamy*. The Johns Hopkins University Press, Baltimore.

Denga, D.I. (1982) Childlessness and Marital Adjustment in Northern Nigeria. *Journal of Marriage and the Family*, 44:799-802.

DeVos, G.A. and Wagatsuma, H. (1969) Minority Status and Deviancy in Japan. In: Caudill, W. and Lin, T.Y. (Eds): *Mental Health Research in Asia and the Pacific*. East-West Center Press, Honolulu.

DeVos, G. and Wagatsuma, H. (1972) Family Life and Delinquency: Some Perspectives from Japanese Research. In: Lebra, W.P. (Ed): *Transcultural Research in Mental Health*. The University Press of Hawaii, Honolulu.

Dilworth-Anderson, P. and McAdoo, H.P. (1988) The Study of

Ethnic Minority Families: Implications for Practitioners and Policymakers. *Family Relations*, 37:265-267.

DiNicola, V.F. (1985) Family Therapy and Transcultural Psychiatry: An Emerging Synthesis. Part II: Portability and Cultural Change. *Transcultural Psychiatric Research Review*, 22:151-180.

DiNicola, V.F. (1986) Beyond Babel: Family Therapy as Cultural Translation. *International Journal of Family Psychiatry*, 7:179-191.

Dissanayake, W. (1982) Newspapers as Matchmakers—A Sri Lankan Illustration. *Journal of Comparative Family Studies*, 13:97-108.

Doi, T. (1973) Omote and Ura: Concepts Derived from the Japanese Two-Fold Structure of Consciousness. *Journal of Nervous and Mental Disorder*, 157:258-261.

Duvall, E.M. (1954) *In-Laws: Pro and Con.* Association Press, New York.

Duvall, E.M. (1971) *Family Development*, 4th Ed. J.B. Lippincott, Philadelphia.

Ebaugh, H.R.F., and Haney, C.A. (1980) Shifts in Abortion Attitudes: 1972-1978. *Journal of Marriage and the Family*, 42:491-499.

Ebigbo, P.O. and Ihezue, U.H. (1982) Neurotic Ties in Families of Nigerians with Psycho-physiologic Disturbances. *International Journal of Family Psychiatry*, 3:345-356.

Ekeda, Y. (1987) *Child Abuse: Distorted Parent-Child Relations.* (In Japanese) Chuou-Kolonsha, Tokyo.

El-Islam, M.F. (1979) A Better Outlook for Schizophrenics Living in Extended Families. *British Journal of Psychiatry*, 135:343-347.

El-Islam, M.F. (1983) Cultural Change and Intergenerational Relationships in Arabian Families. *International Journal of Family Psychiatry*, 4:321-329.

Ellis, A. (1974) Group Marriage: A Possible Alternative? In: Smith, J.R. and Smith, L.B. (Eds): *Beyond Monogamy*. The Johns Hopkins University Press, Baltimore.

Ember, C.R. and Ember, M. (1973) *Anthropology*. Appleton-Century-Crofts, New York.

Erikson, E.H. (1963) *Childhood and Society*, W.W. Norton, New York.

Falicov, C.J. (1982) Mexican Families. In: McGoldrick, M., Pearce, J.K., and Giordano, J. (Eds): *Ethnicity and Family Therapy*, The Guilford Press, New York.

Falicov, C.J. (1983) *Cultural Perspectives in Family Therapy*. Aspen, Rockville, Maryland.

Falicov, C.J. and Brudner-White, L. (1983) The Shifting Family Triangle: The Issue of Cultural and Contextual Relativity. In: Falicov, C.J. (Ed): *Cultural Perspectives in Family Therapy*, An Aspen Publication, Rockville, Maryland.

Falicov, C., and Karrer, B.M. (1980) Cultural Variations in the Family Life Cycle: The Mexican-American Family. In: Carter, E.A., and McGoldrick, M. (Eds): *The Family Life Cycle: A Framework for Family Therapy*. Gardner Press, New York.

Falloon, I.R.H. (1981) Communication and Problem-Solving Skills Training with Relapsing Schizophrenics and Their Families. In: Lansky, M.R. (Ed): *Family Therapy and Major Psychopathology*. Grune & Stratton, New York.

Fengler, A. (1975) Attitudinal Orientations of Wives toward Husband's Retirement. *International Journal of Aging and Human Development*, 6:139-152.

Finkelhor, D. (1979) *Sexually Victimized Children*. Free Press, New York.

Finkelhor, D. (1987) The Sexual Abuse of Children: Current Research Reviewed. *Psychiatric Annals*, 17:233-241.

Fishbein, H.D. (1981) Sibling Set Configuration and Family Dysfunction. *Family Process*, 20:311-318, 1981.

Fleck, S. (1980) Family functioning and Family Pathology. *Psychiatric Annals*, 10:17-35.

Forman, B.D. and Hagan, B.J. (1983) A Comparative Review of Total Family Functioning Measures. *American Journal of Family Therapy*, 11:25-40.

Frantz, T.T. (1984) Helping Parents Whose Child Has Died. In: Frantz, T.T. (Ed): *Death and Grief in the Family*. Aspen, Rockville, Maryland.

Fredman, N. and Sherman, R. (1987) *Handbook of Measurements For Marriage and Family Therapy*. Brunner/Mazel, New York.

Freedman, R., Cooms, L. and Chang, M.C. (1972) Trends in Family Size Preferences and Practice of Family Planning: Taiwan, 1965-1970. *Studies in Family Planning*, 3:281-296.

From-Reichman, F. (1948) Notes on the Development of Treatment of Schizophrenics by Psychoanalytic Psychotherapy. *Psychiatry*, 11:263-273.

Futterman, S. (1954) Personality Trends in Wives of Alcoholics. *Journal of Psychiatric Social Work*, 23:37-41.

Gelles, R.J. (1980) Violence in the Family: A Review of Research in the Seventies. *Journal of Marriage and the Family*, 42:873-885.

Glenn, N.D. and Weaver, C.N. (1981) The Contribution of Marital Happiness to Global Happiness. *Journal of Marriage and the Family*, 43:161-168.

Glick, I.D., Clarkin, J.F., Kessler, D.R. (1987) *Marital and Family Therapy*. 3rd Ed. Grune & Stratton, Orlando.

Goduco-Angular, C., and Wintrob, R. (1964) Folie à Famille in the Philippines. *Psychiatric Quarterly*, 38:278-291.

Goldstein, M.J. (1981) Family Therapy During the Aftercare Treatment of Acute Schizophrenia. In: Lansky, M.R. (Ed): *Family Therapy and Major Psychopathology*. Grune & Stratton, New York.

Goldstein, M.J., and Strachan, A.M. (1987) The Family and Schizophrenia. In: Jacob, T. (Ed): *Family Interaction and Psychopathology*. Plenum Press, New York.

Good, B. and Kleinman, A. (1985) Culture and Anxiety: Cross-Cultural Evidence for the Patterning of Anxiety Disorders. In: Tuma, A.H. and Maser, J. (Eds): *Anxiety and the Anxiety Disorders*. Lawrence Erlbaum, Hillsdale.

Gordon, M. (1972) From a Functional Necessity to a Cult of Mutual Organism: Sex in American Marital Educational Literature, 1830-1940. In: *The Sociology of Sex*. Appleton-Century-Crofts, New York.

Gottman, J.M. (1979) *Marital Interaction: Empirical Investigation*. Academic Press, New York.

Gralnick, A. (1942) Folie à Deux: The Psychosis of Association, A Review of 103 Cases and the Entire English Literature. *Psychiatric Quarterly*, 16:230-263.

Green, A.H., Gaines, R.W., Sandgrund, A. (1974) Child Abuse: Pathological Syndrome of Family Interaction. *American Journal of Psychiatry*, 131:882-886.

Gregory, I. (1959) Husbands and Wives Admitted to Mental Hospital. *Journal of Mental Science*, 105:457-462.

Grotevant, H.D. and Carlson, C.I. (1989) *Family Assessment: A Guide to Methods and Measures*. The Guilford Press, New York.

Guerin, P.J. Jr., Fay, L.F., Burden, S.L., Kautto, J.G. (1987) *The Evaluation and Treatment of Marital Conflict*. Basic Books, New York.

Gupta, G.R. (1976) Love, Arranged Marriage, and the Indian Social Structure. *Journal of Comparative Family Studies*, 7:75-85.

Gurman, A.S., and Kniskern, D.P. (1981) Family Therapy Outcome Research: Knowns and Unknowns. In: Gurman, A.S., and Kniskern, D.P. (Eds): *Handbook of Family Therapy*. Brunner/Mazel, New York.

Haas, L. (1981) Domestic Role Sharing in Sweden. *Journal of Marriage and the Family*, 43:957-967.

Haley, J. (1967) Towards a Theory of Pathological Systems. In: Zuk, G. and Boszormenyi-Nagy, I. (Eds): *Family Therapy and Disturbed Families*. Science and Behavior Books, New York.

Hare-Mustin, R.T. (1978) A Feminist Approach to Family Therapy. *Family Process*, 17:181-194.

Hassen, R. (1980) *Ethnicity, Culture and Fertility: An Exploratory Study of Fertility Behavior and Sexual Beliefs*. Chopmen, Singapore.

Haviland, W.A. (1978) *Cultural Anthropology*, 2nd Ed. Holt, Rinehart, and Winston, New York.

Hawkes, G.R. and Taylor, M. (1975) Power Structure in Mexican and Mexican-American Farm Labor Families. *Journal of Marriage and the Family*, 37:807-811.

Hawkins, J.L. Weisberg, C., and Ray, D.L. (1977) Martial Communication Style and Social Class. *Journal of Marriage and the Family*, 39:479-490.

Herz, F.M., and Rosen, E.J. (1982) Jewish Families. In: McGoldrick, M., Pearce, J.K., and Giordano, J. (Eds): *Ethnicity and Family Therapy*, The Guilford Press, New York.

Herz, S. (1967) The Changing American Family Pattern and Its Effect on Marital Stability. In: Silverman, H.L. (Ed): *Marital Counseling: Psychology, Ideology, Science.* Charles C Thomas, Springfield.

Hetherington, E.M., Cox, M., and Cox, R. (1978) The Aftermath of Divorce. In: Stevens, J.H., and Mathews, M. (Eds): *Mother-Child, Father-Child Relations.* National Association for Young Children, Washington, D.C.

Hill, E.A., and Dorfman, L.T. (1982) Reactions of Housewives to the Retirement of Their Husbands. *Family Relations*, 31:195-200.

Hill, R. (1949) *Families Under Stress.* Harper & Row, New York.

Hill, R. (1958) Generic Features of Families Under Stress. *Social Casework*, 49:139-150.

Hoebel, E.A. (1972) *Anthropology: The Study of Man*, 4th Ed. McGraw-Hill, New York.

Hoffman, L. (1981) The Perverse Triangle in Different Cultures. In: *Foundations of Family Therapy: A Conceptual Framework for Systems Change.* Basic Books, New York.

Holtzman, J.M. and Akiyama, H. (1985) What Children See: The Aged on Television in Japan and the United States. *The Gerontologist*, 25: 62-67.

Housekenecht, S.K. (1979) Childlessness and Marital Adjustment. *Journal of Marriage and the Family*, 41:259-265.

Howells, J.G. (1971) Dimensions of the Family. In: *Theory and Practice of Family Psychiatry.* Brunner/Mazel, New York.

Hsu, F.L.K. (1949) The Family in China. In: Anshen, R.N. (Ed): *The Family: Its Function and Destiny.* Harper, New York.

Hsu, F.L.K. (1972) Kinship and Ways of Life: An Exploration. In: Hsu, F.L.K. (Ed): *Psychological Anthropology.* Schenkman, Cambridge.

Hsu, J. (1983) Asian Family Interaction Patterns and Their Therapeutic Implications. *International Journal of Family Psychiatry*, 4:307-320.

Hsu, J. (1985) The Chinese Family: Relations, Problems, and Therapy. In: Tseng, W.S., and Wu, D.Y.H. (Eds): *Chinese Culture and Mental Health.* Academic Press, New York.

Hsu, J. and Tseng, W.S. (1972) Intercultural Psychotherapy. *Archives of General Psychiatry*, 27:700-705.

Hsu, J., and Tseng, W.S. (1974) Family Relations in Classic Chinese Opera. *International Journal of Social Psychiatry*, 20:159-172.

Hsu, J., Tseng, W.S., Ashton, G., McDermott, J.F. Jr., and Char, W. (1985) Family Interaction Patterns Among Japanese-American and Caucasian Families in Hawaii. *American Journal of Psychiatry*, 142:577-581.

Hsu, J., Tseng, W.S., Ashton, G., McDermott, J.F. Jr., and Char, W. (1986) Cross-Ethnic Study of Normal Family Interactions in Hawaii. *International Journal of Family Psychiatry*, 8:349-361.

Hsu, J., Tseng, W.S., Lum, K.Y., Lau, L., Vaccaro, J., and Brennan, J. (1988) Cross-Ethnic Study of Normal Families in Hawaii. *Asian Family Mental Health Conference Proceedings*, Psychiatric Research Institute of Tokyo, Tokyo.

Hsu, M. (1977) Function of the Male Initiation Ceremony: A Hypothetical Framework. *The Journal of Ethnology and Sociology*, 15:165-174.

Hunt, M., and Hunt, B. (1977) *The Divorce Experience*. McGraw-Hill, New York.

Iamen, J. (1986) Marshalls. In: Tseng, W.S. (Ed): *Culture and Mental Health in Micronesia*. Department of Psychiatry, School of Medicine University of Hawaii, Honolulu.

Inamura, H. (1980) *Violence in the Family: Pathology of Japanese Style Parent-Child Relations*. (In Japanese). *Shinyosha*, Tokyo.

Ingoldsby, B.B. (1980) Emotional Expressiveness and Marital Adjustment: A Cross-Cultural Analysis. *Journal of Comparative Family Studies*, 11:501-515.

Inkeles, A., and Smith, D.H. (1974) *Becoming Modern: Individual Changes in Six Developing Countries*. Harvard University Press, Cambridge.

Izutsu, S., Furukawa, E., and Hayashida, C. (1980) *The Japanese Family*. Presented at the Culture and Family in Hawaii and the Pacific Conference, Honolulu.

Jackson, D. (1968) Family Interaction, Family Homeostasis and Some Implications for Conjoint Family Therapy. In: Jackson, D.

(Ed): *Therapy, Communication and Change.* Science and Behavior Books, Palo Alto.

Jackson, K. (1954) The Adjustment of the Family to the Crisis of Alcoholism. *Quarterly Journal of Studies on Alcohol*, 15:562-586.

Jacob, T. and Seilhamer, R.A. (1987) Alcoholism and Family Interaction. In: Jacob, T. (Ed): *Family Interaction and Psychopathology: Theories, Methods, and Findings.* Plenum Press, New York.

Jacobson, N.S. and Margolin, G. (1979) *Marital Therapy: Strategies Based on Social Learning and Behavior Exchange Principles.* Brunner/Mazel, New York.

Johnson, C. and Flach, A. (1985) Family Characteristics of 105 Patients With Bulimia. *American Journal of Psychiatry*, 142:1321-1324.

Johnson, C.L. (1982) Sibling Solidarity: Its Origin and Functioning in Italian-American Families. *Journal of Marriage and the Family*, 44:155-167.

Jones, G.W. (1980) Trends in Marriage and Divorce in Peninsular Malaysia. *Population Studies*, 34:279-292.

Kandel, D. and Lesser, G.S. (1969) Parent-Adolescent Relationships and Adolescent Independence in the United States and Denmark. *Journal of Marriage and the Family*, 31:348-358.

Kandel, D.B. and Lesser, G.S. (1972) Marital Decision-Making in American and Danish Urban Families: A Research Note. *Journal of Marriage and the Family*, 34:134-138.

Kaslow, F.W. (Ed) (1982) *The International Book of Family Therapy*, Brunner/Mazel, New York.

Kaufman, E. (1985) Families and Family Therapy in Alcoholism. In: Lanksy, M.R. (Ed): *Family Approaches to Major Psychiatric Disorders.* American Psychiatric Press, Washington, D.C.

Kerckhoff, A. (1966) Family Patterns and Morale in Retirement. In: Simpson, I.H. and McKinney, J.C. (Eds): *Social Aspects of Aging.* Duke University Press, Durham.

Khan, M. and Sirageldin, I. (1977) Son Preference and the Demand for Additional Children in Pakistan. *Demography*, 14:481-495.

Khatri, A.A. (1980) Analysis of Fiction—A Method for Intracultural and Cross-Cultural Study of Family Systems. *Journal of Marriage and the Family*, 42:197-203.

Kidwell, J.S. (1981) Number of Siblings, Sibling Spacing, Sex, and Birth Order: Their Effects on Perceived Parent-Adolescent Relationships. *Journal of Marriage and the Family*, 43:315-332.

Killorin, E. and Olson, D.H. (1980) Clinical Application of the Circumplex Model to Chemically Dependent Families. Unpublished manuscript.

Kinzie, D., Tran, K., Breckenridge, A., and Bloom, J. (1980) An Indochinese Refugee Psychiatric Clinic: Culturally Accepted Treatment Approaches. *American Journal of Psychiatry*, 137:1429-1432.

Kitanish, K. and Tseng, W.S. (1989) Social Phobia Among Japanese: Clinical, Family and Cultural Explorations. *Transcultural Psychiatric Research Review*, 26:137-147.

Kluckhohn, C. (1951) Values and Value Orientations. In: Parson, T. (Ed): *Toward a General Theory of Action*. Harvard University Press, Cambridge.

Knodel, J. and Prachuabmoh, V. (1976) Preferences for Sex of Children in Thailand: A Comparison of Husbands' and Wives' Attitude. *Studies in Family Planning*, 7:137-143.

Koch-Nielsen, I. (1980) One-Parent Families in Denmark. *Journal of Comparative Family Studies*, Special Issue: One-Parent Family, 11:17-29.

Kohn, M. (1959) Socialization, Class, and Parental Values. *American Journal of Sociology*, 64:337-351.

Kohn, M.L. (1963) Social Class and Parent-Child Relationships: An Interpretation. *American Journal of Sociology*, 68:471-480.

Korbin, J.E. (1981) Conclusions. In: Korbin, J.E. (Ed): *Child Abuse and Neglect: Cross-Cultural Perspectives*. University of California Press, Berkeley.

Kreitman, N. (1962) Mental Disorder in Married Couples. *Journal of Mental Science*, 108:438-446.

Kubler-Ross, E. (1969) *On Death and Dying*. Macmillan, New York.

Kurian, G. (1976) *The Family in India*, The Hague.

Lambert, W.W., Triandis, L.M., and Wolf, M. (1959) Some Correlates of Beliefs in the Malevolence and Benevolence of Supernatural Beings: A Cross-Societal Study. *Journal of Abnormal and Social Psychology*, 58:162-169.

Lantz, H.R. and Snyder, E.C. (1969) *Marriage: An Examination of the Man-Woman Relationship*. John Wiley & Sons, New York.

Lebra, T.S. (1976) *Japanese Patterns of Behavior*, The University Press of Hawaii, Honolulu.

Lebra, T.S. (1978) Japanese Women and Marital Strain. *Ethos*, 6:22-41.

Lee, G.R. and Stone, L.H. (1980) Mate-Selection Systems and Criteria: Variation According to Family Structure. *Journal of Marriage and the Family*, 42:319-326.

Lee, H.K., Ong, A., and Lee, S.J. (1973) A Comparison of Early and Late Adopters of Family Planning. KIRBS Psychological Studies in Population/Family Planning (No. 1).

Lee, S.H. (1987) Social Phobia in Korea. In: Proceeding of the First Cultural Psychiatry Symposium Between Japan and Korea — *Social Phobia in Japan and Korea*. The East Asian Academy of Cultural Psychiatry, Seoul.

Lefaucheur, N. (1980) Single-Parenthood and Illegitimacy in France. *Journal of Comparative Family Studies*, Special Issue: One-Parent Family, 11:31-48.

Lester, D. (1981) A Cross-Cultural Study of Wife Abuse. *Aggressive Behavior*, 6:361-364.

Levine, N.E. (1980) Nyinba Polyandry and the Allocation of Paternity. *Journal of Comparative Family Studies*, 11:283-323.

Levine, R. (1970) Intergenerational Tensions and Extended Family Structures in Africa. In: Barash, M. and Scourby, A. (Eds): *Marriage and the Family*. Random House, New York.

LeVine, S. and LeVine, R. (1981) Child Abuse and Neglect in Sub-Saharan Africa. In: Korbin, J.E. (Ed): *Child Abuse and Neglect: Cross-Cultural Perspectives*. University of California Press, Berkeley.

Levine, N. and Sangree, W.H. (1980) Conclusion: Asian and African Systems of Polyandry. *Journal of Comparative Family Studies*, Special Issues: Women with Many Husbands: Polyandrous Alliance and Marital Flexibility in Africa and Asia. 11(3):385-410.

Levinson, D. (1988) Family Violence in Cross-Cultural Perspective. In: Van Hasselt, V.B., Morrison, R.L., Bellack, A.S., and Hersen, M. (Eds): *Handbook of Family Violence*. Plenum Press, New York.

Levy, D.M. (1943) *Maternal Overprotection*. Columbia University Press, New York.

Lewis, J.M., Beavers, W.R., Gossett, J.T., and Phillips, V.A. (1976) *No Single Thread: Psychological Health in Family Systems*. Brunner/Mazel, New York.

Lewis, J.M. and Looney, J.G. (1983) *The Long Struggle: Well-Functioning Working-Class Black Families*. Brunner/Mazel, New York.

Li, C., Fang, M., Tseng, W.S., and Hsu, J. (1988) Family Background and Problems: Comparative Study of Normal and Delinquent Adolescents in Beijing. In: *Asian Family Mental Health Conference Proceeding*. Psychiatric Research Institute of Tokyo, Tokyo.

Li, Y.Y. (1968) Ghost Marriage, Shamanism and Kinship Behavior in Rural Taiwan. In: *Folk Religion and the Worldview in the Southwestern Pacific*, The Keio Institute of Cultural and Linguistic Studies, Keio University, Tokyo.

Li, Y.Y. (1982) The Change of the Modern Chinese Family: An Anthropological Investigation. In: The Proceeding of The Change and Development of the Modern China. Taipei, July.

Lidz, T. (1970) The Family as the Developmental Setting. In: Anthony, E.J. and Koupernik, C. (Eds): *The Child in His Family*. Vol. I, John Wiley & Sons, New York.

Lidz, T. (1974) The Family: The Developmental Setting. In: Arieti, S. (Ed): Vol. 1, The Foundations of Psychiatry, *American Handbook of Psychiatry*, 2nd Ed. Basic Books, New York.

Lidz, T., Cornelison, A., Terry, D., and Fleck, S. (1958) Intrafamilial Environment of the Schizophrenic Patient: VI. The Transmission of the Irrationality. *A.M.A. Archives of Neurology and Psychiatry*, 79:305-316.

Lidz, T., Fleck, S., and Cornelison, A., (1965) *Schizophrenia and the Family*. International Universities Press, New York.

Lidz, T., Fleck, S., Cornelson, A., and Terry, D. (1965) The Intrafamilial Environment of the Schizophrenic Patient: IV. Parental

Personalities and Family Interaction. *American Journal of Orthopsychiatry*, 28:764-778.

Lopata, H.Z. (1971) *Occupation: Housewife*. Oxford University Press, New York.

Lupri, E. (1969) Contemporary Authority Patterns in the West German Family: A Study in Cross-National Validation. *Journal of Marriage and the Family*, 31:134-144.

Malinowski, B. (1931) Culture. *Encyclopaedia of the Social Sciences*, Vol. 4, pp. 621-645.

Martin, P.A. and Bird, H.W. (1959) The "Love-sick" Wife and the "Cold-sick" Husband. *Psychiatry*, 22:246-2.

Martin, P.A. (1976) *A Marital Therapy Manual*. Brunner/Mazel, New York.

Mathews, L.J. and Ilon, L. (1980) Becoming a Chronic Runaway: The Effects of Race and Family in Hawaii. *Family Relations*, 29:404-409.

Mathison, J. (1970) A Cross-Cultural View of Widowhood. *Omega*, 1:201-218.

McAdoo, H.P. (1982) Stress Absorbing Systems in Black Families. *Family Relations*, 31:479-488.

McCubbin, H.I., Joy, C.B., Cauble, A.E. Comeau, J.K., Patterson, J., Needle, R.H. (1980) Family Stress and Coping: A Decade Review. *Journal of Marriage and the Family*, 42:855-871.

McCubbin, H.I. and Patterson, J.M. (1983) Family Transition: Adaptation to Stress. In: McCubbin, H.I. and Figley, C.R. (Eds): *Stress and the Family*. Vol. I.: Coping With Normative Transitions. Brunner/Mazel, New York.

McDonald, G.W. (1980) Family Power: The Assessment of a Decade of Theory and Research, 1970-1979. *Journal of Marriage and the Family*, 42:841-854.

McGoldrick, M. and Carter, E. (1980) The Stage of the Family Life Cycle. In: Henslin, J.M. (Ed): *Marriage and Family in a Changing Society*. 2nd Ed. The Free Press, New York.

McGoldrick, M., and Pearce, J.K, (1981) Family Therapy With Irish-Americans. *Family Process*, 20:223-244.

McGoldrick, M., Pearce, J.K. and Giordano, J. (Eds) (1982) *Ethnicity and Family Therapy*. The Guilford Press, New York.

Mead, M. (1928) *Coming of Age in Samoa*. Dell, New York.

Medling, J.M. and McCarry, M. (1981) Marital Adjustment Over Segments of the Family Life Cycle: The Issue of Spouses' Value Similarity. *Journal of Marriage and the Family*, 43:195-203.

Miller, L. (1969) Child Rearing in the Kibbutz. In: Howells, J.G. (Ed): *Modern Perspectives in International Child Psychiatry*. Oliver & Boyd, Edinburgh.

Minturn, L. and Hitchcock, J.T. (1963) The Rajputs of Khalapur India. In: Whiting, B.B. (Ed): *Six Cultures: Studies in Child-rearing*. John Wiley, New York.

Minuchin, S. (1974) *Families and Family Therapy*. Harvard University Press, Cambridge.

Minuchin, S., Baker, L., Rosman, B., Liebman, T., Milman, L., and Todd, T. (1975) A Conceptual Model of Psychosomatic Illness in Children. *Archives of General Psychiatry*, 32:1031-1038.

Minuchin, S., Montalvo, B., Guerney, B.G., Rosman, B.L., and Schumer, B.G. (1967) *Families of the Slums*. Basic Books, New York.

Minuchin, S., Rosman, B.L., and Baker, L. (1978) *Psychosomatic Families: Anorexia Nervosa in Context*. Harvard University Press, Cambridge.

Mirande, A. (1979) A Reinterpretation of Male Dominance in the Chicano Family. *The Family Coordinator*, 28: 473-479.

Moitoza, E. (1982) Portuguese Families. In: McGoldrick, M., Pearce, J.K., and Giordano, J. (Eds): *Ethnicity and Family Therapy*, The Guilford Press, New York.

Momeni, D.A. (1975) Polygyny in Iran. *Journal of Marriage and the Family*, 37:452-456.

Moos, F. (1988) Some Cross-Cultural Perspectives of Change in American, West German, and Japanese Family. In: *Asian Family Mental Health Conference Proceedings*. Psychiatric Research Institute of Tokyo, Tokyo.

Moskoff, W. (1983) Divorce in the USSR. *Journal of Marriage and the Family*, 45:419-425.

Murdock, G.P. (1967) *Ethnographic Atlas*. Pittsburgh.

Myers, G., and Roberts, J.M. (1968) A Technique for Measuring Preferential Family Size and Composition. *Eugenics Quarterly*, 15:164-172.

Nagler, S. (1965) In: Neubauer, P.B. (Ed): *Children in Collectives*. Charles C Thomas, Springfield.

Nanda, S. (1980) *Cultural Anthropology*. D. Van Nostrand, New York.

National Center for Health Statistics (1980) *Births, Marriages, Divorces, and Deaths for 1979*. Monthly Vital Statistics Report, Vol. 28, No. 12, Provisional Statistics. U.S. Department of Health, Education, and Welfare. Hyattsville, Maryland.

Navran, L. (1967) Communication and Adjustment in Marriage. *Family Process*, 1:173-184, 1967.

Nevadomsky, J. (1980) Changes Over Time and Space in the East Indian Family in Rural Trinidad. *Journal of Comparative Family Studies*, 11:433-456.

Offer, D. (1982) Adolescent Turmoil. *New York University Education Quarterly*, 13:29-32.

Offer, D., Ostrov, E., and Howard, K.I. (1981) *The Adolescent: A Psychological Self-Portrait*. Basic Books, New York.

Offer, D. and Sabshin, M. (1974) *Normality: Theoretical and Clinical Concepts of Mental Health*. 2nd eds. Basic Books, New York.

Ohara, K. (1963) Characteristics of Suicides in Japan—Especially of Parent-Child Double Suicide. *American Journal of Psychiatry*, 120:382-385.

O'Leary, K.D. and Curley, A.D. (1986) Assertion and Family Violence: Correlates of Spouse Abuse. *Journal of Marital and Family Therapy*, 12:281-290.

Olsen, D. (1974) Family Structure and Socialization Patterns in Taiwan. *American Journal of Sociology*, 79:1395-1417, 1982.

Olson, D.H., McCubbin, H.I., Barnes, H., Larsen, A., Muxen, M., and Wilson, M. (1982) *Family Inventories*. Family Social Science, University of Minnesota, St. Paul.

Olson, D.H., McCubbin, H.I., Barnes, H., Larsen, A., Muxen, M., and Wilson, M. (1983) *Families: What Makes Them Work*. Sage, Beverly Hills.

Olson, D.H., Portner, J., Lavee, Y. (1985) *FACES III* (Family Adaptability & Cohesion Evaluation Scales). Family Social Science, University of Minnesota, St. Paul, Minnesota.

Orden, S.R. and Bradburn, N.M. (1969) Working Wives and Marriage Happiness. *American Journal of Sociology*, 74:382-407.

Otterbein, C.S. and Otterbein, K. (1973) Believers and Beaters: A Case Study of Supernatural Beliefs and Child Rearing in the Bahama Islands. *American Anthropologist*, 75:1670-1681.

Pakel, E., Prusoff, B., and Uhlenhuth, E. (1971) "Scaling Life Events". Archives of General Psychiatry, 25:340-347.

Palazzoli, M.S. (1974) *Self Starvation: From the Intrapsychic to the Transpersonal Approach to Anorexia Nervosa*. Chaucer Publishing, London.

Palazzoli, M.S., Boscolo, L., Cecchin, G.F., Prata, G. (1977) Family Rituals: A Powerful Tool in Family Therapy. *Family Process*, 16:445-453.

Panitz, D.R., McConchie, R.D., Sauber, S.R., and Fonseca, J.A. (1983) The Role of Machismo and the Hispanic Family in the Etiology and Treatment of Alcoholism in Hispanic American Males. *The American Journal of Family Therapy*, 11:31-44.

Papajohn, J. and Spiegel, J. (1975) *Transactions in Families*. Jossey-Bass, San Francisco.

Parson, T., and Bales, R. (1955) *Family, Socialization and Interaction Process*. Free Press, Glencoe, Illinois.

Patterson, J.M. (1988) Families Experiencing Stress. *Family Systems Medicine*, 6:202-237.

Pebley, A.R., Delgado, H., and Brineman, E. (1980) Family Sex Composition Preference Among Guatemalan Men and Women. *Journal of Marriage and the Family*, 42:437-447.

Pelzel, J. (1970) Japanese Kinship: A comparison. In: *Family and Kinship in Chinese Society*. Stanford University Press, Stanford.

Petersen, A.C. and Offer, D. (1979) Adolescent Development: Sixteen to Nineteen. In: Call, J.D., Noshpitz, J.D., Cohen, R.L., and Berlin, I. (Eds): *Basic Handbook of Child Psychiatry, Vol. I, Development*. Basic Books, New York.

Petersen, L.R., Lee, G.R., Ellis, G.J. (1982) Social Structure, Socialization Values, and Disciplinary Techniques: A Cross-cultural Analysis. *Journal of Marriage and the Family*, 44:131-142.

Poffenberger, T. (1981) Child Rearing and Social Structure in Rural India: Toward a Cross-Cultural Definition of Child Abuse and

Neglect. In: Korbin, J.E. (Ed): *Child Abuse and Neglect: Cross-Cultural Perspectives*. University of California Press, Berkeley.

Pollak, O. (1965) Sociological and Psychoanalytic Concepts in Family Diagnosis. In: Greene, B.L. (Ed): *The Psychotherapies of Marital Disharmony*. The Free Press, New York.

Polloi, T. (1986) Belau. In: Tseng, W.S. (Ed): *Culture and Mental Health in Micronesia*. Department of Psychiatry, School of Medicine, University of Hawaii, Honolulu.

Ponce, D. (1988) Extramarital Affairs: Meaning and Impact on the Filipino Immigrant Family. In: Yoshimatsu, K. and Tseng, W.S. (Eds): *Asian Family Mental Health*. Psychiatric Research Institute of Tokyo, Tokyo.

Popplewell, J.F. and Sheikh, A. (1979) The Role of the Father in Child Development: A Review of the Literature. *International Journal of Social Psychiatry*, 25:267-284.

Prachuabmoh, V., Knodel, J. and Alers, J. (1974) Preferences for Sons, Desire for Additional Children and Family Planning in Thailand. *Journal of Marriage and the Family*, 36:601-614.

Price, G.M. (1945) A Study of the Wives of 20 Alcoholics. *Quarterly Journal of the Study of Alcoholism*, 5:620-627.

Prince-Bonham, S., and Balswick, J.O. (1980) The Noninstitutions: Divorce, Desertion, and Remarriage. *Journal of Marriage and the Family*, 42:959-972.

Purcel, K., et al. (1969) The Effect of Asthma in Children on Experimental Separation From the Family. *Psychosomatic Medicine*, 31:144-164.

Putsch, R.W. (1985) Cross-cultural Communication: The Special Case of Interpreters in Health Care. *Journal of American Medical Association*, 254:3344-3348.

Rabin, A.I. (1958) Infants and Children Under Conditions of "Intermittent Mothering in the Kibbutz." *American Journal of Orthopsychiatry*, 28:577-586.

Rabin, C., Margolin, G., Safir, M., Talovic, S., and Sadeh, I. (1986) The Areas of Change Questionnaire: A Cross-Cultural Comparison of Israeli and American Distressed and Nondistressed Couples. *The American Journal of Family Therapy*. 14:324-335.

Rapoport, R. and Rapoport, R.N. (1976) *Dual-Career Families Reexamined*. Harper & Row, New York.

Reid, J. (1979) A Time to Live, A Time to Grieve: Patterns and Process of Mourning Among the Yolngu of Australia. *Culture, Medicine and Psychiatry*. 3:319-346.

Rhyne, D. (1981) Bases of Marital Satisfaction Among Men and Women. *Journal of Marriage and the Family*, 43:941-955.

Richardson, J.G. (1979) Wife Occupational Superiority and Marital Troubles: An Examination of the Hypothesis. *Journal of Marriage and the Family*, 41:63-72.

Richman, J. (1979) Family Therapy of Attempted Suicide. *Family Process*, 18:131-142.

Ridley, C.A. (1973) Exploring the Impact of Work Satisfaction and Involvement on Marital Interaction When Both Partners Are Employed. *Journal of Marriage and the Family*, 35:229-237.

Rin, H. (1965) A Study of the Aetiology of Koro in Respect to the Chinese Concept of Illness. *International Journal of Social Psychiatry*, 11:7-13.

Rodman, H. (1967) Marital Power in France, Greece, Yugoslavia, and the United States: A Cross-National Discussion. *Journal of Marriage and the Family*, 29:320-324.

Rollins, B., and Cannon, K.L. (1974) Marital Satisfaction Over the Family Life Cycle: A Reevaluation. *Journal of Marriage and the Family*, 36:271-282.

Rosenbaum, M., and Richman, J. (1970) Suicide: The Role of Hostility and Death Wishes from the Family and Significant Others. *American Journal of Psychiatry*, 126:1652-1655.

Rosenblatt, P.C., Walsh, R.P., and Jackson, D.A. (1976) Grief and Mourning in Cross-Cultural Perspective. H.R.A.F. Press.

Ross, A. (1970) The Substructure of Power and Authority. In: Barash, M. and Scourby, A. (Eds): *Marriage and the Family*. Random House, New York.

Rossi, A.S. (1972) Family Development in a Changing World. *American Journal of Psychiatry*, 128:1057-1066.

Rubinstein, D.H. (1986) Micronesian Suicides. In: Tseng, W.S. and Lee, C.A. (Eds): *Culture and Mental Health in Micronesia*. Department of Psychiatry, John A. Burns School of Medicine, University of Hawaii, Honolulu.

Russell, C.S., Olson, D.H., Sprenkle, D.H., and Atlano, R.B. (1983) From Family Symptom to Family System: Review of Family Therapy Research. *The American Journal of Family Therapy*, 11:3-14.

Safilios-Rothschild, C. (1967) A Comparison of Power Structure and Marital Satisfaction in Urban Greek and French Families. *Journal of Marriage and the Family*, 29:345-352.

Safilios-Rothschild, C. (1969) Family Sociology or Wives' Family Sociology? — A Cross-Cultural Examination of Decision-Making. *Journal of Marriage and the Family*, 31:290-301.

Sahlins, M. (1957) Land Use and the Extended Family in Moala, Fiji. *American Anthropology*, 59:449-462.

Salamon, S. (1977) Family Bounds and Friendship Bonds: Japan and West Germany. *Journal of Marriage and the Family*, 39:807-820.

Salts, C.J. (1979) Divorce Process: Integration of Theory. *Journal of Divorce*, 2:233-240.

Sangree, W.H. (1980) The Persistence of Polyandry in Irigwe, Nigeria. *Journal of Comparative Family Studies*, 11:333-343.

Satir, V. (1967) *Conjoint Family Therapy: A Guide to Theory and Technique*, Revised edition, Science and Behavior Books, Palo Alto.

Satorius, N., Jablensky, A., and Shapiro, R. (1977) Two-year Follow-up of the Patients Included in the WHO International Pilot Study of Schizophrenia. *Psychological Medicine*, 7:528-541.

Schneider, D.M. and Gough, K. (Eds) (1961) *Matrilineal Kinship*. University of California Press, Berkeley.

Schram, R.M. (1979) Marital Satisfaction Over the Family Life Cycle: A Critique and Proposal. *Journal of Marriage and the Family*, 41:7-12.

Schwartzman, J. (1982) Normality From A Cross-Cultural Perspective. In: Walsh, F. (Ed): *Normal Family Processes*. Guilford, New York.

Seltzer, W.J., and Seltzer, M.R. (1983) Material, Myth, and Magic: A Cultural Approach to Family Therapy. *Family Process*, 22:3-14.

Shanas, E. (1973) Family-Kin Networks and Aging in Cross-Cultural Perspective. *Journal of Marriage and the Family*, 35:505-511.

Sharp, L. (1970-71) Neglected Entrepreneurs in Thailand. *The Social Science Review Quarterly*, 8:58-63.

Shen, Y. (1985) The Mental Health Home Care Program: Beijing's Rural Haidian District. In: Tseng, W.S. and Wu, D.Y.H. (Eds): *Chinese Culture and Mental Health*. Academic Press, Orlando.

Shey, T.H. (1977) Why Communes Fail: A Comparative Analysis of the Viability of Danish and American Communes. *Journal of Marriage and the Family*, 39:605-613.

Shipman, G. (1982) *Handbook for Family Analysis*. D.C. Heath and Company, Lexington, Massachusetts.

Singer, M. (1974) Delinquency and Family Disciplinary Configurations: An Elaboration of the Superego Lacunae Concept. *Archives of General Psychiatry*, 31:795-798.

Singer, K. (1975) Psychiatric Aspects of Abortion in Hong Kong. *International Journal of Social Psychiatry*, 21:303-306.

Skinner, D.A. (1980) Dual-Career Family Stress and Coping: A Literature Review. *Family Relations*, 29:473-480.

Sluzki, C.E. (1979) Migration and Family Conflict. *Family Process*, 18:379-390.

Sluzki, C.E. (1983) Process, Structure and World Views: Toward an Integrated View of Systemic Models in Family Therapy. *Family Process*, 22:469-476.

Smith, K.C., and Schooler, C. (1978) Women as Mothers in Japan: The Effects of Social Structure and Culture on Values and Behavior. *Journal of Marriage and the Family*, 40:613-620.

Smith, L.G. and Smith, J.R. (1973) Co-Marital Sex: The Incorporation of Extramarital Sex into the Marriage Relationship. In: Smith, J.R. and Smith, L.G. (Eds): *Beyond Monogamy*. The Johns Hopkins University Press, Baltimore.

Spanier, G.B., Lewis, R.A., Cole, C.L. (1975) Marital Adjustment Over the Family Life Cycle: The Issue of Curvilinearity. *Journal of Marriage and the Family*, 37:263-275.

Spanier, G.B. and Furstenberg, F.F. Jr. (1982) Remarriage After Divorce: A Longitudinal Analysis of Well-being. *Journal of Marriage and the Family*, 44:709-720.

Spiegel, J.P. (1957) The Resolution of Role Conflict Within the Family. *Psychiatry*, 20:1-16.

Stabenau, J.R., Tupin, J., Werner, M. and Pollin, W. (1965) A Comparative Study of Families of Schizophrenics, Delinquents, and Normals. *Psychiatry*, 28:45-59.

Stagoll, B. (1981) Therapy with Greek Families Living in Australia. *International Journal of Family Therapy*, 3:167-179.

Stainton, M.D. (1980) The Effect of Ordinal Position or Birth Order on Child Development. *Nursing Forum*, 14:165-179.

Staples, R. and Mirande, A. (1980) Racial and Cultural Variations among American Families: A Decennial Review of the Literature on Minority Families. *Journal of Marriage and the Family*, 42:887-903.

Steinglass, P. (1979) The Alcoholic Family in the Interaction Laboratory. *The Journal of Nervous and Mental Disease*. 167:428-436.

Steinglass, P., Benett, L.A., Wolin, S.J. and Reiss, D. (1987) *The Alcoholic Family*. Basic Books, New York.

Steinmetz, S.K. (1981) Cross-cultural Marital Abuse. *Journal of Sociology and Social Welfare*, 8:404-414.

Stinner, W.F. and Mader, P.D. (1975) Sons, Daughters or Both? An Analysis of Family Sex Composition Preferences in the Philippines. *Demography*, 12:67-79.

Straus, M.A. (1969) Phenomenal Identity and Conceptual Equivalence of Measurement in Cross-National Comparative Research. *Journal of Marriage and the Family*, 31:233-239.

Straus, M.A., Gelles, R.J., and Steinmetz, S.K. (1980) *Behind Closed Doors: Violence in the American Family*. Anchor Books, New York.

Sundberg, N., Sharma, V., Wodtli, T., and Rohila, P. (1969) Family Cohesiveness and Autonomy of Adolescents in India and the United States. *Journal of Marriage and the Family*, 31:403-407.

Suzuki, K. (1987) Family Therapy in Japan. *AFTA Newsletter*, 27:15-18.

Synder, D.K. (1979) Multidimensional Assessment of Marital Satisfaction. *Journal of Marriage and the Family*, 41:813-823.

Szinovacz, M.E. (1980) Female Retirement Effects on Spousal

Roles and Marital Adjustment. *Journal of Family Issues*, 1:423-440.

Tao, K. and Chiu, J.H. (1985) The One-Child-per-Family Policy: A Psychological Perspective. In: Tseng, W.S. and Wu, D.Y.H. (Eds): *Chinese Culture and Mental Health*. Academic Press, Orlando.

Tao, K., Qiu, J., Yu, L., Tseng, W.S. and Hsu, J. (1986) Family Background and Behavior Patterns of Single and Non-single Children. *Zhonhua Senjing-Jingsen-Ko Zazhi* (Chinese Neuro-Psychiatry Journal), 19:321-324.

Tashakkori, A. and Mehryar, A.H. (1982) The Differential Roles of Parents in the Family, as Reported by a Group of Iranian Adolescents. *Journal of Marriage and the Family*, 44:803-809.

Tcheng-Laroche, F. and Prince, R. (1983) Separated and Divorced Women Compared with Married Controls — Selected Life Satisfaction, Stress and Health Indices from a Community Survey. *Social Science Medicine*, 17:95-105.

Terr, L.C. (1970) A Family Study of Child Abuse. *American Journal of Psychiatry*, 127:665-671.

Tharp, R.G., Meadow, A., Lennhoff, S.G., and Satterfield, D. (1968) Changes in Marriage Roles Accompanying the Acculturation of the Mexican-American Wife. *Journal of Marriage and the Family*, 30:404-412.

Thompson, L., Clark, K., Gunn, W. Jr. (1985) Developmental Stage and Perceptions of Intergenerational Continuity. *Journal of Marriage and the Family*, 47:913-919.

Thorman, G. (1983) *Incestuous Families*. Charles C Thomas, Springfield.

Trotzer, J.P. (1981) The Centrality of Values in Families and Family Therapy. *International Journal of Family Therapy*, 3:42-55.

Tseng, W.S. (1969) A Paranoid Family in Taiwan: A Dynamic Study of Folie à Famille. *Archives of General Psychiatry*, 21:55-63.

Tseng, W.S. (1977) Adjustment in Intercultural Marriage. In: Tseng, W.S., McDermott, J.F. Jr., and Maretzki, T.W. (Eds): *Adjustment in Intercultural Marriage*. Department of Psychiatry, School of Medicine, University of Hawaii, Honolulu.

Tseng, W.S. (1986) Cultural Aspects of Family Assessment. *International Journal of Family Psychiatry*, 7:19-31.

Tseng, W.S., and Hsu, J. (1972) The Chinese Attitude Toward Parental Authority As Expressed in Chinese Children's Stories. *Archives of General Psychiatry*, 26:28-34.

Tseng, W.S., and Hsu, J. (1972) Intercultural Psychotherapy. *Archives of General Psychiatry*, 27:700-705.

Tseng, W.S. and Hsu, J. (1986) The Family in Micronesia. In: Tseng, W.S. and Lee, C.A. (Eds): *Culture and Mental Health in Micronesia*. Department of Psychiatry, John A. Burns School of Medicine, University of Hawaii, Honolulu.

Tseng, W.S., and McDermott, J.F. Jr. (1979) Triaxial Family Classification. *Journal of the American Academy of Child Psychiatry*, 18:22-43.

Tseng, W.S., and McDermott, J.F. Jr. (1981) *Culture, Mind and Therapy: An Introduction to Cultural Psychiatry*. Brunner/Mazel, New York.

Tseng, W.S., McDermott, J.F. Jr., Ogino, K., and Ebata, K. (1982) Cross-Cultural Differences in Parent-Child Assessment: USA and Japan. *International Journal of Social Psychiatry*, 28:305-317.

Tseng, W.S., Tao, K., Hsu, J., Chiu, J., Yu, L., and Kameoka, V. (1988) Family Planning and Child Mental Health in China: Nanjing Survey. *American Journal of Psychiatry*, 145:1396-1403.

Udry, J.R. (1966) Social Factors in Mate Selection. In: *The Social Context of Marriage*. J.B. Lippincott, Philadelphia.

Visher, E.B., and Visher, J.S. (1979) *Stepfamilies: A Guide to Working With Stepparents and Stepchildren*. Brunner/Mazel, New York.

Visher, J.S. and Visher, E.B. (1982) Stepfamilies and Stepparenting. In: Walsh, F. (Ed): *Normal Family Process*. The Guilford Press, New York.

Vogel, E.F. and Vogel, S.H. (1961) Family Security, Personal Immaturity, and Emotional Health in a Japanese Sample. *Marriage and Family Living*, 23:161-166.

Wakil, S.P., Siddique, C.M., and Wakil, F.A. (1981) Between Two Cultures: A Study in Socialization of Children of Immigrants. *Journal of Marriage and the Family*, 43:929-940.

Walsh, F. (1982) Conceptualizations of Normal Family Functioning. In: Walsh, F. (Ed): *Normal Family Processes*. Guilford, New York.

Walshock, M.L. (1974) The Emergence of Middle-class Deviant Subcultures: The Cases of Swingers. In: Smith, J. and Smith, L. (Eds): *Beyond Monogamy*. The Johns Hopkins University Press, Baltimore.

Walters, J. and Walters, L.H. (1980) Parent-Child Relationships: A Review, 1970-1979. *Journal of Marriage and the Family*, 42:807-821.

Waltzer, H. (1963) A Psychotic Family—Folie à Douze. *Journal of Nervous and Mental Disease*, 137:67-75.

Ware, H. (1979) Polygyny: Women's Views in a Transitional Society, Nigeria 1975. *Journal of Marriage and the Family*, 41:185-195.

Wellisch, D.K. (1985) Family Therapy and Cancer: Keeping House on a Foundation of Quicksand. In: Lansky, M.R. (Ed): *Family Approaches to Major Psychiatric Disorders*. American Psychiatric Press, Washington, D.C.

Welts, E.P. (1982) Greek Families. In: McGoldrick, M., Pearce, J.K., and Giordano, J. (Eds): *Ethnicity and Family Therapy*, The Guilford Press, New York.

Weiss, R. (1975) *Marital Separation*. Basic Books, New York.

Weiss, R., and Birchler, G. (1975) Areas of Change. Unpublished manuscript, University of Oregon.

Welch, C.E. and Glick, P.C. (1981) The Incidence of Polygamy in Contemporary Africa: A Research Note. *Journal of Marriage and the Family*, 43:191-193.

Wender, P.H., Rosenthal, D., Kety, S.S., Schulsinger, F., and Welner, J. (1974) Crossfostering: A Research Strategy for Clarifying the Role of Genetic and Experiential Factors in the Etiology of Schizophrenia. *Archives of General Psychiatry*, 30:121-128.

Westermeyer, J. (1985) Psychiatric Diagnosis Across Cultural Boundaries. *American Journal of Psychiatry*, 142:798-805.

Westermeyer, J. and Neider, J. (1985) Cultural Affiliation Among American Indian Alcoholics: Correlations and Change Over a Ten Year Period. *Journal of Operational Psychiatry*, 16:17-23.

Whitaker, C., Felder, A., and Warkentin, J. (1965) Countertransference in the Family Treatment of Schizophrenia. In: Boszormenyi-Nagy, I. and Framo, J. (Eds): *Intensive Family Therapy*. Harper & Row, New York.

Whitehurst, R., Frisch, G.R., and Serok, S. (1980) A Comparison of Canadian and Israeli Separation and Divorce. *International Journal of Family Therapy*, 2:3-21.

Whiting, B.B. and Whiting, J.W.M. (1975) *Children of Six Cultures: A Psycho-Cultural Analysis*. Harvard University Press, Cambridge.

Whiting, J.W.M. (1967) Sorcery, Sin, and the Superego: A Cross-cultural Study of Some Mechanism of Social Control. In: Ford, C. (Ed): *Cross-Cultural Approaches*. CT:HRAF Press, New Haven.

Whiting, J.W.M., Kluckhon, R., and Anthony, A. (1958) The Function of Male Initiation Ceremonies at Puberty. In: Maccoby, E.E., Newcomb, T.M., and Hartly, E.L. (eds): *Readings in Social Psychology*, Henry Holt, New York.

Williams, J.H. (1977) Middle Age and Aging. In: *Psychology of Women: Behavior in a Biosocial Context*. W.W. Norton and Company, New York.

Williamson, N.E. (1976) *Sons or Daughter: A Crosscultural Study of Parental Preferences*. Sage, Beverly Hills.

Willie, C.V. (1988) *A New Look at Black Families*. 3rd Ed. General Hall, Dix Hills.

Willie, C.V. and Greenblatt, S.L. (1978) Four "Classic" Studies of Power Relationships in Black Families: A Review and Look to the Future. *Journal of Marriage and the Family*, 40:691-694.

Wimberger, H.C. (1965) Counseling in Parent-Child Problems. In: Klemer, R.H. (Ed): *Counseling in Marital and Sexual Problems: A Physician's Handbook*, The Williams & Wilkins, Baltimore.

Winch, R.F. (1963) *The Modern Family*. Holt, Rinehart and Winston, New York.

Winkler, I. and Doherty, W.J. (1983) Communication Styles and Marital Satisfaction in Israeli and American Couples. *Family Process*, 22: 221-228.

Wolf, A.P. (1966) Childhood Association, Sexual Attraction, and the Incest Taboo: A Chinese Case. *American Anthropologist*, 68:883-898.

Wolin, S.J., Bennett, L.A., Noonan, D.L., and Teitelbaum, M.A. (1980) Disrupted Family Rituals: A Factor in the Intergenerational Transmission of Alcoholism. *Journal of Studies on Alcohol*, 41:199-214.

Woon, T. (1976) Epidemic Hysteria in a Malaysian Chinese Extended Family. *Medical Journal of Malaysia*, 31:108-112.

World Health Organization (1976) II. Special Subject—Suicide, 1950-1971. *World Health Statistics Report*, 29:396-413.

Wynne, L.C., Ryckoff, I.M., Day, J., and Hirsch, S.I. (1958) Pseudo-Mutuality in the Family Relations of Schizophrenia. *Psychiatry*, 21:205-220.

Wynne, L.C., and Singer, M.T. (1963) Thought Disorder and Family Relations of Schizophrenics. *Archives of General Psychiatry*, 9:191-32,33-40.

Xu, D., Cui, Y., Tseng, W.S., Hsu, J. (1988) Family Background and Stress: Comparison Among Neurasthenia, Anxiety and Depression in Beijing. In: Yoshimatsu, K., and Tseng, W.S. (Eds): *Asian Family Mental Health*. Psychiatric Research Institute of Tokyo, Tokyo.

Yamao, A. (1986) Truk. In: Tseng, W.S. (ed): *Culture and Mental Health in Micronesia*. Department of Psychiatry, School of Medicine, University of Hawaii, Honolulu.

Yanagisako, S.J. (1979) Family and Household: The Analysis of Domestic Groups. *Annual Review of Anthropology*, 8:161-205.

Yoder, J.D. and Nichols, R.C. (1980) A Life Perspective Comparison of Married and Divorced Persons. *Journal of Marriage and the Family*, 42:413-419.

Yoshida, S. (1985) Women and Drinking in Japan. Presented at the Japanese Culture and Mental Health Conference, East-West Center, Honolulu.

Yoshimatsu, K. (1984) Parent Abuse in Japanese Culture. Presented at the Japanese Culture and Mental Health Conference. East-West Center, Honolulu.

Young, F.W. (1962) The Function of Male Initiation Ceremonies: A Cross-Cultural Test of an Alternative Hypothesis. *The American Journal of Sociology*, 67:379-396.

Zuk, G.H. (1978) A Therapist's Perspective on Jewish Family Values. *Journal of Marriage and Family Counseling*, 4:103-110.

Subject Index

Author Index